WORLD YEARBOOK
OF EDUCATION 1994

WORLD YEARBOOK
OF EDUCATION 1994

THE
GENDER GAP
IN HIGHER
EDUCATION

Edited by Suzanne Stiver Lie, Lynda Malik and Duncan Harris (Series Editor)

KOGAN
PAGE

London • Philadelphia

First published in 1994

Kogan Page Limited
120 Pentonville Road
London N1 9JN

© 1994 Kogan Page and named contributors

British Library Cataloguing in Publication Data

A CIP record for this book is available from the British Library.

ISBN 0 7494 1079 5
ISSN 0084-2508

Typeset by DP Photosetting, Aylesbury, Bucks
Printed and bound in Great Britain by
Biddles Ltd, Guildford and King's Lynn.

Contents

List of contributors

Feride Acar, Middle East Technical University, Ankara, Turkey — *Chapter 15*

Felicity Allen, Monash University, Australia — *Chapter 2*

Helen S Astin, University of California, Los Angeles, USA — *Chapter 17*

Julia Balaska, Panteion University of Athens, Greece — *Chapter 8*

Jacqueline Feldman, Centre National de la Recherche Scientifique, Paris — *Chapter 6*

Malgorzata Fuszara, University of Warsaw, Poland — *Chapter 13*

Susanne Grimm, University of Munich, Germany — *Chapter 7*

Beata Grudzinska, University of Poznan, Poland — *Chapter 13*

Unni Hagen, DISE, Institute of Education, London — *Statistical Appendix*

Tahereh Alavi Hojjat, Allentown College, St Francis de Sales, USA — *Chapter 9*

Neelam Hussain, Lahore, Pakistan, currently Brunel University, London — *Chapter 12*

Suzanne Stiver Lie, University of Oslo, Norway — *Chapters 1, 11, 19, Statistical Appendix*

Grace C L Mak, Chinese University of Hong Kong — *Chapter 5*

Lynda Malik, Villanova University, Pennsylvania, USA — *Chapters 1, 12, 17, 19, Statistical Appendix*

P T M Marope, University of Botswana — *Chapter 3*

Uta Meier, German Youth Institute, Munich and Ludwig Maximilians University, Munich, Germany — *Chapter 7*

Annie Morelle, Centre National de la Recherche Scientifique, Paris — *Chapter 6*

Marina Yu Morozova, Russian Academy of Sciences, Moscow — *Chapter 14*

Railiya Mukhsinovna Muqeemjanova, Russian Academy of Sciences, Moscow — *Chapter 18*

Greta Noordenbos, Leiden University, The Netherlands — *Chapter 10*

Gulnara Tukhlibaevna Quzibaeva, Tashkent Medical Paediatrics Institute, Uzbekistan — *Chapter 18*

Nicolina Sretenova, Bulgarian Academy of Sciences, Bulgaria — *Chapter 4*

Margaret B Sutherland, University of Leeds, UK — *Chapter 16*

Mari Teigen, Norwegian Research Council for Science and the Humanities, Norway — *Chapter 11*

Acknowledgements

This volume represents the efforts of 24 scholars from 17 different countries. The project began in the summer of 1990 when a group of six scholars met in Paris to plan a comparative study on the situation of women in higher education. It is a continuation of the issues addressed in *Storming the Tower: Women in the Academic World* (Lie and O'Leary, 1990).

A cooperative venture of such magnitude owes thanks to many for their support. Special thanks are due to the Institute for Educational Research at the University of Oslo and the Department of Sociology, Villanova University, Pennsylvania, USA for the use of their facilities and resources. The Programme for Research on Education, the Research Council of Norway, along with the Institute for Educational Research provided partial funding for several workshops in connection with the project and also provided travel grants for the East European contributors. The contributors' institutions provided funds for research in connection with their respective countries' studies and also funds in the form of grants for travel to the various seminars. Other funding agencies include the Mediterranean Women's Institute of Athens, Greece.

Many of the contributors participated in one or more workshops. In addition to the initial meeting in Paris there was a workshop in the summer of 1991 in Råssö, Sweden, where Suzanne's cottage was put at the disposal of eleven scholars from nine countries, all of whom shared in the housekeeping. An editorial meeting was held in Leiden, The Netherlands in the summer of 1992, with four participants, and a workshop in Warsaw, Poland in the autumn of the same year had seven participants from six countries. These seminars proved helpful to our efforts to develop a common framework and in discussion of draft chapters and general trends. We also gained insight into the common and special problems of women academics from many different countries and, most important, we developed firm friendships with like-minded scholars. The success of the seminars was also due in no small measure to the efforts of Jacqueline Feldman and Annie Morelle, Paris; Greta Noordenbos, Leiden; and Beate Grudzinska, Poznan, who were responsible for the local arrangements and in addition gave valuable editorial assistance. We would also like to acknowledge the editorial help of Felicity Allen, Australia, who went through a number of drafts at an early stage of the project.

Without the frequent use of a facsimile machine this project could not have been completed. Special thanks to the staff of the University of Oslo – to Unni Hagen for preparing the statistical appendix, Betty Nicolaisen for typing the final manuscript of the volume, Mari Anne Ramstad for converting the many disks and Yngvil Mortensen, Marianne Bryn and Siri Ytrehus for their administrative help. Thanks also to David W Schlosser for preparing the common bibliography, Lisa Ferraro Parmelee for her editorial assistance, and Joan Lesovitz for typing the tables, all from Villanova University.

We would like to thank Helen Carley and Dolores Black at Kogan Page and series editor Duncan Harris, Brunel University, for their encouragement and support.

A final word of thanks is due to our families who for extended periods over the past three summers fended for themselves while Lynda and Suzanne worked on the volume in Oslo and Sweden.

Part 1: Introduction

1. The gender gap in higher education: a conceptual framework

Lynda Malik and Suzanne Stiver Lie

Introduction

One of the most widely reported findings of the post-war era has been the ubiquitous presence of gender[1] stratification. Although its occurrence is almost universally recognized, fundamental questions about its causes and development remain unanswered. The most important of these concern the reasons why every society appears to have an (implicit or explicit) hierarchy based on gender and the relative position of men and women within these hierarchies.

The first question is beyond the scope of this volume. Suffice it to say here that the combination of high maternal/infant mortality rates and short life expectancies which characterized our species for most of its life on this planet was undoubtedly related to the early development of gender role differences. In the post-industrial world these conditions no longer prevail and yet male and female gender roles are still everywhere differentiated.

Concerning the relative position on the hierarchy of men and women, a remarkable consistency appears to exist. In every society for which we have data, men occupy a disproportionate share of superordinate positions. This is true regardless of the criterion of classification (ie, income, prestige, power, etc.) and across national and ideological frontiers. Gender-based inequalities are marked in capitalist, socialist and formerly socialist societies, in rich and in poor ones, in religious societies and in secular ones and in cultures where values of equality are cherished as well as in those committed to inequality.

The gender gap in higher education: the problem defined

In this volume we propose to examine the relative position of men and women, ie, the gender gap, in higher education in 17 countries throughout the world: Australia, Botswana, Bulgaria, China, France, Greece, the Federal Republic of Germany, Iran, The Netherlands, Norway, Pakistan, Poland, Russia, Turkey, the United Kingdom, the United States, and Uzbekistan.

3

Our focus is on women, particularly their changing position in higher education as students, faculty and administrators. In many societies the images, roles and behaviour of women are changing – in some countries this change is dramatic, in others it is not. The definition of higher education varies considerably from country to country. We have chosen to concentrate primarily on universities and research institutions because of their power as selecting, licensing and gate-keeping institutions. More importantly, they greatly influence and control definitions of knowledge and much, though not all, of the ideological machinery of the state and of society (Rendel, 1984). Academic women are of particular interest because they have the potential to play a critical role in shaping women and men of the future and, in addition to influencing the form and content of knowledge, they also serve as role models for female students.

We describe the gender gap in higher education as having both vertical and horizontal dimensions. The vertical aspects consist of rank, salary, and power differentials among faculty and administrators. The horizontal dimension relates to field of study among students and faculty. This gender gap is our dependent variable; we are interested in studying its size, characteristics and development in various historical and cultural contexts.

Our underlying aim is twofold. First, we hope to develop a picture of the dimensions of the gender gap in each country (in the individual chapters) along with a description of its history and relationship to significant aspects of the relevant cultural milieu. Second, in the conclusion we identify similarities and differences between countries and thereby attempt to arrive at low-level theoretical propositions which can be tested in the future.

More specifically, the following questions will be investigated:

- Is there a gender gap in higher education in the countries under investigation?
- Is it increasing or diminishing and under what conditions?
- How is the gender gap connected with economic, legislative, political and religious conditions of each country under study?
- Are current trends best explained by particular combinations of cultural, societal or individual level characteristics?
- Are there national or university policies which aim at gender equality in the countries under study? What have been their effects?
- Is there any relationship between the changing size of the gender gap and the development of the women's movement and Women's Studies?

Comparative analysis: some considerations

The above-mentioned countries were selected for inclusion in the study because they are theoretically interesting as their cultures and social structures vary greatly. Many are very much in the news these days (eg, Iran, Pakistan, Russia, Uzbekistan and Eastern Europe) but accurate information about them is hard to come by. One of the principal aims of this volume is to see whether structural/cultural variations are related to variations in the nature and extent of the gender gap.

Most comparative studies focus on the *similarities* between countries. Our approach will also include, as suggested by Erik Allardt (1990), an explanation of cultural *differences* and unique historical developments characteristic of the individual countries.

Comparative studies have many inherent difficulties; these include lack of comparable information, variation in the quality and reliability of statistics and lack of uniform definitions of the factors and conditions included in the analyses. For example, higher education may be defined differently in different countries, academic degrees and ranks have different nomenclature and requirements and even substantive fields of study may not be uniformly structured. With the assistance of the authors we have attempted to define academic terminology and structures so that the resultant categories are homogeneous with respect to the factors considered, regardless of national, cultural or political variations.

Theoretical framework

Contemporary research on gender stratification in higher education has emphasized the structural characteristics of the university system (Chamberlain, 1988; Hicks and Noordenbos, 1990; Kyvik, 1988; Luukkonen-Gronow, 1987); the importance of individual motivation (Astin, 1984); cultural and societal barriers to the advancement of women (Acar, 1990; Cass *et al.*, 1983; Lie, 1990); the influence (or lack thereof) of marital status on the productivity of female scientists (Cole, 1987; Cole and Zuckerman, 1987; Kyvik, 1990), and the interaction of cultural, social and personality factors on women's professional careers (Acker *et al.*, 1984; Harding, 1986; Stolte-Heiskanen *et al.*, 1991). Most of the studies in this area have focused on individual countries. Notable examples of comparative studies include those done by Kelly and Slaughter, 1991; Lie and O'Leary, 1990; Moore, 1987; Stolte-Heiskanen *et al.*, 1991; and Sutherland, 1985a.

Attempting to find a framework sufficiently broad to encompass situations in a wide range of countries and yet providing enough standardization to make meaningful comparisons possible, we decided to combine a comparative and integrative approach.

We were convinced, above all, of the centrality of the concept of culture in a paradigm which stresses the differentiation between culture, personality and society (Alexander, 1988). In our view the symbolic system (culture) provides a vital link between structure and action. (We owe a profound debt to Talcott Parsons, 1951 for this formulation.) In addition to a consideration of culture at the national level, we recognize that cultural sub-systems (eg, class, gender, religion) are also internalized. Although this process provides the background for the individual's feelings, actions and thoughts, the individual is not a passive receiver. Each person negotiates a unique interpretation of the symbolic system, based on his or her own positions, abilities, interests and relational network.

Most observers would agree that any particular normative system generally furthers the interest of those holding power in that system. Therefore any discussion of the importance of culture must also include a consideration of power, which not only is inherent in normative systems, but also in social structures and interpersonal relations. Pierre Bourdieu's (1988) analysis of the mechanisms whereby power is accumulated, maintained and legitimated is particularly relevant to the analysis of gender stratification within the university. Bourdieu maintains that the right to speak, ie, legitimacy, is granted to those possessing 'cultural capital' (recognized resources and values). Such individuals become spokespersons for the prevailing system and attempt to marginalize challengers and minimize their influence.

Although our theoretical framework appears to be two-dimensional, we are not presenting a static model in which homeostasis is the ultimate value. Rather it is clear to us that all three systems (cultural, social and personality) are constantly changing. Change may be stimulated by new circumstances, as in the case of invention, discovery and diffusion, or economic developments, and is also initiated by clashes of interest and the circulation of élites. Individuals involved in these processes are influenced by, and turn around and influence, their milieu. As Berger and Luckmann (1987) argue, human beings are products of society and at the same time society is a human product.

Even though we recognize the importance of sub-system categories, in this volume when we discuss culture we are referring primarily to situations in which the 'nation is context' (Scheuch, 1966). There are two primary aims in this regard. We wish to compare, across national boundaries, the relationship of selected factors (for example, political or economic patterns) to our dependent variable, and we also attempt to describe, within each country, the relative importance of the various institutions. The former is important if

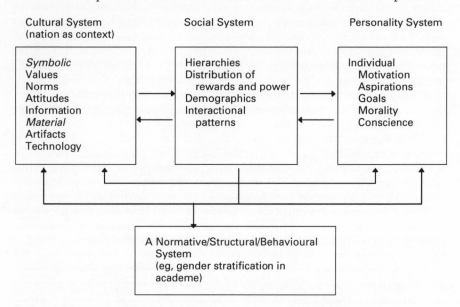

* The arrows refer to the influence of each category on the other, currently and over time.

Figure 1.1 *Multi-dimensional model explaining inequalities in higher education*

we are to have a meaningful framework within which to interpret our empirical information, the latter because we also need to know whether the priority accorded a particular institution itself becomes a significant independent variable.

Although a cultural system contains various ideational and material aspects, as indicated in Figure 1.1, these are largely derived from a core of values which provide the underlying inspiration. One of the most interesting by-products of our investigation has been the identification of core values in various countries and a description of their effect on higher education in general and on gender stratification in particular.

Discussing the social system, we refer essentially to the Weberian hierarchies of class (income), status and power. In addition to the emphasis on cultural background, we recognize that structure significantly affects historical processes and contemporary developments (Skocpol, 1979, cogently makes this point). Currently dramatic structural realignments have been occurring in many of the countries discussed in this volume. These structural changes have had profound effects in every area of life. We are particularly concerned with the effect of political, economic and religious changes on life in the university. Although these may appear, on the surface, to be gender neutral, in reality they often affect the lives of academic men and women in radically different ways.

At the level of the individual we are particularly interested in motivations, aspirations and goals and the behaviour which actualizes them. We view the individual as having internalized the fundamental norms and values of the relevant cultural contexts and interacting with significant others in terms of these guidelines. Each person, however, creates his or her own cultural synthesis, which is shaped by the individual's needs and circumstances. We believe that most behaviour is goal-directed, although this does not necessarily imply that the goals are rationally selected or that the means employed to attain them are rational. Furthermore, we think that in some fundamental way human behaviour must be understood as each individual's solution to the problem of adjusting to competing (and sometimes contradictory) goals while at the same time maintaining an acceptable 'presentation of self' (Goffman, 1959).

When Figure 1.1 is applied to our topic of gender stratification, the cells appear as in Figure 1.2.

The higher education sub-cultures in the countries under consideration may be descibed in terms of their universal and particularistic aspects. Universal values include rationality, intellectual activity and the search for and transmission of knowledge. These values (Bourdieu's *doxa*) are so widely accepted and fundamental that they are rarely questioned. Particularistic aspects of the higher education sub-culture, by contrast, refer to values derived from the specific culture of the nation. Examples of these might include the stress placed on 'serving the people' in China, obedience to religious regulations in societies where these have been institutionalized, and the union of university and capitalist endeavours (eg, biotechnology) in many Western (and now also formerly Communist) countries.

Other values (which appear to be universal rather than particularistic) are more closely related to the behaviour of individuals. Bourdieu calls these

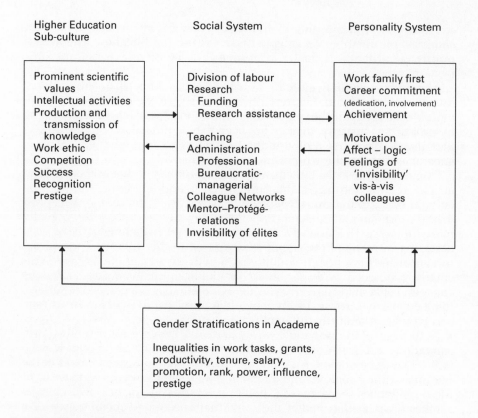

Higher Education Sub-culture	Social System	Personality System

Prominent scientific values
Intellectual activities
Production and transmission of knowledge
Work ethic
Competition
Success
Recognition
Prestige
	Division of labour
	Research
	  Funding
	  Research assistance
	
	Teaching
	Administration
	  Professional
	  Bureaucratic-managerial
	Colleague Networks
	Mentor–Protégé-relations
	Invisibility of élites
		Work family first
		Career commitment
		(dedication, involvement)
		Achievement
		
		Motivation
		Affect – logic
		Feelings of 'invisibility' vis-à-vis colleagues

Gender Stratifications in Academe

Inequalities in work tasks, grants, productivity, tenure, salary, promotion, rank, power, influence, prestige

* The arrows refer to the influence of each category on the other, currently and over time.

Figure 1.2 *Concepts related to gender inequality in higher education*

constituents of the 'scientific habitas'; they include such values as competition, prestige, the work ethic and recognition.

The social system within the university (or research institute) is hierarchically organized. Advancement within the hierarchy is based on the accumulation of academic capital, primarily research productivity. Other criteria can also be important (eg, teaching ability, seniority, etc.), depending on the particular institution and the country in which it is located.

Generally, academic personnel at universities divide their time between research, teaching and administrative tasks. The emphasis and extent of these tasks often vary within and between countries. For instance, countries under the influence of the former Soviet Union have organizational patterns in which research is primarily concentrated in Academies of Science and teaching is the main function of universities. A similar division of labour is also found in France, where CRNS has developed as a centre of research.

In some countries (mainly in the West) academics themselves control advancement within the hierarchy. In others the state, whether for religious or political reasons, makes the major decisions. (See Hojjat, Mak and the chapters concerning former Communist countries in this volume.) In all countries the distribution of resources such as funding for research and research assistance is being decided increasingly by outside sources including foundations and quasi-governmental agencies such as UNESCO and the World Bank. Even in these situations, however, the distribution of resources is mediated by recommendations from influential academics. Individuals also may gain power and influence within an informal network of colleagues. Usually, but not always, these networks are organized according to discipline. Within disciplines different schools of thought often arise which compete for power and legitimacy. Side by side with the professional structure is the bureaucratic-managerial (administrative) structure, which controls the operational and support aspects of the institution. Recruitment into the entire system is controlled by the award of advanced degrees and mentor-protégé relationships.

The university has been described as a 'greedy institution' (Acker et al., 1984). Advancement in the hierarchy requires a major commitment of time and effort and an insider's insight into the rules of the academic game. Both of these conditions are fraught with difficulties for many academic women. The 'gender system' which runs through cultural, societal and individual circumstances (Harding, 1986) dictates that men and women prioritize their varying role obligations differently. In most societies a woman who is also a wife and mother is supposed to consider her family as her top priority, particularly when her children are young. In situations where household and childcare assistance are limited this problem becomes particularly acute, as university women attempt to juggle family and profession (Lie, 1990). Although certain studies (Cole, 1987) have shown that marital status does not significantly affect publication, others have pointed out that the age of a woman's children is a good predictor of publication rates (Kyvik, 1990; Lie, 1990). Women with young children publish less than others, and women in general advance more slowly than men along the academic hierarchy. These situations are rooted in the choices individual women make about the relative priority of family and professional obligations and of course these choices are rooted in fundamental values in the culture, which dictate that men do their duty to their families by succeeding in their careers.

In every social situation, but particularly in those characterized by a high degree of instrumentalism, knowledge of (and ability to manipulate) the rules is as important to success as skill. In the academic sub-culture many of the rules (such as the importance of publication) are clearly and forthrightly presented. However, others which are equally critical to an individual's career progress remain unwritten and often not comprehended. Understanding and manipulation of the informal norms require initiation into the powerful collegial networks (often aptly called 'old boy networks') which control the profession. For a variety of reasons women are much less likely than men to be sponsored by influential, established scholars (O'Leary and Mitchell, 1990) and this reduces their access to powerful collegial networks.

Lack of self-confidence and feelings of alienation which result from overt discrimination as well as from exclusion from informal networks, also influence the career choices and progress made by academic women (Davis and Astin, 1990). Some feminist scholars have reacted against these conditions by challenging the objectivity and rationality which are assumed to underlie the scientific canon. These scholars advocate structural changes and affirmative action programmes which would make the system more 'woman friendly'. Implementation of these recommendations has resulted in the establishment of Women's Studies programmes and research centres throughout the world.

Conclusion

In this chapter we have attempted to integrate functionalist and post-functionalist concepts into a framework which would direct our inquiry. These theoretical guidelines enabled us to identify categories of variables which might be importantly related to the gender gap in higher education and thereby to suggest that each contributor consider these factors in her own chapter. Current information about various countries is presented, summarized and compared. On this foundation we aim, ultimately, to formulate theoretically interesting propositions which may be subject to empirical verification.

The information available on gender differences in higher education is somewhat uneven. Most countries have detailed information concerning student enrolment, but less for faculty and administrators. In some countries like the United States, The Netherlands, Norway and the United Kingdom this issue has been on the research agenda for many years, resulting in a wealth of information regarding differences in research productivity, wages, etc. In a number of formerly Communist countries covered in this volume, information was not aggregated by gender for the university faculty, since problems of gender discrimination had been officially viewed as having been solved. This was also true in China. In cases where information was not available on a nation-wide basis the authors were asked to describe the vertical and horizontal aspects of gender stratification in a typical university.

Note

1. 'Gender' is often used to refer to the socially constructed roles of males and females.

Part 2: National profiles

2. Academic women in Australia: progress real or imagined?

Felicity Allen

SUMMARY: Over the last decade Australian universities have changed structurally and increased their student intake more than tenfold. Women's qualifications have improved considerably during this time. These changes have not been matched by any great increase in women's opportunities to become academics or to reach high academic rank. Where women do enter universities, they are virtually limited to the sub-lecturing ranks. Only one in eight of Australian academics is a tenured woman, but one in two of them is a tenured man. The usual reasons advanced for this were considered, but did not account for the pattern of employment found. The stability of women's under-representation over time suggested that leaving the matter to the universities themselves will not result in any useful change. One option may be to change the existing Affirmative Action legislation to include some penalties for non-compliance.

Introduction

Australian history and society

First settled by Europeans in 1788, Australia is the youngest of the English-speaking countries. The first phase of its history was taken up with major developmental tasks such as clearing farmland and building cities. At first settlement, sex ratios were markedly skewed in favour of men because of its origins as a convict colony. Australia is a vast country geographically, consisting of eight States or Territories with a population of approximately 20 million people. Most Australians live in five large coastal cities. Each state has its own government, but despite this, the country is reasonably homogeneous; movement across state boundaries is free and most qualifications are nationally recognized. There are two major political parties: Liberal Coalition and the Labour party. Although the majority of Australians are nominally Christians, organized religion plays only a minor role in cultural life. Although Australian culture has historically emphasized the importance of equality and a 'fair go', other conflicting values have included male bonding in the form of 'mateship', freedom of choice and hard work.

13

Sympathy and assistance for those unable to work, whatever the cause, have been limited at times.

There is now a reasonably well-developed network of pensions and welfare services, including subsidized childcare, medical care and education. Many welfare initiatives reflected the policies of the Labour party; however, both major parties have now moved to the right and means-testing has been widely adopted. Fees for tertiary education have been reintroduced.

Women's role in the paid work-force has changed dramatically over the past 30 years. In the 1960s and 70s, the occupational status of women declined. The Australian work-force had the greatest degree of sex segregation of all the countries surveyed by the OECD in 1977 (Sawer, 1984). The major responsibility for childrearing rests with the mother, although it is now acceptable for mothers to work for money as well (Young, 1989). Women undertake the major burden of caring for dependants, young and old. This is increasing with 'deinstitutionalization' of the elderly and chronically ill (Simons *et al.*, 1991) who are now often cared for at home.

During the 1970s and 80s interest in fostering equal opportunity for both women and members of minority groups, including Aboriginals, increased. The Affirmative Action (Equal Opportunity for Women) Act, 1986 was introduced to compel organizations to eliminate discrimination but there are no real penalties for nonconformity, and its effectiveness has been questioned. Male behaviour became more resistant as women achieved more powerful positions in the Public Service (Ziller, 1986) and in university administration (Wienecke, 1988).

Women were approximately 40 per cent of all professional workers during the 1970–1980 period (Australian Bureau of Statistics, 1982), but were only 17.8 per cent of the doctors and dentists and 1.8 per cent of the architects/ engineers in 1982, while predominating in nursing and teaching. Women were more likely to enter relatively low-status professions than men.

Women and girls in the education system

Compulsory education was introduced by the 1880s. Primary level education was compulsory for both sexes from the first. Australian women entered university courses as students in 1879.

Private primary and secondary education exist alongside the government system. Approximately 27 per cent of schoolchildren attend private schools, which attract a more upper-class clientele. Almost all (90 per cent) of private school students complete secondary schooling, compared with 50 per cent of government school students. Over half (53 per cent) of the private school students continue to tertiary education compared to 15 per cent of government school students (Williams and Carpenter, 1990). These figures partly reflect the social origins of the private school students. Until the 1980s, fewer girls than boys went to university (Anderson, 1992). This changed so abruptly that among those born between 1960–66, the proportion of women who are graduates exceeds that of men.

The change from an élite to a mass system of tertiary education happened very rapidly. In 1921, 1.4 per cent of 17–22 year-olds were university

Table 2.1 *Higher degrees by sex, 1977, 1982 and 1990*

	1977*	1982*	1990#
Doctorate			
Male	86.3	78.1	65.5
Female	13.7	21.9	34.5
	n=800	n=960	n=9503
Master's			
Male	80.9	72.3	58.8
Female	19.1	27.7	41.2
	n=1940	n=2240	n=26814
Bachelor's			
Male	60.9	56.3	49.0
Female	39.1	43.7	51.0
	n=23810	n=25210	n=340598

* Source: ABS Cat No. 4208.0: 11.
\# Source: *Higher Education Series Update No. 1* (1991) DEET.

students, and this rose to 12 per cent by 1981. By 1990, 20 per cent of this age group were university students. Between 1950 and 1980, women's share of bachelor's degrees rose from 18.3 per cent to 43.9 per cent and their post-graduate enrolment rose from 6.9 per cent to 28.0 per cent (Jones and Castle, 1983).

Ten years ago, women made up only one in five PhD students and one in four Master's students. In 1990, women had achieved near parity at the Master's level but were still only one in three of the PhD students. Post-graduate degrees awarded to women still cluster in humanities and law (Powles, 1986).

Two important considerations for postgraduate students are finances and entry qualifications. Jones and Castle (1989) found that women were less likely to receive first class bachelor-level degrees than men, which meant that they were less likely to win a postgraduate scholarship. They speculated that this might contribute to the lower enrolment rates of women in higher degree programmes. It is clear, however, that women's qualifications have shown a marked recent improvement.

The Australian tertiary sector

Recent changes in organization

The recent history of the tertiary sector can be described as 'boom or bust'. In 1960 Australia had ten universities, four of which dated from the nineteenth century. Between 1960 and 1977 another nine were founded. Ten years of relative quiet ensued. Since 1987, tertiary education has undergone major structural changes. To appreciate the current status of women in academia, it is important to understand how employment opportunities have altered. In

1985, tertiary education included universities, Colleges of Advanced Education (CAEs) and the Tertiary and Further Education sector (TAFE). The TAFE sector was rarely funded for higher education courses and will not be discussed further. The 19 universities contained 172,000 students (Birt, 1985). The university sector had the highest prestige and was considered to prepare students to enter the major professions. The proportion of women employees was very low; in 1987, out of 15,215 university academics, only 26 per cent were women, lower than 40 per cent in the professions (Allen, 1990). Little is known about the proportion of women administrators, but women were rare in the top positions (eg, Registrar). The 45 CAEs catered for 184,000 students; the ratio of male to female academic staff varied widely between CAEs.

Tertiary education changed abruptly in 1987 with publication of the 'Green Paper' (Dawkins, 1987). This set out the government's intention to abolish distinctions between universities and CAEs, to create a small number of large institutions and to shift research funds from the universities. The aim of these changes was to create the 'Unified National System'.

The focus of this chapter is women in universities. For the purposes of analysis, a university is any tertiary educational institution supplying data to the Department of Education, Employment and Training (DEET) and containing professors in 1991. Twenty-seven institutions now conform to this definition.

Women academic staff

Women's pattern of employment as academics is distinctive (see Table 2.2). The typical female academic is a tutor or demonstrator; the typical male is a senior lecturer. Women are less likely than men to enjoy tenure with its associated benefits. The importance of tenure becomes clearer when it is understood that untenured academics may not apply for promotion in their own university (Hobson, 1991) and are not acceptable to many funding bodies as leaders of research teams.

Women are under-represented among academics both by comparison with other professions and in their enrolment as university students (see

Table 2.2 *Full-time and permanent part-time staff in Australian universities, 1972–91*

	1972*	%F	1982	%F	1991#	%F
Professor	925	1.5	1089	2.4	1723	7.31
Reader	968	2.8	1365	5.2	2799	10.29
Sen Lecturer	2245	5.5	3644	8.9	6037	17.24
Lecturer	2883	12.7	2921	20.9	9726	38.71
Below Lect.	2679	39.2	2861	42.9	4937	51.29
Total	9699		11880		25222	

* Calculated from Ryan and Evans (1984).
# Calculated from DEET printouts (1992).

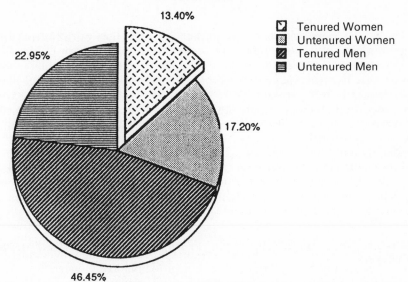

Figure 2.1 *Tenured and untenured male and female faculty (as a per cent of total)*
(1991)

Table 2.1). This situation has been stable since 1972, although there has been a recent increase in access to employment.

In 1972, women were only 16.3 per cent of all university academics. Ten years later, the proportion had risen to 19.2 per cent (Ryan and Evans, 1984) and it reached 26 per cent by 1987 (Allen, 1990). The proportion of women reached 30.8 per cent in 1991 (DEET, 1991), but some of this increase is due to amalgamation of CAEs with universities. (These figures include all academic staff, including those below the rank of lecturer.)

The different meaning of a university career to the two sexes could be seen most clearly in the comparison of the proportions in full-time, secure employment in universities and part-time, unstable employment.

Only 13.4 per cent of Australian academics were tenured women in 1991, compared to 46.45 per cent who were tenured males (see Figure 2.1).

At present the 'career entry-level rank' is that of lecturer. This is one of the few ranks with sufficient numbers of each sex for comparisons to be meaningful. The number of tenured lecturers in 1991 was obtained from the DEET 1992 printouts. Overall, 51.8 per cent of female lecturers were tenured, compared to 57.9 per cent of the males. Marked inter-university variations were found (female range: 23.5–76.5 per cent; male range: 28.9–81.5 per cent), suggesting that universities have no consistent policy on awarding tenure.

Although the male advantage was apparently small, once it is multiplied by the numbers of each sex at the lecturer level nationwide, a marked difference in the number of male and female academics with their feet on the first rung of the career ladder can be found. Table 2.2 shows that there were 9,726 lecturers in Australia in 1991. Of these, 1,949 (20.0 per cent) were both female and tenured, but 3,452 (35.5 per cent) were both male and tenured. The reasons for granting tenure at this level have not been studied and the causes of the inter-university variations are unknown.

Under the same legislative requirements and, theoretically, the same appointment system, considerable variation in the proportions of senior women occurs between universities. Three universities have no women professors. The percentage of senior academics who are female ranges from 7.4 per cent to 26.1 per cent. There were no obvious relationships between the proportion of women at the senior level with the age of the university or its technical emphasis. The University of Adelaide, for example, was among the first universities in the country to admit women students, yet only 7.4 per cent of its senior academics are women.

Professional opportunities for women academics are worse than those for men. While this problem is now well known (eg, Mack, 1990), there is disagreement about the causes, whether women's opportunities are changing or even whether they can be changed (Over, 1981).

Reasons for women's poor career opportunities in Australian universities

Investigations into women's employment conditions conducted at many universities have reached similar conclusions (eg, Sawer, 1984; Wilson and Byrne, 1987). Several explanations have been advanced for the findings, including the following:

- selection and promotion procedures,
- low levels of turnover,
- women's reluctance to apply for positions,
- incompatibility of academic employment and domestic responsibilities
- sex-based differences in academic merit.

While most writers have focused on these, others have raised the issue of discrimination (eg, Jones and Lovejoy, 1983; Mack, 1990). They suggested that few women are senior academics because of deliberate decisions by male policy makers. The evidence for these reasons will now be considered.

Selection and promotion procedures

Opportunities for promotion vary according to the rank and appointment that the individual currently holds.

As a rule, applicants for advertised positions submit written applications. While studies of individual universities (eg, Poiner and Burke, 1988) found a gradual progression towards more rigorous advertising rules, these requirements may not be standardized, particularly for junior positions. Harper (1987) found that 54 per cent of academics learned about a position by invitation. Under these circumstances, recruitment may not be entirely open.

Even when positions are advertised, details of the position requirements may be very sparse, allowing shifts in emphasis to develop during the recruitment process (Poiner and Burke, 1988). There is no universal requirement to justify short lists without female applicants, although some universities do require an explanation. Even if one is on the short list, interviews are not inevitable (Harper, 1987). Although they are usual for senior appointments, practice with junior appointments varies. All-male selection committees are not unusual. The selection committee is rarely required to explain its decision. Lack of uniform selection procedures may explain geographic variations in the proportions of senior academic women.

Low levels of turnover in universities

As described earlier, 1960 to 1980 was a period of expansion. This major expansionary phase occurred at a time when the sex difference in qualifications was more marked than it is today. One explanation for the slow increase in the proportion of women academics has been that a large cohort of tenured men, recruited during this period of expansion, is now blocking women's promotion. Over (1981) asserted that little change in women's position in academia could be expected in the next 20 years because there would be few openings.

The idea of a low employment turnover in academia is now widely accepted (eg, Wilson and Byrne, 1987), although Over (1981) gave no evidence and his predictions are counterintuitive. Many academics are qualified to practise another profession (eg, engineering) and many academics do not reach the top until they are near retirement. Both factors theoretically should lead to high turnover.

Over and Lancaster (1984) followed up two cohorts of lecturers (1962–4 and 1975–6) for six years from the time of their appointment. Their data show an annual turnover of 7.3 per cent and 5.3 per cent respectively. The authors called this 'low', but even if the lower figure were typical, half of all lecturing positions would be vacated every ten years. Slightly lower figures have been found in more recent studies; Sloan et al. (1990) found an annual outflow of 2.44 per cent of all tenured academic staff (based on 1989 data) but a turnover of 3.88 per cent per annum of all academic staff. They commented that 'This turnover rate, not surprisingly, is low when compared to manufacturing industry.' (p. 64). However, vacating one quarter of all tenured positions every ten years should have allowed substantial alterations in the proportions of female academics.

The explanation of the low numbers of women by allegedly low turnover rates in academia is called into question by Poiner and Burke's (1988) study at the University of Sydney. Women increased their numbers by a factor of 17 during the expansionary period, but men increased theirs by a factor of 50.

Academic turnover is not particularly low and men gain more than women from periods of expansion. This explanation is not sufficient to explain the poor representation of women.

Women's reluctance to apply for positions

There is evidence that when women apply for a position, they are more likely to succeed than men (Harper, 1987; Wilson and Byrne, 1987). This raises the question of why women rarely attain senior rank. One explanation has been that women are reluctant to apply.

Some evidence indicates that women make fewer applications than men

(Harper, 1987). Poiner and Burke reported a woman who did not apply for a chair because 'It never occurred to me that they would appoint a woman.'(1988, p. 39). However, it is unknown whether women make fewer applications than men of similar rank. Very little is known about the role of applications as few researchers have gained access to them.

The role of interpersonal politics in applications needs to be considered. Women are less likely than men to acquire mentors (Sawer, 1984) and have less access to informal networks. The lack of standardization of procedures means that informal networks are important in determining the 'inside track' to promotion or selection.

Personal invitations continued to be important. Images of each sex may determine the type of invitations they receive. Allen (1990) found that not one of 51 senior women (1984 data) had begun their careers above the lecturer level. By contrast, 33 per cent of a random sample of senior men at the same university had begun their careers as senior academics. Under these circumstances, referring to 'women's reluctance to apply' is misleading.

Incompatibility of academic employment and domestic responsibilities

The relative scarcity of senior female academics has been attributed to career interruptions or to reduced research output when their children are small (eg, Baldwin, 1985). While this is widely believed, the university sector's response to the needs of women burdened with a double shift could be described as 'too little – too late'. Three institutional responses which could help considerably are:

- maternity leave,
- adequate childcare facilities, and
- flexible working hours.

Maternity leave was first instituted in 1973 for tenured academics. Table 2.2 shows that few women could claim maternity leave as a right even today. Crèche facilities are now available at most universities, but the number of places is often below the demand (Sawer, 1984). Flexible time positions with pro rata benefits have been available for many years but are usually held by men in faculties concerned with clinical studies (eg, medicine).

Neither Sawer (1984) nor Harper (1987) found large numbers of women academics taking maternity leave, but the reasons for this are unclear. Some may time the arrival of children to coincide with the main vacation. Sawer reported women who felt obliged to choose between career and either having fewer children than they wanted, or none. While the hypothesis that the combined demands of teaching and motherhood leave little time for research is compelling, evidence is contradictory (Cole and Zuckerman, 1987; Kyvik, 1990; Lie, 1990; Luukkonen-Gronow, 1987).

Sex-based differences in academic merit

The remaining explanation is that there are true differences in academic merit, with men having more and women less.

What is 'academic merit'? It is usually held to refer to some amalgam of the following:

- qualifications,
- type and/or rate of publications,
- teaching ability, and
- administrative work.

These four issues are examined below.

Qualifications

If postgraduate qualifications were major determinants of rank, senior academics without them would be rare. Lecturers would have doctorates on appointment and women's qualifications would be lower than those of men.

Although Over (1981) maintained that '... a postgraduate degree is typically a necessary qualification for a university appointment ...' (p. 170), Baldwin (1985) found that only 51 per cent of lectureships at Monash between 1980 and 1984 went to candidates with PhDs. Sloan *et al.* (1990) asked, 'What do we know about the qualifications profile of academic staff? The short answer is that we know very little.' (p. 21).

The most recent national information had been collected in 1980. These data showed variations in qualifications across rank; 51 per cent of lecturers held doctorates compared with 78 per cent of professors. The University of Melbourne Calendar revealed that professors were appointed without doctorates in the 1980s. The question then arises, if men can profess a subject without a doctorate, why not women?

Publications

If publications are a major determinant of academic rank, senior academics publish more than juniors. Women should have consistently lower rates of publication than men.

The number of publications is an inadequate estimate of research productivity, and the problems of assessing quality are formidable. Given the emphasis on publication in selection and promotion (eg, Wilson and Byrne, 1987), it is surprising to find there are no normative data by discipline. In their absence, no selection committee can know whether a candidate's record is reasonable, yet judgements about whether candidates have published 'enough' are regularly made.

Studies of publication rates usually rely on self-report data, but the weight of evidence (eg, Cass *et al.*, 1983) suggested that men publish more than women. However, it was impossible for them to determine the relationship between publication rate and rank. Davies (1982) found women were not promoted in the same proportions as men with similar publication records. Wilson and Byrne (1987) found a sex difference in the relationship between rank and publication: senior men published more than junior men. By contrast, many of the most productive women were in the junior ranks.

The evidence available on publication rates is consistent with at least two explanations:

- high publication rates are rewarded by promotion, and
- promotion makes high publication rates possible.

A study of the relationship between publication rates and promotion may clarify this issue.

Teaching ability

If teaching ability were an important determinant of rank, academics would be required to demonstrate ability on appointment, followed by regular evaluations.

There are no requirements that academics hold teaching qualifications, and they are rarely required to provide independent evidence of teaching ability. A notable exception to this is Macquarie University whose guidelines for promotion to senior lecturer state: 'Applicants should ensure that their teaching has been evaluated.' (1986, p. 3).

Participation in administration

If participation in administration is an important determinant of academic rank, then men should play a greater role in administration than women and administrative activities should be rewarded by promotion.

Less is known about this area than all the other areas. There are two forms of administration: the work of coordinating courses, particularly laboratory-based courses, and participation in administrative committees. Virtually nothing is known about the former.

The powerful administrative committees have been found to be male-dominated by those who have studied them (eg, Wilson and Byrne, 1987). However, membership in many committees is a *consequence* of rank, rather than a *cause* for promotion. Convincing evidence that participation in administrative activities and membership in committees leads to promotion has not yet been obtained.

Discussion

It is easy to show that women in academia are limited to low positions, but it is difficult to discover why. In fact, one of the most striking aspects of this knowledge-based industry is how little academia knows about its own staff and their career patterns.

The selection and promotion procedures of most Australian universities are sufficiently under-regulated to permit considerable latitude. With few requirements to justify their decisions, most committees continue to appoint or promote people like themselves – usually men. While there is no need to postulate deliberate discrimination to explain this phenomenon, there are few safeguards to protect women against powerful misogynists. Davies (1982) successfully brought an action against the University of New England under their state-based Equal Opportunity legislation. At the Australian National University, the appointment of a male on the basis that he was a 'scholar of international repute' was challenged when the Science Citation Abstracts demonstrated that a woman competing for the same position had been cited more frequently (Sawer, 1984).

The combination of promotion bars between tutor and lecturer and the ban on applications from non-tenured staff combines with women's concentration into these two areas to create a vicious circle. If universities were serious about equal opportunity, they could end these barriers by changing the legislation. There is no reason why this cannot be done.

The argument that women's poor representation in senior positions is the inevitable result of low turnover may be untenable. Postulating a reluctance to apply on women's part sounds like blaming the victim. Even if it could be shown that women were reluctant to apply, is that sufficient? Should there not be some attempt to rectify this?

The effect of domestic responsibilities on rank remains unclear. In any event a great deal could be done to mitigate the impact of these responsibilities on women's careers. Such actions are being undertaken slowly, if at all. The marked geographic variation in the proportions of senior women argue against the view that family responsibilities are a major barrier.

The arguments about the relative academic merit of the two sexes again have very little evidence to back them. The view that women are not promoted or appointed because they lack doctorates is frequently heard, yet this is not a barrier for men. Even the necessary rates of publication have not been established for many disciplines so that there are no benchmarks to guide committees. Teaching skills and administrative activities have been virtually ignored.

This review of women's conditions of work and access to senior positions has shown that women are markedly less likely to reach senior ranks than men. This situation has been explained away as due to reasons beyond the universities' control. While there are simple steps which would redress the balance considerably, there is no sign that these will be taken. There is a lack of will to promote women's success so that women's talents are grossly under-used. Australia must decide whether a small country can continue to waste half of its highly trained intelligence.

The stability of women's under-representation over time suggests that leaving the matter to the universities themselves will not result in any useful change. One option may be to change the existing Affirmative Action legislation to include penalties for noncompliance.

3. Batswana women in higher education: from systematic exclusion to selective engagement*

P T M Marope

SUMMARY: Factors underlying gender-related inequality in access to higher education from the pre- to the post-independence era are outlined. During the two and a half decades of independence university enrolments reached near-parity along gender lines. Notwithstanding tremendous gains that women have experienced in the post-independence era, female students are still sparse in scientific, mathematics, and technological fields. As faculty, women are equally rare in the above-mentioned fields, as well as in top echelons of the university's decision-making bodies.

Introduction

For eleven years the institution remained a citadel of male education, not opening its doors to women.... The late inclusion of women reflected the attitude of both Batswana and missionaries concerning the position of women in society. Both male Batswana and missionaries regarded women as inferior. Their place was in the home ... careers and positions were incompatible with the 'proper' role of women (Mgadla, 1986, pp. 208–9).

Women account for 40 per cent of the total enrolment each year, and this proportion is constant for both Batswana and non-Batswana students (Ministry of Finance and Development Planning, 1984, pp. 7/11).

The above vignettes echo one of the themes which pervade this volume, that globally, women are latecomers to the field of higher education. Within the specific context of Botswana, they map the road Batswana[1] women have travelled towards gender parity in access to higher education. Like a road in a desert, it has been long and hard with frustrating mirages and promising oases. In terms of access, the destined oasis is nigh. There is hope that the 'womenfolk' will quench their century-long thirst for higher education. From a state of complete denial of entry into higher education institutions in

* In keeping with usage in Botswana itself, the word 'Batswana' has been retained when referring to the citizens of that country.

the early twentieth century, currently they compare favourably with their counterparts in developed countries. By 1990, women constituted 49 per cent of university enrolments. Beyond enrolment figures, however, many a road leads to a mirage; women are still under-represented in scientific, techno-logical and mathematical fields, the higher echelons of the university's academic hierarchy, and the university's high administrative and decision-making bodies.

Socioeconomic, political and cultural profile

After 80 years of British rule, Botswana gained political independence in 1966. Since independence, multi-party politics and rapid economic growth have proceeded in a peaceful and stable environment. The new government was founded on principles of democracy and social justice, including equity in the distribution of all social services and amenities. The constitution affords all citizens freedom of speech, association and religion, universal adult suffrage and in most areas equal rights for all. The country covers approximately 582,000 square kilometres – about the size of France. It has a population of 1.3 million, 52 per cent of which are women. Although the population is small relative to the size of the country (1.7 persons per square kilometre), economic planning and development advantages associated with small populations are frustrated by its rapid 3.4 per cent annual growth rate.

Although at independence Botswana was one of the poorest countries in Africa, it now has one of the fastest growing economies in the sub-Saharan region. In 1987 the Gross National Product (GNP) per capita was $1,050, comparing highly favourably with a $330 average for sub-Saharan Africa. Over the past two and a half decades of independence, the Gross Domestic Product (GDP) has, in real terms, grown at an annual average of 13 per cent, resulting in a GDP per capita of approximately $2,160 by 1989. This pros-perity is due mainly to the transformation from a predominantly agrarian to a mining economy. Between 1967 and 1988 the contribution of the mining sector to GDP rose from 2 per cent to 50 per cent while that of agriculture declined from 41 per cent to 3 per cent (Republic of Botswana, 1991)

Botswana society comprises eight Tswana[2] tribes which are ethnically related and speak related languages. Twenty per cent of the population speaks languages belonging to non-Tswana ethno-linguistic groups. The society is nominally Christian although most people also practise indigen-ous tribal religions. Tribal and religious divides have had no significant impact on the conditions and status of women; manifestations of female inferiority have, rather, differed mainly along urban/rural divides.

About 70 per cent of Batswana live in rural areas where arable farming and cattle rearing remain the primary ways of life. The decline of the agri-cultural sector has meant that the majority of the population has not bene-fited from the economic growth as much as their urban counterparts, who draw higher cash incomes from their participation in the modern labour market (Republic of Botswana, 1985).

In addition to rural/urban distinctions, economic and social inequalities exist along gender lines. Although the numerical majority, women remain economic minorities in both urban and rural settings. In urban centres, the economic inferiority of women is expressed through their low-to-middle rank positions in the labour market, and consequently their relatively low earnings. As recently as March 1991, women constituted 38 per cent of the civil service[3] and yet only filled 13 per cent of the executive-level positions which are either secured by promotion, or require postgraduate entry-level qualifications (Republic of Botswana, 1991). Across the government, para-statal[4] and the private sectors, men outnumber women by a factor of 5 to 1 in such top-level positions as members of parliament, cabinet members, permanent secretaries, company directors and company boards of directors (Mannathoko, 1991). Women remain scarce in these positions because of their low educational attainments and gender-biased job promotions which tend to favour men.

In rural settings, women are less likely than men to own farming land, cattle and other traditional sources of wealth. The few women who own property have the smallest plots of farming land, and the smallest number of cattle. This lack of the traditional means of production is due mainly to traditions which dictate that sons inherit and control the family wealth while daughters are expected, through marriage, to inherit their husbands' family wealth. Other contributing factors are the traditional and modern marriage laws under which women's property rights are reduced to those of minors.

Women are solely responsible for home chores including taking care of children and the elderly from both their own families and their husbands' families. This lopsided division of labour persists to a lesser extent even in urban centres as women increase their participation in the modern labour market. In rural areas, farming and taking care of small livestock are an additional female responsibility.

In both rural and urban centres, the inferior status of women is maintained by a variety of mechanisms, including sex-role differentiation, traditions of control and inheritance of property, marriage laws and citizenship laws, all of which favour men (Molokomme, 1987; 1989). Thus, despite the egalitarian ideals expressed in formal policy documents, informal value systems rooted in patriarchy and reinforced by male-dominated modern institutions continue to deny women equal rights.

Primary education for women: the circumstantial beneficiaries

Since the mid-1800s when Christian missionaries introduced western formal schooling, female enrolments have always outnumbered those of males at the primary level. Until 1930, girls accounted for 75 per cent of primary school enrolments. However, currently there is a move towards parity; female enrolments have dropped to 51 per cent in 1989 (Bechuanaland Protectorate, 1939; Republic of Botswana 1991).

Though often misconstrued as indicative of lack of discrimination against women, the preponderance of girls was purely circumstantial (Parsons, 1984). Traditionally, boys and young men look after cattle while girls take care of home chores. Because cattle are kept in cattle posts far removed from villages (where the schools are), boys could not combine cattle herding with schooling, while girls could combine their daily home chores (in villages) with schooling.

The situation of boys was aggravated by the introduction of hut tax and an education levy in the early 1900s which forced Batswana men to migrate to South African mines in pursuit of cash employment. This meant that younger boys had to take on more of their fathers' duties, which made it even more difficult for them to enrol in school (Parsons, 1984). It is also possible that for young Batswana males, prospects of employment in South African mines with no formal education requirement acted as a pull factor, making formal education irrelevant and thereby (Craig, 1981) further deterring them from enrolling in school. Today the overall illiteracy rate is 26.4 per cent (having declined from 67.3 per cent 25–30 years ago). The illiteracy rate among females amounts to 35 per cent (World Bank, 1992).

Post-primary education for women: the systematic exclusion

Other than the incidental advantage which accrued to girls at the primary level, there is no evidence of any deliberate efforts to educate them. On the contrary, existing literature is replete with evidence of discrimination against girls in terms of both access and curricula differentiation. The pseudo-advantage which accrued to girls at the primary level disappeared as they reached the post-primary level. Here a deliberate commitment was required in terms of paying expensive fees and releasing them from home chores to attend boarding secondary schools which, until 1944, were available only outside the country.

The few girls who made it to secondary school were discriminated against through the curriculum. They were trained in such home-oriented skills as baking, mending, washing, starching and ironing clothes. Boys, on the other hand, especially the sons of royals, were trained for careers, mainly as teachers, evangelists and employees of Tswana States secretariats (Chirenje, 1977; Gustafsson, 1987; Parsons, 1984). The boys' curriculum increased their opportunities for public careers and further education while that of girls mainly increased their opportunities for marriage.

Even after completion of secondary school, girls had virtually no access to higher education. For instance, Tiger Kloof, one of the South African higher education institutions accessible to Batswana at the time, did not admit women until 1915, 11 years after its opening in 1904. The exclusion of women from higher education institutions was deliberate and systematic and reflected the attitudes of both male Batswana and missionaries towards women as inferiors (Chirenje, 1977; Mgadla, 1986).

Because exclusionary policies took place outside the borders of Bechuanaland, and also before independence, one could argue that they were not direct policies of the Bechuanaland education system. However, historical literature provides ample evidence that those policies were condoned by the same Batswana chiefs, missionaries and colonial education officers who vehemently opposed the circumstantial exclusion of boys from primary schools, and later encouraged their enrolment in post-primary and higher education institutions (Chirenje, 1977; Mgadla, 1986). They are also the same policies underlying the deficit of Batswana females in secondary and higher education which endured more than a decade after independence.

Women in higher education: selective engagement

Three factors explain the sparcity of women in higher education during the first decade of independence. First was parental reluctance to spend money on the secondary education of their daughters (Bechuanaland Protectorate, 1939). Because of the selective nature of the education system, the under-participation of girls at the secondary level directly corresponded to their under-representation at university level. Second was the girls' post-primary curriculum, which did not provide adequate preparation for higher educa-tion. Third were regulations that directly denied women access to higher education. Table 3.1 presents trends on the representation of women in higher education from the immediate post-independence period up to 1991.

For Botswana the general theme of this volume, gender disparities in higher education, breaks new ground on two fronts. First, higher education institutions are a fairly recent phenomenon. Although Batswana have been acquiring university education outside the country since the early 1900s, it was not until 1971 that the first university campus of Botswana enrolled its first cohort. The 1971 campus gained full university status – University of Botswana – in 1982, and remains the only one in the country. Being a young university, it offers mainly undergraduate degrees, and is limited in capacity and range of course offerings. For most Batswana, university education is a rare opportunity. In 1991, approximately 2.4 per cent of men and 2 per cent of women of eligible age gained entrance to university.[5]

Second, concern over gender disparities in post-primary education has developed only in the late 1980s to early 1990s. Peculiar to the history of Botswana's education therefore has been the gender blindness of education policies as a whole.

Several indicators attest to this gender blindness, especially in higher education. First, higher education enrolment statistics are rarely and inconsistently disaggregated by gender and field of study. As in Table 3.1, lack of such statistics makes it hard to keep track of the progress and set-backs women have had over the years. Second, in contrast to universities in most of the countries represented in this volume, the University of Botswana has not yet instituted a gender studies department or a gender research programme. It was not until 1991 that the university began drafting policy in this area. Third, the gender-blindness is manifest in the paucity of literature and empirical investigations of gender disparities, especially in higher education.

From Table 3.1, general and field-specific figures show that after a decade of independence, higher education remained pretty much a male preserve. It was not until the early 1980s that female enrolments began to show sub-stantial gains, and, in some fields, even surpassed those of men by 1991. An

Table 3.1 *Student enrolment by field and gender: selected years*

Field	1968			1970			1972			1975			1983			1991		
	M	F	%F	M	F	%F	M	F	%F	M	F	%F	M	F	%F	M	F	%F
Soc. Sci.	24	5	17	38	6	14	42	11	21	104	38	27	199	149	42	757	853	53
Education	4	2	33	17	10	37	33	21	39	76	54	41	191	170	47	273	314	53
Arts	14	4	22	5	5	58	4	1	20	4	1	20	4	1	20	120	342	55
Math/Sci.	25	5	16	49	10	17	40	16	28	96	22	19	122	25	17	294	97	25
Total	67	16	19	109	31	22	119	49	29	280	115	39	632	456	42	1729	1640	49

Sources: Republic of Botswana, Education Statistics (1968, 1970, 1972, 1975, 1983) Gaborone, The Government Printer. Figures for 1991 are compiled from the University of Botswana admissions records.

Note: Enrolment figures do not include foreign students. Figures for 1968 to 1975 comprise Batswana students in local and foreign universities. Figures for 1983 to 1991 include students only at the University of Botswana.

obvious exception to these gains has been in science and mathematics.

The under-achievement of Batswana in science, mathematics and related fields cuts across both genders. This generally poor performance is manifest in the country's unsuccessful attempts to recruit local people to fill high-level positions in mathematics and science-oriented professions such as medicine, mathematics, statistics and engineering (Colclough *et al.*, 1988; Republic of Botswana, 1985; 1991).

As discussed above, the historic under-representation of women in higher education partially explains their middle-to-low rank status in the labour market and in salary scales. Although a prestigious academic institution, the university has been no exception to this trend. Table 3.2 presents the distribution of the university faculty by gender, field of study and rank.

This table shows that women constitute 18 per cent of the university faculty. There is near equal gender representation in the faculty of education, but a gross under-representation of women across all other faculties. Also conspicuous is the absence of women in the senior lecturer, associate professor and professor ranks.

Although no empirical evidence exists, the absence of women in the higher ranks may derive from two of the university's promotion criteria: publications and 'within-rank' duration of service. Owing to time spent on home-related activities, women's overall publication rates are likely to be lower than those of men, reducing their chances of upward occupational mobility. In addition to publications, the university has a minimum number of years of service within each rank before which one cannot proceed to the next rank. Criteria for promotion also include teaching quality and community service. Men generally have longer university teaching experience than women, therefore they move up faster than even those women with a comparable number and quality of publications.

For women, being in the lower ranks of the university academic hierarchy has also meant lack of representation in the higher echelons of the university's decision-making bodies. Selection to such bodies is based mainly

Table 3.2 *Academic staff by field, gender, rank and academic year 1991/2*

Field	Professor		Asst prof.		Snr Lecturer		Lecturer		SDF	
	M	F	M	F	M	F	M	F	M	F
Education	2	–	–	–	9	3	16	20	2	1
Arts/Hum	4	–	–	–	14	–	27	6	3	3
Soc Sci	3	–	3	–	13	–	27	13	8	1
Math/Stat	3	–	1	–	10	–	24	1	5	2
Nat Sci	3	–	5	–	22	–	55	6	5	1
Total	15	0	9	0	68	3	149	46	23	8

Source: Sefe, F T K and Rasebotsa, N (eds) (1991) *University of Botswana Calendar, 1991–2.*

Note: SDF refers to Staff Development Fellows, ie, staff members awaiting training for their Master's Degrees.

Table 3.3 *University governance by gender and citizenship academic year 1991/2*

Governing body	Citizens		Non-citizens		% Citizens		Overall percentages	
	M	F	M	F	M	F	M	F
University Council	17	0	2	0	89	0	100	0
University Senate	10	3	35	1	20	6	92	8
Deans of Faculties	0	0	5	0	0	0	100	0
Department Heads	3	2	8	0	23	15	85	15

Source: Sefe, F T K and Rasebotsa, N (eds) (1991) *University of Botswana Calendar, 1991–2.*

on seniority. Table 3.3 presents the distribution of women and men on the university governance by citizenship. Notice that governing bodies are arranged in order of decision-making power, and therefore status and prestige.

It is interesting to note the disparities in the representation of women and citizens across Table 3.3. The University Council is the ultimate governing body of the university, and its membership includes 'leading figures from the national community as well as senior personnel from within the University' (Sefe and Rasebotsa, 1991, p. 44). On the basis of such criteria, council members are exclusively male and are almost all citizens. Even mere recognition as a leading community member is a rarity for a Batswana woman.

The University Senate is the academic authority of the university. Except for representatives of students and faculty and for heads of departments, senate membership is based on academic seniority. Criteria for faculty deanship are based on a combination of seniority and election by members of the relevant faculty. Heads of departments are selected by departmental boards and then appointed by the university administration. Seniority also plays a role in this selection.

The exclusion of women from university governance can thus be explained through three factors. Most important is the lack of recognition of women's accomplishments as community leaders. Council appointments are made by men, who choose not to see women's accomplishments in the community. Second, women, especially from the Senate, generally have middle-to-low rank status within the university academic hierarchy. Third, some women may be reluctant to stand for offices of responsibility as faculty deans.

Conclusion

In conclusion Batswana women have come a long way in terms of general access to higher education. Beyond this, the situation of women can be described as one of selective engagement. As in the larger labour market, women remain in the middle-to-low echelons of the university academic, administrative and governance hierarchy. They also continue to be under-represented in scientific and technical fields.

Notes

1. 'Batswana' refers to citizens of Botswana and 'Motswana' refers to the singular form: citizen of Botswana.
2. The noun root 'Tswana' is a generic reference for ethnicity, citizenship, culture and language. It can be used alone in sentences, or with prefixal inflections: Mo- to denote singular citizen; Ba- to denote plural citizens; and Se- to denote language, culture and/or manner of doing things.
3. The civil service remains the main employer of Botswana's labour force.
4. 'Parastatal' refers to companies and other departments whose ownership is shared by government and the private sector.
5. Most Batswana students enter university between 19 and 20 years of age and complete their studies between ages 23 and 24 years. The percentage of the population (by gender) that enters university is calculated by dividing the total 1991 population aged 19 to 24 by the total 1991 university enrolment. The estimate is therefore gross since the numerator is not based on university enrolment aged 19 to 24, but includes mature entry students who mostly enter the university beyond the age of 24. Information for calculating net estimates was not available. (Note: The formula used here follows that used by Botswana Central Statistics Office. Estimates include Batswana students only, and exclude those in the pre-entry science programme)

4. The nation's showcase: Bulgarian academic women, between the Scylla of totalitarianism and the Charybdis of change

Nicolina Sretenova

SUMMARY: The chapter outlines the image of traditional Bulgarian women and their struggle to enter higher education. It attempts also to show how the Soviet model of equality has affected women's position in Bulgaria, in particular women's place in the academy. A thesis of hidden and non-apparent discrimination against women in higher education, illustrated by the formula 'equality of end results with unequal conditions at the start' is advanced. The chapter also briefly traces the peculiarities of the current transition period in Bulgarian society.

A historical and cultural profile

Contemporary Bulgaria is a small country located in the centre of the Balkan peninsula. Bounded by the former Yugoslavia, Greece and Turkey, the river Danube divides Bulgaria from Romania and the Black Sea separates it from the former USSR. According to preliminary census data (1992) the population numbers 8,472,742, of which women comprise 51 per cent. This represents a 5.3 per cent decrease since 1985. The Eastern Orthodox faith is professed by 86 per cent of the population, with most of the remainder identifying themselves as Muslims.

The traditional Bulgarian woman

The Bulgarian state was founded in the seventh century on the basis of cultural dualism consisting of the nomadism of the proto-Bulgarian Turkic Central Asian tribes and the agricultural patterns of southern Slavonic tribes. By the ninth century Bulgarian culture had contributed literacy and Christianity to the Slavonic world community. These two developments became focal points of Bulgarian culture, enabling her to preserve her identity during the centuries of turbulence which followed. During the tenth century a socio-religious development known as the Bogomil movement arose, and its ideology spread to western Europe, primarily northern Italy and southern France. One of the key points in this ideology was the equality of men and women under God, which contrasted sharply with official church dogma.

In the fourteenth century Bulgaria was invaded by Turkey, whose rule lasted until 1878. During these five centuries of Turkish occupation Bulgaria lost its spiritual leadership in the Slavonic world and became a *village* society as the aristocracy and existing cultural institutions were destroyed (Genchev, 1988). In spite of the duration of Turkish rule there was very little intermarriage between Turks and Bulgarians and the heart of Bulgarian culture remained intact.

Since the Bulgarian feudal state did not fully develop serfdom, peasants continued to own land and live in democratic village communes where the family was the basic economic productive unit. The autonomous and closed Bulgarian family, consisting of several generations, had the character of an association where women worked on equal terms with men. The traditional Bulgarian woman did not follow the pattern of the European woman, who was subjected to a more rigid patriarchal form of social organization. Bulgarian women shared the heavy farm work with men and at the same time were conscious of their importance and power in the immediate social environment (Dinkova, 1978).

Women's education and the role of the university in rebuilding Bulgaria

The cultural shift towards Europe at the beginning of the nineteenth century was reflected in the field of education by the borrowing of European experience and educational models and, in particular, the incorporation of conceptions of women's education. A number of Bulgarian intellectuals published articles in favour of women's education, resulting, in 1840, in the establishment of the first (non-religious) public primary girls' school in Bulgaria. Before the Liberation in 1878 their number had increased to 100. At this time Bulgarian women and men received their secondary and higher education abroad.

A belated enlightenment commenced as the University of Sofia aimed to train teachers for secondary schools and to educate government officials who were desperately needed by the restored state. During the early years of the new nation key positions in higher education and science were occupied by Bulgarian men who had received their higher education in Germany (then the science centre of Europe), Russia, Austria and Switzerland. These men transferred the Western European model of organization of higher education to Bulgaria and, along with it, opinions about the place of women in science (Arnaoudov, 1939).

Women's struggle to enter higher education

Although European women paved the way for Bulgarian women's access to higher education, the European woman of culture was traditionally from the upper classes and, for her, education was not necessarily connected with professional employment. In contrast, Bulgarian women entered education and science with vocational goals.

Seven years after the university was founded, several women teachers sent applications to the National Assembly and the Ministry of Education, asking to be admitted as students to the university, only to have their applications turned down. The next year 600 women petitioned Parliament requesting that the admission of women to Sofia University be regulated by law. The fight for women's admission to higher education received wide public support.

Arguments against women's admission to the University were not unlike those used in other countries. One argument, however, was peculiar to Bulgarian conditions. Among educated men there was already a discernible trend towards the formation of an intellectual proletariat and some feared that they would now have their circumstances exacerbated by competition from women with diplomas. Nevertheless, women won the right of admission to higher education in 1901 despite opposition from government and university authorities. In 1901, 12 women enrolled in the faculty of history and philology, and four in the faculty of physics and mathematics. By 1912 these figures rose to 428 in history and philology and 113 in physics and mathematics (Arnaoudov, 1939).

By the end of the Second World War Bulgarian women represented 23 per cent of those with higher education, 17 per cent of medical doctors, 39 per cent of dentists, 53 per cent of pharmacists, 54 per cent of teachers, 10 per cent of agronomists and 3 per cent of architects (Dinkova, 1978). However, in higher education the picture was quite different. In the teaching staff of Sofia University for the first half century of its existence (1888–1938) there was only one woman associate professor and only 25 women assistant professors and lecturers, all of whom were appointed on short-term contracts (*Almanac of the Kliment Ohridski University of Sofia 1888–1939*, 1988).

During this period (in 1937) Bulgarian women were also given a limited regional and national franchise (*Gazette*, 1937). Complete equality of rights between the sexes (including full electoral rights for women) was guaranteed by law in 1944 (*Gazette*, 1944).

Women's position in Bulgaria after the Second World War

Following the Soviet Union, equality of rights between the sexes was guaranteed by law. Bulgarian women had equal rights with men including equality before the law, an equal right to work and equal political rights. In Bulgaria women traditionally had composed nearly half of the labour force. Of the total employed in 1965 the percentage of women was 41, in 1975, 47, and in 1989, 50. Bulgaria ranked third in Europe (after the former USSR and the former German Democratic Republic) in the percentage of employed women (Ilieva, 1991). This situation was due to the great demand for labour, the characteristic traits of the traditional Bulgarian woman who always was treated as a 'worker' and saw herself as such, and the legally guaranteed right of women to work on equal terms with men. In addition this was made possible by the well-developed system of nursery schools. In 1980 there were an average of 92 places per 100 children applying for the kindergartens and in 1986–7 the number of places increased to 99 per 100 children.

However, figures alone do not tell much if they are not analysed in a cultural context. According to official propaganda, the Bulgarian woman has rights that should be the envy of women in the West – she has possibilities for professional fulfilment in every sphere of social, cultural and political life. While the problem of the Western woman in the 1970s was to escape from her home and to gain opportunities for a professional career, Bulgarian women already comprised 43 per cent of the labour force. However, women's issues were never raised in the totalitarian state. There were no women's movements in Bulgaria or Eastern Europe. According to the party line, the existence of a feminist movement in Bulgaria was made meaningless by the institutionalized equality guaranteed by the constitution. Western feminist movements were considered identical with 'sexual licence'.

The essence of a totalitarian state is the total dominance of the state over the individual and full control over all forms of social activity. From this point of view, the policy of full employment of women meant, in practice, increased possibilities for state control. It also functioned as partial compensation for the absence of a social security system. In a totalitarian state all persons, including women, who do not 'practise socially useful labour' are regarded as parasites, as immoral, degraded people, and are stigmatized. Consequently many women's lives were overburdened by employment, hours spent standing daily in food lines, and the obligation to take care of the daily tasks of the household and children.

The structure of Bulgarian universities after the Second World War

Since professional women were better situated than others, Bulgarian women flocked to higher education and science. The proportions of female to male graduate and undergraduate students were approximately equal. At the faculty level, women represented about one-third of the staff in universities and institutions of higher learning and about one-third of the scientists of the Bulgarian Academy of Sciences. Here again the principle 'equal pay for equal work' operated, so that academic women received exactly the same salary as their male colleagues at the same level of the faculty hierarchy.

It would thus appear that empirical data confirm that sex equality existed in higher education and science. However, neither judicial definitions nor figures alone have any relevance when the hidden mechanisms of the social system are examined. A rather grim reality is hidden behind the official policy and data.

A shift of the scientific centre from Western European countries/Germany to the Soviet Union occurred when the Soviets imposed their rule over Bulgaria and other Eastern European countries. It would perhaps be more correct to say that there was a shift in both the scientific and political centres. For nearly half a century the USSR determined the norms of the scientific community in Bulgaria and other Eastern European countries. As part of the 'scientific periphery', Bulgaria sent students in large numbers to the USSR for advanced degrees, particularly in the natural sciences and technology.

Generally speaking, the organization of higher education and the Academy of Sciences follows the 1930s Soviet model.

The strategy of strict government planning and control was true in higher education and science as well as in other spheres of life. It was not the universities but the state (a so-called 'government commission') which controlled the number of students who entered higher education. Market forces did not distribute the educated work-force; rather, the operative principle was that every graduate had a guaranteed work place based on yearly labour estimates. This, together with the absence of alternatives for professional and intellectual expression and a condescending attitude towards the intelligentsia as a whole, explains why young people flocked to higher education.

In addition to financing the teaching of students, the state also gave the majority of them grants. The number receiving grants increased from 31 per cent in 1970 to 55 per cent in 1989. The entire organizational structure of the university, including funding, hiring of staff and even curricular content was regulated and controlled by the state. (The usual duration of Bulgarian higher education is four and a half to five years, ending with a defence of a thesis and 'state' examinations.)

Student enrolment and hidden mechanisms of discrimination

Table 4.1 shows an increasing number of women enrolling in higher education; in 1960, women comprised 40 per cent of the student body. Since 1970 women students have constituted a higher proportion of the student body than male students. In 1987 they reached a high of 56 per cent.

Table 4.2 shows that women students have dominated at the universities, teacher training and economic institutions since the 1980s, and they are near parity with male students at medical and technical institutes. Upon the basis of these statistics it has often been maintained by the Bulgarian government that a trend towards the 'feminization' of higher education is proof that there is no discrimination against women with respect to their enrolment in higher education.

Since the demise of Communism, quotas based on parents' occupation, region and ethnic background have been eliminated. However, I will argue that the system still allows hidden discrimination against women with respect to their entrance into higher education.

Although the Constitution declares that education is free, the Bulgarian system of higher education cannot be characterized as 'open'. Every year there are about 90,000 candidates, but only 25,000 to 30,000 are admitted. Acceptance is determined by results on anonymous competitive examinations. Following the Soviet pattern, a central governmental body decides on the number of students to be admitted to each institute in each specialty. It also determines a 'quota for men' and a 'quota for women' for every speciality. Usually the ratio is 50:50, but in some technical institutes the proportion is 60:40 and in Dramatic Arts 70:30 (men:women). The quotas are not constant, but change every year. Practically, this means that women compete against women and men against men. The examination is, of

Table 4.1 *Total number of higher educational institutions, students, students per 10,000 population and graduates in Bulgaria (1960–92)*

	1960	%F	1970	%F	1976	%F	1980	%F	1987	%F	1991	%F	1992	%F
Number of higher educational institutions	20		26		26		28		30		40		40	
Students – Total Female	54,965 21,834	39.7	89,331 43,508	48.7	103,662 55,480	53.5	85,330 45,363	53.2	116,407 64,034	55.0	144,043 75,362	52.3	154,714 87,267	56.0
Students per 10,000 population	70		105		118		96		130					
Women students per 10,000 women	55		102		126		102		141					
Graduates	5,789		12,409		16,556		19,072		16,929		22,825			

Source: Statistical guide for higher education in Bulgaria, Sofia, 1989; *Higher and College Education*, National Institute of Statistics, 1992, Sofia.

Table 4.2 Student enrolment by type of higher education institution

Type of institution		Number (total and female)								Relative Share (total and female, percent)		
		1980	%F	1985	%F	1987	%F	1991	%F	1980	1985	1987
Universities and Teacher Training	– Total	19,898	68.2	26,955	73.6	36,569	72.9	50,644	67.9	21.8	26.5	31.4
	– Female	13,578		19,834		26,650		34,372		29.9	36.8	41.6
Economics	– Total	14,162	58.4	15,324	52.0	17,384	50.9	22,538	54.3	16.6	15.1	14.9
	– Female	8,273		7,965		8,859		12,244		18.3	14.8	13.9
Technical	– Total	30,059	38.7	35,845	43.6	41,668	45.3	47,795	43.6	35.2	35.3	35.8
	– Female	11,623		15,643		18,855		20,840		25.6	29.1	29.4
Medicine	– Total	12,218	60.0	12,539	45.3	11,566	48.6	9,183	50.9	14.3	12.4	9.9
	– Female	7,321		5,685		5,624		4,676		16.1	10.6	8.8
Agriculture	– Total	3,815	47.7	3,693	68.9	6,212	40.2	5,230	42.4	4.5	5.6	5.4
	– Female	1,818		2,548		2,497		2,217		4.0	4.7	3.9
Arts	– Total	3,110	49.7	2,618	51.4	3,008	51.5	2,152	45.3	3.7	2.6	2.6
	– Female	1,545		1,345		1,549		974		3.4	2.5	2.4
Total	– Total	85,330	53.2	101,507	53.0	116,407	55.0	144,043	52.3	100.0	100.0	100.0
	– Female	45,363		53,816		64,034		75,362		100.0	100.0	100.0

Source: Statistical guide for higher and college education in Bulgaria, Sofia, 1989. *Higher and College Education*, National Institute of Statistics, Sofia, 1992.

course, the same. Because the applications of women are more numerous and they generally score higher than men on the examinations, their competition is more severe.

Thus, the statistical data in Table 4.1 show, in essence, equality of end results and not equality of opportunity. There is clearly discrimination against women regarding their entrance to higher education. The formula, *equality of end results with unequal conditions at the start*, is reproduced at every step in the career of academic women.

The gender gap in postgraduate education

As in the Soviet model of higher education there are two levels after completing a first university degree – a postgraduate degree and a doctorate. After defending a dissertation on both these levels, one receives the scientific degree of Candidate of Science and Doctor of Science, respectively. The doctorate of science is rarely taken. The Bulgarian Academy of Sciences and other academies provide educational opportunities for postgraduate study, along with other institutes for higher education.

Table 4.3 shows that at the postgraduate level one can no longer speak about the 'feminization' of science, since the proportion between the sexes appears more balanced. In 1987 the male:female ratio among postgraduate students was 57:43; among those who received an advanced degree it was 55:45. In the fields of medicine and humanities there still appears to be a higher proportion of women. Here the picture reflects the end result, and not conditions at the start.

As at the undergraduate level, the number of postgraduate students in different specialities in the universities and academies is centrally determined. Universities and academies are obliged to employ the number of postgraduate students they 'order' after these students defend their dissertations. Thus market forces do not determine the distribution of the workforce with diplomas. Without a postgraduate degree students cannot pursue a scientific career but can only act as assistant lecturers or research associates if they are lucky enough to win the competition for those positions.

At the postgraduate level there are no quotas, but the general formula outlined for undergraduate students is reproduced in a more complicated fashion. Theoretically the candidate with the best examination results obtains a three-year grant at the university or academy. In that period he or she must write a dissertation. However, in the totalitarian state several other 'written' and 'non-written' forms of selection were mandatory, and in some cases preceded the 'scientific' selection.

A basic principle for selection in the past was the 'class-party check-up'. The intelligentsia were 'tolerated' because they had to pass through several mandatory 'check-ups' in order to filter out those who were themselves, or whose families were, 'foreign to the regime'. Even if such people did succeed in getting a position, every step of their professional development was carefully monitored by the state party. Those deemed 'unsuitable' got stuck at a low level and remained there until retirement.

After the 'party' and 'genetic' selection came a 'gender selection,' which has been retained to the present day, although this does not appear in any

Table 4.3 *Postgraduate students trained in Bulgaria and abroad during the period 1980–87 having a scientific degree in Bulgaria and abroad during 1987, by gender and discipline*

Science Branches		Number of trained postgraduate students						Number of postgraduate students with a scientific degree			
		1980	%F	1985	%F	1986	%F	1987	%F	1987	%F
Technical	– Total	800	43.6	1,113	32.0	1,256	32.4	700	30.3	89	33.7
	– Female	349		356		407		212		30	
Medicine	– Total	102	100.0	85	64.7	123	52.0	85	52.9	14	57.1
	– Female	102		55		64		45		8	
Natural	– Total	453	54.8	691	39.1	763	39.7	714	41.0	64	39.1
	– Female	248		270		303		293		25	
Agriculture	– Total	109	60.6	136	45.6	163	46.4	132	49.2	20	50.0
	– Female	66		62		71		65		10	
Humanities	– Total	541	66.2	727	53.0	759	56.8	721	56.0	71	57.8
	– Female	358		391		431		404		41	
Totals	– Total	2,005	56.3	2,752	41.2	3,054	41.8	2,352	43.3	258	44.6
	– Female	1,128		1,134		1,276		1,019		115	

Source: Statistical guide for higher and college education in Bulgaria, Sofia, 1989.

official document. Though its effect was smaller than those of 'party' and 'genetic' selections, the chances for a woman to become professionally prominent in the humanities were zero if she were not a party member or a protégé of someone in a powerful position. Even today, a woman is always accepted first as a woman and second as a professional in scientific circles (Domozetov, 1985).

The three forms of 'non-scientific selection' were less powerful in the natural sciences and technology. Probably this is an additional reason why so many women specialized in these fields (see Table 4.3). The so-called 'exact' sciences, with their more specific criteria, provided better chances for equal conditions at the start, and better opportunities for professional development. These fields have also been given the highest priority in the USSR and Eastern Europe.

Women faculty

Table 4.4 shows that women academics represent a third of university staff. Although there are variations according to speciality, on average only 9 per cent of women were full professors and 22 per cent associate professors in 1987. More recent data show a slight increase, up to 12 per cent women professors and up to 25 per cent women associate professors (National Institute of Statistics, 1992).

The mechanisms for obtaining academic promotion are similar to those for postgraduate study. 'Non-scientific selection' criteria are important because the positions of associate and full professor are positions of power in the faculty hierarchy.

Although the percentage of women students in undergraduate and postgraduate education is substantial, the percentage of women who succeed in obtaining the ranks of associate and full professor is small. It appears that the difficulties academic women in Bulgaria have in reaching top positions are not unlike those of Western women, though many of the mechanisms differ.

Further thoughts on higher education and science in the transition period in Bulgaria

The process of transition in post-totalitarian Bulgaria could be defined as contradictory and indeterminate. The deep crisis in all social institutions has had a particularly strong impact on the educational system, which is facing a virtual collapse.

The key terms of the transitional period are *privatization* and *decommunization*. The changes towards a market economy and privatization in the economic sector affect the educational system, since paid education has been widely introduced at all educational levels. Since 1991 primary language schools, colleges and three formerly free universities (including the American University in Bulgaria) have been requiring tuition fees. Table 4.5 indicates that the percentage of paid education students has increased from 35 in 1991 to 47 in 1992.

Table 4.4 *Gender stratification in academe during 1987–8 in types of institutes of higher education and scientific titles*

Type of Institution		Total	%F	Full Professor	%F	Associate Professor	%F	Assistant Professor	%F	Lecturer	%F
Universities and Teacher Training	– Total	3,091	42.2	238	7.6	628	28.3	1,407	54.5	818	41.7
	– Female	1,304		18		178		767		341	
Economics	– Total	1,181	36.4	103	3.9	282	19.9	551	37.6	245	66.5
	– Female	430		4		56		207		163	
Technical	– Total	5,631	25.5	351	4.8	1,158	16.2	2,352	29.6	1,770	30.1
	– Female	1,433		17		187		696		533	
Medicine	– Total	4,224	46.5	187	13.5	387	23.5	2,416	48.8	1,234	54.0
	– Female	1,962		25		91		1,180		666	
Agriculture	– Total	537	28.9	116	7.8	115	20.9	219	26.9	123	51.2
	– Female	155		9		24		59		63	
Arts	– Total	916	51.1	113	22.1	126	38.9	159	50.3	518	60.6
	– Female	468		25		49		80		314	
Sports	– Total	325	28.9	24	16.7	57	35.1	162	24.7	82	36.6
	– Female	94		4		20		40		30	
Total	– Total	15,941	36.7	1,132	9.0	2,753	22.0	7,266	41.7	4,790	44.1
	– Female	5,846		102		605		3,029		2,110	

Source: Statistical guide for higher and college education in Bulgaria, Sofia, 1989.

Table 4.5 *Student admission in 1991–2, 1992–3 and percentage of paid education students*

	1991	%F	1992	%F
Admission				
Total	33,388	59.7	41,511	63
Female	19,923		26,150	
Percentage of paid education students out of total	35		47	

Source: *Higher and College Education*, National Institute of Statistics, Sofia, 1992.

Though statistics do not track paid education by gender, the 3 per cent increase in total female university admissions may at least partially be explained by the expansion of paid education, which has increased by 12 per cent in the same period.

The transitional period in Bulgaria is characterized by a strong wave of emigration; between 1989 and 1991 400,000 people left Bulgaria. Unofficial estimates indicate that these represent one-quarter of the research staff of the Bulgarian Academy of Sciences between 31 and 40 years of age. Thus Bulgaria is witnessing a great *brain drain*.

Drastic cutbacks in the university and research institute budgets will certainly also entail *freezing* of scientific activity as the access of Bulgarian researchers to international meetings, conferences, contacts, etc. is limited. Given the dynamic development of modern science, even a year of inaction can be crucial for a scientist. Therefore, in the transitional period Bulgaria faces the dilemmas of *brain drain* and *frozen brain* (Sretenova, 1993).

The third major problem of the transitional period is unemployment. (It must be underlined that unemployment data become out of date each month.) According to official statistics 15.6 per cent of the country's work force is unemployed. The situation is particularly acute among specialists with higher education in engineering and technology and especially among those who are under 30. Women of the intellectual professions are not exempt from the general rule; about 57 per cent of the total unemployed with higher education are women. The most severely affected are women with technical specialties (40 per cent of the total unemployed are women with higher education), followed by those with university degrees in economics, teaching, etc. (Mikhova, 1991).

It is clear, then, that higher education and science are subject to a subtle pressure in the transitional period: on one hand, there is fiscal stagnation, on the other a flow of specialists towards the private sector and foreign countries. In this situation it is almost impossible to predict the future professional opportunities of women in educational and scientific institutions.

Conclusion

The major issue of current Bulgarian society is to develop a *survival strategy;*

this edges out gender problems. Unfortunately, when all is said and done, the problem boils down to individual and not to social survival; the current brain drain has been accompanied by a religious, political and economic fragmentation of the Bulgarian community.

5. Higher education in the People's Republic of China

Grace C L Mak

SUMMARY: The success of the Communist revolution in 1949 brought about significant expansion in women's access to higher education. However, inertia followed the initial spur and women never exceeded about a third of enrolment in undergraduate studies and a fifth in graduate school. Their representation is heavy in arts and humanities but light in science and technology. A similar pattern is found in academe, where, in addition, women are disproportionately represented in low ranks. Discrimination at the institutional level and in daily practice, which is shaped by conventional gender role stereotypes, has blocked the actualization of women's full potential in higher education.

Introduction

The People's Republic of China (hereafter China), occupying a vast area in Asia, is home to a population of 11.6 billion, of which 48.6 per cent is female, and 74 per cent is rural (Guojia, 1992). It is one of the oldest civilizations in the world. For 4,000 years, from the twenty-first century BC to the early twentieth century AD, the country was run on a cyclical dynastic pattern. Modern ideas, including women's rights, began to develop in the nineteenth century and China became a republic in 1911, when revolutionaries overthrew the last emperor of the Qing dynasty. During this time the weakness of China prompted its intellectuals to search for ways to strengthen the nation. One of the ways, according to reformers Liang Qichao (1873–1929) and Kan Yuwei (1858–1927), was to educate women.

Chinese values and attitudes have been heavily influenced by Confucianism. Originally one of many competing schools of thought in the Eastern Zhou dynasty (770–221 BC), Confucianism has among its central themes the necessity of hierarchy among social groups and the importance of the subjects' loyalty to the emperor. It was adopted as the official political ideology from the Han dynasty (206 BC–220 AD) onwards and since then has had an important role in shaping Chinese national culture. The Confucian concept of appropriate behaviour for women is captured in such sayings as 'women without knowledge are virtuous'. In this tradition women are relegated to the domestic sphere, thus making them economically dependent on men. The extent to which this idea was translated into reality hinged on a woman's social class and geographical background. Women from poor families always had to work for income; it was a sign of affluence for women not to have to work. Today some men still consider it a loss of 'face' for wives to work for wages.

The status of women emerged from a non-issue to a social concern in the early twentieth century when educated men, and later educated women as well, began to fight for women's rights. Improving women's status, particularly freeing them from forced arranged marriages and allowing them to participate in the paid labour force, were important issues (among others) widely discussed in journals and the press. While such rights were granted in government policy documents, they had not actually been implemented. Although the women's movement had begun to take shape, it never went beyond a small urban élite.

During the same period, nascent industrialization acted as a catalyst to change women's social status. Factories in major cities like Shanghai and Tianjin began to employ meaningful numbers of women, who had become a significant social group by the 1930s. Employment gave them economic independence; many of them delayed marriage to their mid-20s. Divorce began to appear and although the numbers were small they signalled an alternative lifestyle hitherto unknown to Chinese women. Political events also spurred women's involvement in the public sphere. During the Sino-Japanese War (1937–45), men joined the army and women's labour filled their vacancies in the economy. Thus the combined effects of the women's movement, industrialization and political events in the first half of the century provided the impetus for changing the Chinese woman's role from traditional to modern (Mak, 1991).

There had been no tradition of educating women in Confucian China. A route for male social mobility (Ho, 1964), education was often deemed not only unnecessary but undesirable for women. Education for females consisted of training in domestic skills. In rare cases women, often from the aristocracy, were taught the classics, but educated women were not expected to assume a role in economic life.

Organized education for women was initiated by Christian missionaries when five ports were open for trading with the West after China's defeat by Britain in the Opium War in 1842. Such education was free and attracted boys and girls from very poor families. Missionary schools were to exert a great influence on the development of modern education in China (Lutz, 1971). This was a milestone in the history of education for females; girls' schools were set up by private indigenous groups in 1898 and by the government in 1907 (Mak, 1991). Education enabled women to seek employment even if they were not driven by economic need, as in the case of women in the professions and public service in the early decades of the century.

Early beginnings of women in higher education

The development of primary and secondary education generated a demand for higher education. Although modern government-sponsored higher education was introduced to China in 1898, for women it could only be sought abroad (Burton, 1912). As was the case in primary and secondary schooling, missionaries were pioneers in extending higher education to females. Coeducational Lingnan College in Guandong province first admitted women in 1905, and three women's colleges followed suit (Cheng, 1936). In 1912 a government edict called for the establishment of teachers' colleges for women; however not until 1919 did one appear. These colleges prepared women to teach in the expanding number of girls' secondary schools (*ibid.*).

In 1920 National Beijing University, the first modern government university in China, set a precedent for coeducational public higher education by admitting women (*Quanguo fulian*, 1986). However, higher education was accessible only to a very small upper stratum of the population, of which women were a tiny minority. Women were also distributed unevenly among the disciplines, concentrating on education and medicine. This was related directly to sex segregation in life outside the home. Girls' schools and female patients created the demand for women teachers and doctors (Lutz, 1971).

On this weak base women's participation in higher education was to soar. The impetus came from the Communist takeover in 1949 which brought about structural changes in education and many other facets of life in China.

The Communist revolution and the rise of women's status

The victory of the revolution enabled the Chinese Communist Party to extend its attempts at social transformation from the fragmented areas they had occupied before 1949 to the entire nation. A new constitution was promulgated, guaranteeing equality between males and females in education, marriage, employment and politics. The marriage laws of 1950 and 1953 institutionalized freedom of marriage for women and declared polygamy illegal. Newly established minimum ages for marriage (18 for women and 20 for men) aimed at preventing child marriage. In the mid-1950s fertility was encouraged, but since 1978 the state has imposed a rigid 'one child per couple' policy which has reportedly resulted in the widespread abortion of female foetuses. These low birth rates combined with the availability of daycare centres (in urban areas) has freed women, enabling them to participate in the economic sphere. In rural areas agrarian reform (in 1950) granted women equal title to land in the hope of encouraging women's support for the new government. However, women's land still came under the control of the male head of household, and divorced women and unmarried women were barred from obtaining land (Johnson, 1983).

Less educated women still encounter difficulties in their attempts to find factory work or other unskilled labour. By contrast, the entry of educated women to the professions has been facilitated by an acute shortage of skilled labour. Women have made least progress in the political sphere. While they are rather active at the grassroots level, such as the street committee, they are not visible at higher levels. In sum, the revolution has consolidated and expanded the struggle for equal rights (Mak, 1991); however, the gains made by women took place only when male interests had already been satisfied.

Communist ideals were mediated by traditional Chinese patriarchy in such a way that liberation for women seldom achieved prominence as a cause in its own right.

Women in higher education since 1949

As in most countries, the Chinese education system operates at the primary, secondary and tertiary levels. The compulsory basic law of 1986 aimed at guaranteeing a nine-year basic education for all school-aged children. Although full implementation of the law remains elusive, almost all children have at least a primary education. Upper secondary education takes four forms: grammar school, specialized school (including technical education and teacher training), agricultural vocational school and workers' training school. At this level girls comprised some 45 per cent of the enrolment in 1991 (*Guojia tongjiju*, 1992). At the tertiary level the increase in females is less impressive than at lower levels.

Students

Since 1949 higher education has generally been expanding, notwithstanding fluctuations due to shifting political and educational policies. The Great Leap Forward (1958–9), a rash expansionist experiment, saw a great increase in higher education enrolments, only to be followed by contractions in the aftermath of the campaign in the early 1960s. A more devastating campaign, the Cultural Revolution (1966–76) led to the closure of schools for two years (1966 to 1968) after which they gradually reopened. This was a period of chaos in China, as reflected by the absence of statistics on higher education enrolment. Since 1978 China has returned to pragmatism and stability, and higher education, like other aspects of life in China, has been characterized by growth. This erratic pattern is reflected in the absolute figures of female students in higher education (Table 5.1). In general, however, the Communist revolution put higher education within the grasp of women.

Table 5.1 shows that the increase in women's enrolment has been significant. A 30-fold increase (in absolute numbers) has been registered over the past four decades. This progress has been repeatedly cited by the government as an achievement of Chinese Communism; however, the picture thus presented is incomplete. In relative terms, women's share has less than doubled, from a fifth to a third of the total, and this percentage has not increased for 20 years. Thus progress has really been rather modest, especially considering that educational access is supposedly non-discriminatory.

It is clear that in recent years institutions of higher education have tended to discriminate against female applicants. All things being equal, female applicants are rejected at a higher rate than males; those who are admitted have to have higher scores than the male candidates. The phenomenon has become so widespread that it has been the subject of repeated reports in the press (*Zhongguo funubao*, 22 September 1986; 18 December 1989; *Renmin ribao*, 23 February; 16 June 1990). Admissions personnel attempt to justify their

Table 5.1 *Women's enrolment in regular institutions of higher education in China, 1947–91 (in 10,000s)*

Year	No.	%
1949	2.3	19.8
1950	2.9	21.2
1951	3.5	22.5
1953	5.5	25.3
1956	10.0	24.6
1957	10.3	23.3
1958	15.4	23.3
1959	18.3	22.6
1960	23.6	24.5
1961	23.4	24.7
1962	21.0	25.3
1964	17.6	25.7
1965	18.1	26.9
1973	9.7	30.8
1974	14.5	33.8
1975	16.3	32.6
1976	18.7	33.0
1977	18.2	29.0
1978	20.7	24.1
1979	24.6	24.1
1980	26.8	23.4
1981	31.2	24.4
1984	40.0	28.6
1985	51.1	30.0
1987	64.7	33.0
1988	68.9	33.4
1989	70.2	33.7
1990	69.5	33.7
1991	68.2	33.4

Source: *Zhonghua quanguo*, 1991, p. 168; *Guojia tongjiju*, 1992, p. 719.

The figures include enrolment in first degree programmes and post-secondary non-degree programmes.

behaviour by pointing to new constraints in the employment of women in the economy.

Since the early 1980s local governments and hiring units have had some discretion when school or university graduates are recommended to them, and this has often resulted in discrimination against women graduates even when the latter were academically sound (*Zhongguo funubao*, 27 February 1985; 10 August 1988; 6 June 1990). Those who make hiring decisions give assorted reasons for their behaviour, most of which are gender based and speculative. Some feel that since women's conjugal and maternal roles distract them from giving full attention to work, female job applicants should be rejected. Public opinion on this issue tends to be contradictory. Intending to be critical of discrimination against women, the press often attributes it (among other reasons) to a lack of determination on the part of women to strengthen their own abilities. This is a classic 'blame the victim' approach, which has damaging consequences for women's self-esteem; it also provides a convenient excuse for institutions of higher education to discourage the admittance of women. While the government recognizes the problem, it does not make it a priority. These factors undoubtedly explain the lack of a percentage increase in female enrolment in institutions of higher learning in the past two decades.

At the graduate level, women constitute 12 per cent of those (16,717) who completed the master's degree and 19 per cent of those (75,167) working towards it and a mere 7 per cent of those (287) who completed their doctoral studies and 8 per cent of those working towards it (calculated from Zhonghua quanguo, 1991). Satisfactory explanations for these low percentages are not easily available. Discrimination in admitting women at this level is a possibility, although it is not widely reported. Occasional reports of hiring units rejecting females who have completed graduate education are just beginning to surface. Another possible explanation is cultural. Many Chinese women 'marry up' to men who are older, better educated and better employed. Since only a very tiny segment of the population has graduate education, many women worry that 'too much' education may diminish their marriage prospects. Such gender role stereotyping does not permit women to fulfil their own potential. Married women who may desire graduate education tend to give priority to their husbands (Mak, 1991). Women fare equally poorly in overseas education. They reached a maximum of 23 per cent of Chinese students sent abroad to study (usually at graduate level) in 1976 and 13 per cent in 1981 (calculated from Zhonghua quanguo, 1991).

Available data on female students in higher education are heavy on numbers, reflecting the Chinese definition of equality as mainly numerical. Data on the distribution of women across various disciplines are scattered. What little we know suggests that women tend to dominate in disciplines deemed suitable for them, such as education (Zhongguo funubao, 14 December 1988). Chinese stereotypes of what 'suits' women seem to have been revived in the present era of opening to the West, after decades of revolutionary challenge. Women are assumed to be talented in languages, education, fashion design and food science, and tertiary level courses for them are designed in that light (Guangming ribao, 26 March 1989). This uneven distribution is found also among Chinese students pursuing studies abroad. In 1987, women made up 19 per cent of the total (3,178), but 45 per cent of those in fine arts (29), 36 per cent in liberal arts (708), 32 per cent in education (129), 18 per cent in medicine (299), 13 per cent in engineering (602), 12 per cent in pure sciences (633), and 11 per cent in agriculture (198) (Zhonghua quanguo, 1991). Gender stratification among students is mirrored in the vertical and horizontal stratification of the faculty.

Faculty

The social status of college faculty can be assessed in two ways. While college faculty command respect for the knowledge and expertise they possess, they are never among the best paid in China. Their ranking has dropped further on the national salary scale in the current reform era as the average salary of workers has soared (*China Daily*, 9 November 1992).

Women comprise a minority of college faculty, but their representation has increased over time, as Table 5.2 demonstrates. At the beginning of the Communist era, women made up a mere 11 per cent of faculty at regular institutions of higher learning, but in 1991 they constituted nearly 30 per cent. In 1988 females constituted 10 per cent of all college faculty of the age of 60 or above, but 34 per cent of those aged 30 or below (*Zhonghua quanguo*, 1991), showing that expanded access to higher education since 1949 has benefited women.

While the increase has been substantial, the figures beg further investigation. A breakdown of statistics by rank reveals that there is little room at the top for women. For example, of all faculty at institutions of higher education in 1988, 28 per cent were women, but they made up 34 per cent of the teaching assistants, 36 per cent of the instructors, 29 per cent of the lecturers, 19 per cent of the associate professors, and only 11 per cent of the full professors (calculated from *Zhonghua quanguo*, 1991). This pattern of unequal distribution by rank is found in institutions of higher education in major

Table 5.2 *Women as a percentage of faculty at regular institutions of higher education in China, 1950–91 (in 10,000s)*

Year	No.	%
1950	0.2	11.0
1954	0.7	17.6
1956	1.1	19.2
1957	1.4	20.4
1958	1.6	19.1
1959	2.0	20.2
1961	3.4	21.2
1962	3.0	21.1
1965	2.8	20.6
1973	3.0	22.7
1974	3.2	23.5
1975	3.8	24.4
1976	4.1	24.7
1977	5.0	26.8
1978	5.2	25.4
1980	6.3	25.3
1983	7.8	25.9
1985	9.2	26.7
1991	11.6	29.7

Source: *Zhonghua quanguo*, 1991, p. 174; *Guojia tongjiju*, 1992, p. 719.

cities like Shanghai (Zhu and Jiang, 1991; Wang, 1991) and also in other skilled professions in China (*Guojia kewei*, 1986).

Graduate schools continue to employ few female faculty. In 1988 women faculty made up 8 per cent of advisers for master's students and 3 per cent of advisers for doctoral students (*Zhonghua quanguo*, 1991). The disparity between the numbers of women doctoral advisers and female full professors reflects the difficulty that women encounter at the top levels of higher education. This disparity may be due in part to discrimination by the State Council, which acts as a gatekeeper. However, since many women faculty also suffer discrimination from their male superiors (which will be discussed later in this section), the latter also almost certainly accounts for some of the difference.

Academic research in China is conducted in research centres in tertiary institutions as well as in separate institutes such as the prestigious Chinese Academy of Sciences and the Chinese Academy of Social Sciences. Women constituted 28 per cent in the former group in 1988, which paralleled their representation in tertiary teaching. Administrators tend to assign supportive roles in teaching and research to women and leadership roles to men. For example, of 170 research projects conducted at Central China Normal University in 1987, women acted as principal investigators for only 8 projects (4 per cent) (Wang, 1991). This situation adversely affects women's prospects for promotion because research and publication are weighted more heavily than teaching. While women faculty are found to be competent in teaching, they lag behind in research and publications (*ibid.*) for which they are not given equal opportunities.

In contemporary China, science and technology courses are emphasized over arts and humanities because of an official development policy focusing on heavy industry. Women constitute a minority of students and subsequently of professionals in science and technology. However, the perceived advantages of these two fields are weakening, with courses like English, computer science and economics becoming more popular because they tend to lead to more lucrative jobs today. In 1986 women made up 30 per cent of scientific researchers. Inequality in ranking is also evident. For example, at the Chinese Academy of Sciences women occupied 17, 30 and 36 per cent of senior, intermediate and beginning positions, respectively. At the uppermost echelon of the same Academy, women are rare. For example, of 379 members of the academic committee (*xuebu weiyuan*) in 1984, women were a mere 4 per cent (*Guojia kewei*, 1986).

The low proportion of women is partially due to the retirement system. Until recently the compulsory retirement age, except for those in top positions, was 60 for men and 55 for women. Originally intended to protect female manual workers (*Zhongguo funubao*, 21 September 1990), this law has met with resistance from many female professionals because women after the age of 50 enjoy greater freedom from family obligations and are likely to desire more activity. Retirement at 55 drastically reduces the number of female professionals. Of 170,000 women with senior professional titles, eg, engineer, professor, associate professor and researcher, a recent study found that 24 per cent were approaching retirement (*China Daily*, 25 February 1991).

A 1990 regulation entitled senior professional women to postpone retirement to the age of 60 (*Zhongguo funu*, n.9, 1990), but it was found that top management manipulated other regulations so that the effect of the new decree was nullified. For instance, a government department exercised its newly gained discretion in hiring senior professionals to keep male professionals and fire their female colleagues who had reached age 55, although they were reported to be in good health and had demonstrated competence in work (*Zhongguo funubao*, 6 July 1992). Therefore it is clear that regulations alone cannot always defend women's rights.

An unequal gender-based division of labour at home also contributes importantly to the low rank held by most women in the education hierarchy. The increase in women's participation in education and the economy has not been accompanied by a fundamental change of the responsibility pattern at home. An academic woman typically marries at the age of 25.6 and gives birth to her child at 27 (Wang, 1991); childrearing overlaps with the early phase of her career. The academic woman spends more time than her male counterpart on household chores. She spends 4.4 hours daily on housework during the week and 9.1 hours on Sundays, compared with 3.5 hours and 6.7 hours respectively for men (*Zhonghua quanguo*, 1991). In addition, care for her parents or parents-in-law, when needed, falls on her shoulders. This explains why a recent survey indicates that the youngest group of male academics with senior titles were 26 years old, while their female counterparts were 44 years old (Wang, 1991). The problem is aggravated by insufficient technological support. Academics are so poorly paid that they can afford few electrical appliances and little domestic help. When women are finally freed from maternal obligations, they are made to retire earlier than men. The spirit of traditional patriarchy lives on, only it has a modern and Communist facade.

An ideology of pragmatism and efficiency guides China's current move toward the market economy. Tertiary institutions have to demonstrate they are cost-effective. Faculty are requested not only to conduct research and publish, but also to generate income-producing services and consulting which are not necessarily directly related to research and teaching. Given women's burdens at home and limited opportunities to perform in academe, their male colleagues are in a better position to meet the new demands and thus to contribute to their institutions' 'cost-effectiveness'.

Another strategy by which tertiary institutions demonstrate efficiency is to weaken job security. An academic appointment traditionally has been a lifetime sinecure, but this will gradually be replaced by a contract system. Similarly, promotion, which had been in part based on length of service, will now adopt measurable performance as its major criterion (*Zhongguo funubao*, 22 September 1986). These new standards work to the disadvantage of women, squeezing female faculty out to support services and administrative work, which are deemed inferior to research and teaching. In Wuhan, 80 per cent of librarians in tertiary institutions are women, many of whom have been redeployed from teaching (Wang, 1991). Although women's disadvantages in academe are largely caused by inequality at home and unfair stereotyping of their ability at work, the government and the public attribute it to women's own incompetence. The view that 'women should strengthen themselves' and 'overcome their inferiority complex in order to face up to new challenge' surfaces repeatedly in the press (*China Daily*, 9 March 1984; *Zhonghua quanguo*, 1984). Rather than tracing the root of the problem the victim is blamed.

Administrators

In 1988 women constituted 35 per cent (58,194) of administrators in institutions of higher learning (*Zhonghua quanguo*, 1991), but little information is available about their relative positions. In higher education, administrative work generally ranks lower than research and teaching, hence the reassignment of women faculty to administration; however, where administration represents power and status, for example presidency of tertiary institutions, women are few and far between. Xie Xide, the president of Fudan University in Shanghai, is a prominent exception.

Conclusion

Even with the initial dramatically expanded access to higher education, the advances Chinese women have made are slight given the long span of four decades. Their experience suggests that an increase in women's participation in higher education is not necessarily incremental. Government policy shapes it considerably. Its erratic pattern shows just how precarious any improvement in women's status is. Gains are easily taken away as policy changes. Although, despite adversity, the proportion of women students and faculty has increased, the discrimination they are facing has never been more blatant. If and when the experimental contract system in higher education hiring is fully adopted, the self-esteem and actual status of female faculty will be damaged. Moreover all this is taking place when the value of teaching and research at the tertiary level is declining in monetary terms and when means to accumulate wealth are expanding in the current economic boom in China. These trends will exacerbate the difficulty in recruiting quality faculty in tertiary institutions. Even under these conditions, however, as long as tertiary institutions have a choice, they favour men. The declining proportion of women researchers at the Chinese Academy of Sciences, from 43 per cent in 1980 to 35 per cent in 1985, is a warning signal (Mak, 1991).

6. 'Les femmes savantes' in France: under the glass ceiling[1]

Jacqueline Feldman and Annie Morelle

SUMMARY: The participation of women in the university and in research is investigated in the context of French culture, with its trend towards élitism and its ambivalence towards feminism. Data for students, university teachers, researchers and administrators show that women are found mainly in the humanities (especially language subjects) and least in the sciences (especially physics and technical subjects). An extreme hierarchy – the 'glass ceiling' effect – means that women are still the exception in the highest grades of prestige and power.

France: a country of oppositions

Abstract ideas beyond gender

The tradition of France inclines towards generous, abstract ideas, but often shows a lesser concern for their actual fulfilment. Some authors characterize it as being above all a 'republican' country, compared for example to Great Britain or the USA, which are judged to be more 'democratic', with an emphasis on the pragmatic organization of people. France is a centralized country, with an often heavy bureaucracy, where the ideas of universality and *laïcité*[2] are important. It is interesting to note that great and abstract ideas such as these (and others like *république, démocratie, nation, France*, to name but four) are all of the feminine grammatical gender. This seems to illustrate the contradictory position of women in France: praised in theory and too often ill-treated in fact, with a sometimes coarse, at other times subtle, misogyny.

Although the word 'feminism' originated in France, the feminist movement has always had difficulty being recognized in a country where a lively cultural tradition likes to emphasize, in the relationship between the two genders, the game of sexual seduction.

France is a country of harsh oppositions, with outbursts of violence leading to revolutions and, until recently, a strong class struggle, with a marked opposition between the right and the left. In this often dramatic climate, most of the time the women's issue appears secondary, depending upon the good will of the left to take up the cause of gender equality. Gender

56

equality, including the right to vote, was included in the constitution only at the end of World War II; it took some decades more to erase discrimination from the legal texts.

After World War II, the main feminist activities of women concerned the right to birth control, obtained in 1967, then to abortion, obtained in 1975 as a result of the women's liberation movement in the 1970s. This very lively and creative movement followed the strong and provocative student movement of May 1968. Spectacular actions succeeded in modifying, in a drastic manner, the mental and cultural atmosphere in France. The hypocritical 'double standard' of morality has now been eradicated and the right of women to lead their own lives established. We have at last come out of the nineteenth century with its militant misogyny, but gender roles are still marked, if in a more attenuated way. In 1974, the creation of a *Secrétariat d'Etat à la condition féminine* denoted the will to apply systematic state action to help promote real equality, although this ministry remains marginal and lacks financial resources.

Women at work: work ideology versus home tradition

Historians credit France with having been, in the last century, one of the countries in Europe which employed most women (Marchand and Thélot, 1991). In opposition to the 'bourgeois' ideology of the 'woman's place at home', an ideology of the working woman indeed also exists. The influence of Marxism, which insists upon material independence as the basis of women's emancipation, is clear. Another important ideological influence has been that of the republican *laïque* school, which takes charge of children for the major part of the week, thereby making working easier for mothers.

In 1989, women represented 42 per cent of the actively employed population; among women aged 25 to 54 years, 72 per cent were employed. Twenty-four per cent of employed women worked part time (versus 3.5 per cent of employed men); part-time jobs have been especially encouraged since 1982 (INSEE, 1991). There has been a *structural change* in women's employment during this century. At the beginning of the century, employed women were found mostly in agriculture; currently they are mostly (76 per cent) in the tertiary sector where, in 1989, they represented 52 per cent of the employees. A strong concentration characterizes women's occupational structure: in 1982, 20 occupations out of 455 in all accounted for 45 per cent of all working women, and most of these occupations are rather unskilled (INSEE, 1991).

Another aspect of the situation is the impressive increase in unemployment as a consequence of the crisis affecting economies in the West. Women are particularly affected; the unemployment figure for 1989 is 13 per cent for women and 7 per cent for men (INSEE, 1991). Until recently, women were considered as a reserve labour force for the economy as a whole. It is all the more remarkable then that the official discourse on unemployment (through the government or the media) no longer discriminates between the genders. The right for women to work seems to have been definitely won, at least among officials. This was symbolized by the passage, in 1983, of a law mandating occupational gender equality.

Access to responsibilities

France is gradually becoming used to competent women in jobs of responsibility. The proportion of female executives and professionals has increased in the last few decades, from 16 per cent in 1962 to 26 per cent in 1985 (INSEE, 1987). In 1981, one out of five women working was an executive (APEC, 1981). There is, however, for the same job, an overqualification of women in comparison to men. Women hold lower jobs and have lower salaries than men with the same qualifications. This phenomenon is reinforced by the 'choice' of women towards less recognized occupations.

Women are also very much under-represented on the political scene. Although they constitute 53 per cent of the voters, they are less than 6 per cent of *députés* (MPs) and mayors, and 4 per cent of senators. They are a little better represented at the local level (17 per cent of the Municipal councillors) (INSEE, 1991). At the national level, in 1992 there were five women out of approximately 40 members of the government.

Education: a feminine job

Education, an important part of the tertiary sector, has been completely coeducational in France for only 20 years. Education is provided mostly in state schools, although there are also private (mainly Catholic) schools, which are attended by about 17 per cent of children. In state schools, the *laïque* ideology has, until the present day, rather successfully facilitated the integration of successive immigrant waves.

Education is compulsory and free for children aged 6 to 16 years, but *écoles maternelles* (nursery schools) accept children from the age of 2. Most families take advantage of this opportunity: nearly all 3 year-olds and 35 per cent of 2 year-olds attend them. Ninety-six per cent of the teachers in *écoles maternelles* and 74 per cent of the teachers in primary school are female. At the age of 11, children enter secondary schools where 55 per cent of the teachers are female (*Minisètre de l'Education Nationale*, 1989). At 14, children are tracked along one of two paths: a shorter one, leading to technical qualifications, and a longer one leading to the *baccalauréat*. The short path is unfavourable to girls and leads them to traditional feminine jobs which are highly sensitive to unemployment; boys in the short path often receive useful technical training.

The *baccalauréat* provides entrance to the university and as such represents an important diploma. The increase of *bacheliers* in the last decades is an impressive phenomenon in French society, and shows the increased need for highly educated people. In 1945, 4 per cent of girls and 5 per cent of boys obtained the *baccalauréat*. In the 1980s, this figure rose to 30 per cent of girls and 22 per cent of boys (INSEE, 1991). There are different types of *baccalauréat*. The most prized, which affords the greatest number of opportunities, is the one where mathematics is decisive. A quarter of the boys and a tenth of the girls received this degree in 1988[3] (*Le Monde de l'Education*, 1990).

Higher education and research: a changing status

Two dual systems

The French higher education system is complex (Clark, 1986). Students can either study at the university or at the *Grandes Ecoles*.[4]

The *Grandes Ecoles* represent the élite path. Students are admitted after a competitive examination for which they prepare during two or three years of special classes. The most prestigious *Grandes Ecoles* are the *Ecole Normale Supérieure* (founded in 1795), the *Ecole Polytechnique* (1794), and the more recent *Ecole Nationale d'Administration* (1945). Although the first trains teachers and the second engineers, graduates from these schools can easily be found as higher executives throughout the financial, administrative and industrial worlds. The total number of students in the *Grandes Ecoles* is 90,000, compared to the 1,100,000 who comprise the total number of university students.

Research can take place either at the university or in a number of research centres. The most important research centre is the *Centre National de la Recherche Scientifique* (CNRS, created in 1939) with 11,100 researchers, approximately one-fifth of the number of university teachers (54,600) (CNRS, 1990; MEN, 1991b). Careers duplicate those in the university, although a university professor still enjoys higher prestige. There is close cooperation between CNRS and the universities. Other institutions also undertake teaching and/or research, such as the prestigious *Collège de France* created in 1543.

The university crisis

The democratization of higher education which took place in the 1960s signified for the university a kind of mutation (Feldman, 1984).[5] Once an élite system, with faith in progress, education and science, the university is having some difficulty keeping up its intellectual tradition while at the same time educating students who will mainly become employees and technicians. The climate has correspondingly changed inside universities and research institutions. Once a rather small and convivial milieu, it is now an increasing bureaucratized environment, where scholars are judged by their quantitative output and their 'visibility'.[6]

It is worthwhile noting that, in this climate of change, nobody seems to want to question the status of the *Grandes Ecoles*.

Women in higher education and research

The entrance of women into higher education

In the seventeenth century, Molière mocked women's aspiration to culture in his play *Les femmes savantes*. At that time women exercised their influence through the 'salons' they held (until the nineteenth century) which 'competed with academies for the attention of the learned' (Schiebinger, 1989).

In spite of this, until the latter part of the nineteenth century, higher education for women was exceptional and of a private character. From the end of the nineteenth century onwards, women started to seek university diplomas which would enable them to get jobs. In the general universities (sciences or humanities), there was no official exclusion,[7] but secondary schools did not teach girls mathematics, philosophy, Latin or Greek, which were necessary for the *baccalauréat*, which in turn was required for entrance to the universities. From 1905, private schools did prepare girls for the *baccalauréat*. A 'feminine' *baccalauréat* was created in 1919. Only since 1924 have the two genders had an identical syllabus for this basic examination.

The prestigious *Académies* have most strongly resisted the entrance of women. Marie Curie, in spite of her double Nobel prize, was never admitted to the *Académie des Sciences*, but the *Académie de Médecine* did accept her in 1922. The *Académie Française*, the oldest and the most prestigious of the *académies*, elected a woman, Marguerite Yourcenar, for the first time only in 1980.

Coeducation in the Grandes Ecoles

Entrance to the prestigious *Grandes Ecoles* has been obtained very progressively. In the *Ecole Polytechnique*, where mathematical subjects are essential, coeducation dates back to 1972.[8] The last *Grande Ecole* to accept girls was the military one, *Saint-Cyr* (founded in 1802, coeducational in 1983). The *Grandes Ecoles* founded during the present century were coeducational from the start.

The French tradition of single-sex schools led to teacher-training schools having a somewhat different history. The *Agrégation*, a competitive examination instituted in 1767, and open only to men until 1880, was separate until the 1970s. Only in 1986 were the two most prominent *Ecoles Normales Supérieures* (*Ulm* for the boys, and *Sèvres* for the girls) unified.

Gender stratification among the students

In the universities

A dominant feature of recent trends has been the constant and smooth progression of women in higher education since the beginning of the century (Baudelot and Establet, 1992). At that time, only 2.3 per cent of the students were girls; they are presently 54 per cent.

Two other dominant features are the very different distributions of women according to subject (horizontal stratification) and according to level of studies (vertical stratification).

In the traditional universities, women are predominant in the humanities (around 70 per cent) and in pharmacy (65 per cent), whereas they amount to only 36 per cent in sciences and odontology (dentistry). Approximate equality is achieved in law, economics and medicine (INSEE, 1991). Table 6.1 shows also the evolution of the choice of different subjects. One can note the increase in economics (16 per cent), in law (10 per cent), in medicine and dentistry (7 per cent) and a stagnation in science.

Table 6.1 *The percentage of female university students*

Years	Law	Economics	Literature	Sciences	Medicine	Pharmacy	Dentistry	Total
1974–5	45.7	32.6	68.5	36.4	39.4	62.2	29.0	48.9
1984–5	56.4	48.6	71.5	36.3	46.9	65.4	36.3	54.5
Variations	+10.7	+16.0	+3.0	−0.1	+7.5	+3.2	+7.3	+5.6

Source: Delavault (1986).

On this horizontal stratification is superimposed a vertical stratification: the higher the diplomas, the higher the proportion of male students. For example, in 1989 55 per cent of female students received diplomas which corresponded to four years of study; one year later, this proportion, corresponding to five years of study, dropped to 44 per cent. This effect is more marked for the humanities than for the sciences (MEN, 1992).

Data from Table 6.1 aggregate different kinds of subjects and tend to smooth out the horizontal stratification. This stratification is more marked if one considers more basic subjects. For example, the sciences include biology, where women students are a majority, and mathematics, where they are much fewer. One should also distinguish, in the humanities, between philosophy, with fewer women, and languages, where they are numerous. In the case of the *Agrégation*, 40 per cent of the students in 1986 were women; we find 62 per cent of them in languages, but only 34 per cent in philosophy, 53 per cent in biology but only 27 per cent in mathematics and 3 per cent in engineering (MEN, 1988).

In the Grandes Ecoles

Girls tend to choose the university rather than the *classes préparatoires* to the *Grandes Ecoles* which represent the élite track. In the humanities, the figures are 74 per cent versus 69 per cent, in sciences 37 per cent versus 20 per cent. Again, one will find that biology seems more attractive to girls than the mathematical subjects (MEN, 1991a). In the corresponding engineering schools, girls comprised only 9 per cent of the student body in 1973, while they were 19 per cent in 1988. In *Ecole Polytechnique*, they comprise around 8 per cent, and in *Ecole Nationale d'Administration* 22.5 per cent (in 1986).

Coeducation, which was instituted only in 1986 for *Ulm-Sèvres*, has been hard for girls. If they are approximately equal in the humanities, their percentage in the mathematical sections has drastically decreased (unpublished data from ENS).

Gender stratification: teachers and researchers

University teachers

Table 6.2 shows how the two stratification structures extend to university teachers.

Horizontal stratification (according to field) is noticeably flatter than it is among the students (Table 6.1): the percentage of female teachers varies between 20 per cent and 35 per cent, the maximum being in literature (47 per cent for the lower grade), the minimum in sciences. Change in the choice of field in this decade has also been much less marked than among the students. The increase in the presence of women is particularly slow in the health universities. Although women are gaining ground in the hierarchy little by little, vertical stratification is still very marked. Women get most professorships in the humanities (22 per cent) and least in the health universities (7 per cent).

Table 6.2 *The percentage of female university teachers*

	Years	Law	Humanities	Sciences	Health	Total
Professors	1980–81	7.4	16.4	7.4	5.8	8.6
	1985–6	7.3	18.4	7.1	6.3	9.1
	1989–90	9.4	21.7	8.2	7.2	10.7
'Maîtres de conférences'	1980–81	21.6	37.9	22.4	44.2	29.5
	1985–6	25.2	38.5	23.5	45.0	30.9
	1989–90	26.3	40.5	26.0	46.0	32.7
Assistants	1980–81	31.2	40.8	28.5	28.5	30.8
	1985–6	33.6	44.2	29.9	33.8	34.3
	1989–90	37.2	47.4	33.3	35.8	36.7
Total	1980–81	21.5	33.2	20.5	24.0	24.3
	1985–6	23.1	34.5	20.5	26.8	25.6
	1989–90	23.4	35.4	20.1	28.0	26.3

Source: Ministère de l'Education Nationale, *Notes d'information*, 1981 to 1991.

The CNRS researchers

The CNRS, which developed after World War II in a climate of economic expansion, provides, relatively speaking, a rather good place for women. One notes however a decrease in female researchers in the last few decades (from 35 per cent in 1960 to 30 per cent in 1989), due to more competitive economic conditions (Bataillon *et al.*, 1991).

One can notice the usual horizontal stratification with, in 1987, women accounting for 42 per cent of the positions in the life sciences (including natural sciences and psychology) and only 13 per cent in physics. Although the hierarchical structure shows the usual trend, with (in 1990) only 6 per cent of women in the highest grade of *Directeur de Recherches* (the equivalent of university professor), a comparison with the university is clearly in favour of the CNRS, which presents a more flattened hierarchy, especially for the social sciences (CNRS, 1990). A detailed examination of the career promotion patterns in CNRS shows that women are older than men in the same grade, and wait longer than men to be promoted (Cachelou, 1979).

Administration

One can distinguish two types of administrative functions (managerial and non-managerial) in the running of the university system. The main functions, such as teacher appointments, are performed by committees, which are constituted according to set procedures. They are composed of teachers and also, since 1968, students and other university employees, as well as 'outside' members. The committees take 'political' decisions, whereas the everyday running of the university is done by the administrative staff. We are not surprised to find that the gender gaps are very different in these two groups. Apart from a few technical jobs where three-quarters of the staff are men, or the infirmary services with 99 per cent female nurses, we find that most of the administrative staff are women, and that their presence is inversely related to rank, from 98 per cent in the lower grades to 61 per cent in the higher ones (MEN, 1991b). There are far fewer women in the managerial positions, as can be seen from Table 6.4, which shows the percentage of women on the committees which decide faculty appointments

These numbers are, in general, noticeably lower than the actual presence of women in the university or CNRS. Exceptions are grade B in law, and grade A in sciences. Nevertheless, these figures do represent an increase from 1978. A woman *président* of a university is quite exceptional: three out of 78 in 1985, only one in 1991. We find no women among the 17 general directors of the CNRS, in a period of 50 years.

Prestige and rewards

Within university and research careers, recognition by peers and prestige titles are very important. Every year, the CNRS awards one gold and several silver and bronze medals. From 1954 to 1988, there were 40 gold medals, of

Table 6.3 *The percentage of female researchers in CNRS*

	Years	Mathematical Sciences	Physics	Chemistry	Earth Sciences[1]	Life Sciences[2]	Total Sciences	Social Sciences	Total
Directeurs de recherche	1977	13.3	6.0	19.5	21.5	34.5	21.6	28.4	22.5
	1987	14.3	6.7	15.3	17.5	33.8	19.8	30.6	21.0
Chargés de recherche 1*	1977	21.9	14.4	30.3	29.8	56.1	35.8	40.2	36.5
	1987	20.7	16.0	31.2	29.6	46.5	33.0	37.4	33.6
Chargés de recherche 2*	1977	16.8	9.5	17.1	20.0	37.7	23.3	29.7	24.6
	1987	17.9	19.7	35.3	22.4	40.1	30.0	37.5	31.5
Total	1967	15.8	18.7	30.1	30.5	52.1	33.8	34.2	33.9
	1977	21.9	10.6	23.8	25.0	45.2	28.4	33.9	29.3
	1987	18.1	13.5	26.4	25.0	41.8	28.0	35.7	29.4

1. Includes astrophysics, geology.
2. Includes biology, psychology.
* Corresponds more or less to senior and junior researchers.

Source: Unpublished data from CNRS.

Table 6.4 *The percentage of females on university/CNRS committees and their percentage as university teachers/CNRS researchers*

1985 University	Law		Humanities		Sciences		Total 1985		Total 1978	
	Committee members	University teachers	Committee members	University teachers	Committee members	University teachers	Committee members	University teachers	Committee members	University teachers
Grade A	3.1	7.7	9.6	17.4	6.0	7.2	7.6	10.3	6.3	10.0
Grade B	25.0	23.9	27.9	38.7	16.8	22.9	23.1	28.2	15.6	27.0
Total	14.0	22.8	18.8	34.2	11.3	20.5	15.3	25.3	8.6	21.0

1985 CNRS	Social Sciences		Sciences		Total 1985		Total 1978	
	Committee members	CNRS researchers	Committee members	CNRS researchers	Committee members	CNRS researchers	Committee members	CNRS researchers
Total	28.4	35.4	16.6	28.4	20.0	29.8	15.5	29.3

Source: Delavault (1986) and UNESCO (1987).

which two were awarded to women (an archeologist and a biologist); that makes 5 per cent. The percentage increases for silver medals (11 per cent in humanities and biology) and bronze medals (19 per cent). In the prestigious *Collège de France*, we had, in 1992, two women out of 48 professors. In the *Académies* fewer than 5 per cent are women.

Women's Studies

The feminist movement is not too active in the universities at the present time. In the 1970s, its more radical elements opposed the idea of integration into a system which was considered as basically inegalitarian. However, some university feminist study groups were started in 1975, including one in an English department. In 1982, a year after the Socialists came to power, a national women's colloquium on research was organized; that was the first official recognition of the legitimacy of Women's Studies.

Women's Studies is also known as feminist, feminine, or sex social relationships studies. The word 'gender' is not entirely recognized, and subject to some criticism. However, much related work is also done without specification, especially in sociology, history and philosophy. There are now five teachers in Women's Studies in four out of 78 universities, and only one recognized group in the CNRS, in sociology. The subject is, however, to a certain extent recognized as important, although a very active feminist involvement is considered undesirable in an institution which is supposed to be ideologically neutral.

Conclusion: between equality and difference

Legal equality has now been achieved in France, however, established patterns of gender roles are deep-rooted. The statistics are striking: climbing the professional ladder, 96 per cent of women teach in the *écoles maternelles*; women account for 11 per cent of university full professors. In university committees, only 8 per cent are women and in the *académies*, fewer than 5 per cent. In a sense, women still relate first to *nature*, and are in charge of the youngest children, and men to *culture*, which leads to prominence in the social organization, honours and large salaries.

A horizontal stratification is superimposed on this vertical one: female students tend to choose the humanities, which will often lead them to secretarial jobs; however, a recent trend shows them doing biological sciences, law and the rather new management studies. This will make women participate more directly and, it is hoped, with efficiency, in the public arena. By contrast, women's presence in the physical and technical sciences, where there is little unemployment, seem to be decreasing slightly.

Two trends are clearly at work in today's society. An egalitarian ideology encourages women to develop all their potentialities and fully participate in the responsibilities of society. On the one hand, at the government level, the *Secrétariat d'Etat chargé des droits des femmes* has tried to encourage girls to choose traditional 'masculine' jobs, in order to avoid unemployment. On the other hand, there is some desire to maintain traditional gender roles, especially among males. This expresses itself through the *habitus*, or unwritten law (Bourdieu, 1984), with its patron-protégé relationships which favour men.[9] Some young women who prefer values such as personal self-fulfilment and relational quality rather than occupational success and competition also support traditional gender-role ideology. The result of these opposite trends is that, although our data show the continuous increase of women in university and research institutes, the upper positions of the ladder still strongly resist this increase, supporting the idea of a 'glass ceiling' (Morrison, 1987), invisible but nevertheless real.

What about quotas to break the ceiling? Cautiousness prevails in France on this question. People are afraid that a woman promoted because of a quota will not get as much consideration as she would otherwise – a position which combines the French élitist culture and an ambivalence towards feminism.

When trying to draw some conclusions about this moving and complex picture, one can either have an optimistic or a pessimistic view. One can notice all the obstacles which are still on the road towards equality. Prominent among these is the increase in the competitive aspect of today's society. One may also note that women are going into occupational sectors which are neglected by men. Higher education, which has suffered a considerable loss of prestige, compared to newer, economically vital sectors such as computing, finance, international industry, where the scarcity of women is striking, might be one of these.

However, one may also note that, beyond formal equality, women have acquired the right to be themselves for the first time in history. It will be fascinating to see what their future choices may be. One may also consider that the educational sector is still a fundamental one, as in any society, and notice, as a philosopher has pointed out, 'the extreme desire to learn' on the part of women (Le Doeuff, 1991). This has prompted two male educational sociologists to call the twentieth century 'the century of the women' (Baudelot and Establet, 1992).

Notes

1. 'Glass ceiling' refers to the presence of an invisible barrier (see Morrison, 1987).
2. *Laïcité* means secularity, non-religious, and stems from the opposition of republicans to the influence of the Catholic church in the French educational system.
3. Girls have a better success ratio than boys. This means that the lower percentage of girls comes more from their choice than from their ability.
4. The French *Grandes Ecoles* are on the university level.
5. The 1968 student movement clearly was a result of this tension. One may also relate to it the women's liberation movement of the 1970s: as marginal newcomers in the cultural world, women were particularly sensitive to the contradiction between its official aims and its realities.
6. Headlines from newspapers or book titles are eloquent: 'The submerged university', 'To save university', 'The collapse of the university', 'The university adrift'.
7. At that time many female foreigners came to attend courses in France. Such was the case of Marie Curie, who was the first woman to get a chair at the Sorbonne, in 1906, when she succeeded her husband. The philosopher and scientist Clémence Royer was, in 1884, the first woman to teach at the Sorbonne.

8. The same year, 1972, a girl was placed first in the entrance examination and hit the headlines.
9. In 1982, commenting on the functioning of university committees, a man mentioned 'sexist prejudices' and 'discriminatory attitudes' (towards women) which resulted more from 'insufficient awareness' than 'militant machismo' (Delavault, 1986 p. 102). This author notes that, wherever the marital situation is taken into account in the discussion of a promotion, the traditional role of the man as supporting his family is still predominant.

7. On the disparity of the sexes in German universities

Susanne Grimm and Uta Meier

SUMMARY: Germany as a nation is a newcomer; late with respect to its industrialization and late in its development of a stable democracy. In spite of different ideologies women were under-represented in leading positions in both German states because of patriarchal structures. Progress will be made towards realizing equality of opportunity between the sexes only when the labour market structure (more part-time jobs for men and women), family structure and career structure (all of which are dependent on the economy and the state) are changed. During their socialization girls and women must be educated about the social construction of gender identity.

Sociocultural profile of the Federal Republic of Germany

The Federal Republic of Germany lies in the heart of Europe, at the crossroads of East and West, North and South. Germany as a nation is a latecomer; late with respect to its industrialization, late also with respect to the establishment of democracy. In comparison with England and France, Germany's industrialization was not only late, but also rapid, so that patriarchal structures of rank and authority were maintained longer (Dahrendorf, 1965). It took the military defeats of 1918 and 1945 to permanently establish democratic structures. The Wall between the Socialist East and the Capitalist West Germany fell in 1989; after 40 years (1949–89) both parts of Germany were reunited. Until 1945 East and West Germany had a common past:

1870–1918: *Imperial Germany*; World War I.
1918: active and passive voting rights 'granted' to women. High unemployment among academics. Women teachers and women academics admitted to professions only in limited numbers.
1919–32: *Weimar Republic*; first democracy; world economic crisis. Open discrimination against women; edict mandating dismissal of women whose husbands had jobs.
1933–45: *National Socialist dictatorship*; World War II. Fascist antifeminism; ideology of femininity, women reduced to birth machines (Mohr, 1987).

1945–48: Allied occupation.
1949: Founding of the *Federal Republic of Germany (BRD)* and the *German Democratic Republic (DDR)*.
1961: construction of the Wall.
1989: the Wall comes down: *Unification of the two Germanys.*

Values and norms

BRD

Central goals are striving for individual success, competition, social equality of opportunity (between the sexes, classes and social groups) and dominance of the performance principle (Schäfers, 1990).

In reality women are disadvantaged in every respect. The more centrally important an area is in society, the fewer women are represented in it. This is true in politics, economics, universities and the mass media. Gender is a structural category under which unequal chances applying to society as a whole are predicated. The BRD is not only a capitalist, but also a patriarchal society in which professional position and therefore group and class membership are unequally divided (Bammé *et al.*, 1983). The image of 'women's self-sufficiency' is increasingly the standard by which more and more women plan their lives (Grimm, 1987). Gender constitutes the dominant dividing-line in the division of labour: horizontally (male and female professions) and vertically (gender hierarchy). In addition the system of values and rights is structured around the family. It is only since 1977, with the reform of family law, that wives have had the right to employment. At the level of the cultural and political system there is a continuous attempt to reproduce gender stereotypes via gender-specific socialization and curricula (rejection of reform of curricular contents, sexism in schoolbooks, etc.).

DDR

The DDR's central social goals included an emphasis on social justice, defined as closing the gaps in living conditions among all classes and social groups as well as between the sexes. In the 1970s and 80s the performance principle became increasingly important and somewhat at odds with the Socialist demand for equality and justice.

The average DDR citizen was expected to be continually employed from school graduation until retirement. Employment represented the central State strategy for the integration of the population (see Chapters 4 and 13 in this volume). This officially proclaimed social goal was to be implemented by the right to education and employment and the obligation to work, as well as by the installation of a multiplicity of state and private systems of regulations, supports and controls. Among these were labour, family and social policy regulations governing the labour of women, especially in the second half of the 1970s and in the 1980s.

In this sense working mothers were taken for granted in the culture of the DDR. However, the patriarchal character of DDR society led to obvious discrimination against women in employment and in public life. In the DDR the following rule also held true: the more important an area of economics, politics or science was held to be, the less women were represented in it (Meier, 1991).

Women in the labour market

BRD

In the capitalist welfare state, employment represents the central source of life opportunities for the members of society. However, the participation of women in employment is influenced by patriarchal structures in the labour market and the ideology of the 'culture of the two genders'. The labour market is separated into 'female' and 'male' areas of employment and linked to gender-specific lines of differentiation. In addition, women are refused entry into traditional male domains and in particular to high levels of the hierarchy and to opportunities in economics, politics and culture. The percentage of women working full or part time in 1990 was 40.8 per cent; 41 per cent of women with pre-school children were in the labour force and daycare facilities were available for 87 per cent of pre-school children (82 per cent half daycare). Most women were concentrated in low-level positions (58 per cent), 37 per cent are in middle-level positions and only 5 per cent occupy top positions. These conditions in the labour market lead to serious disadvantages for women (salary, job security, opportunities for further training and for promotion). Furthermore, the cultural system of the two genders assigns paid labour to men and leaves the unpaid labour in the home and family to the women. Conflicts between employment and family labour are defined as a woman's and not as a man's problem. The combined effects of the family and marketplace gender hierarchies creates the preconditions for the replication of the social order (Maier, 1991).

DDR

In the DDR, just as in the BRD, employment represented the central access to material well-being and social recognition. This was true for women as well as men. By the end of the 1980s more than 90 per cent of the female population between the ages of 15 and 60 was either employed or in training, only 14 per cent of women were working in part-time jobs. However, in the DDR (as in the BRD) women were integrated into a gender-specific labour market. Women in industry had the unattractive jobs, worked under less favourable labour and health conditions (Nickel, 1990) and were more frequently assigned jobs below their levels of qualification.

The gender-specific recruitment and allocation mechanisms in the training and employment system of the DDR led to economic disadvantages for women. In 1988 full-time employed women earned only 78 per cent of men's earnings. Within the 15–25 year-old cohort, 65 per cent were concentrated in the lower income group (up to 700 marks per annum), although only 6 per cent held part-time jobs. Males in the labour force in this age group made up only 27 per cent of this income group (*Statistisches Bundesamt*, 1990b).

Women in politics

BRD

Although women received the right to vote in 1908 in Germany, the centuries-old exclusion of women from politics makes itself felt even today. Women vote and men are voted for. Women represent a minority in the political parties (in 1988, 38 per cent of the Greens, 26 per cent of the SPD, 24 per cent of the FDP, 23 per cent of the CDU and 14 per cent of the CSU). The same holds true in the unions, where only a quarter of the members are women (in 1989).

A discussion of quotas is beginning to bear fruit. Women are now more frequently represented in leading positions than among the party rank and file: in 1989, in the Federal Government, up to 90 per cent, in the governments of the *Länder* (provinces) up to 18 per cent (Geißler, 1992).

DDR

In the DDR discrimination against women was particularly severe in politics. In spite of all the equality programmes, women were hermetically sealed out of the centre of power. No woman was ever admitted to the inner leadership circle of the *Politbüro* as a voting member. Only two were on the waiting list for acceptance as full *Politbüro* members; one waited 26 years, the other 16 years (Geißler, 1992).

The strikingly obvious under-representation of women in leading positions in industry, science and politics makes one point clear. Attempts at equality included formal statements of equality of the sexes, the raising of the educational level and qualifications of women, their full integration into a gender-specific segmented employment system and the availability of a daycare system for children. These measures, however, did not lead to greater participation of men in household and childcare activities. The patriarchal essence of structures in all areas of life were not affected in any way by these attempts.

Women in education

BRD

In spite of formal equality, open and subtle disadvantages to women and girls in schools remain to this day. Despite success in performance, girls are unable to compensate for their lack of faith in themselves (Horstkemper, 1987). The hope that the social inequalities between men and women could be evened out by means of education has proved to be illusory although social inequality between men and women has lost its formal legitimacy. Family, school and employment continue to function as institutions for the reproduction of the cultural system of the two genders, for the hierarchical ordering of gender relations and for the attribution of gender-specific abilities.

Because of the federal structure of the BRD the *Länder* exercise autonomy in the area of culture and education. Since 1973 this has led to a 'polarization of educational policy' (Grimm, 1987) between social-liberal *Länder* governments (*A-Länder*) and CDU/CSU-governed *Länder* (*B-Länder*). This polarization is reflected in the area of women's policy and in the current state of women's rights in the universities.

DDR

The integration of DDR women into the employment system was accompanied by various strategies for qualifying women. These included special study programmes for women, management training and state appeals for the participation of women in specialized technical professions and technical study programmes. The goal was to overcome traditional educational deficits and to create better employment opportunities for women.

In 1988, 87 per cent of all employed women in the former DDR had completed either a special training programme or higher-level professional training. Although approximately 80 per cent of all employees in the educational system were women, only one in four schools was headed by a woman director. However, every second position of assistant director, a much more labour-intensive position, was filled by a woman.

Historical situation of women in the universities

Empire and Weimar Republic

Silent struggle for the realization of rights gained.

1900–1909: admission of women to university, different policies in the various *Länder*.

Women had a formal right to study, but in practice a climate of hostility to women studying was created by the ideology of femininity.

The social climate in the universities was dominated by the fear of downward mobility of students of middle- and upper-class origins. Women were regarded as competition by male students and therefore as an additional threat to their *Lebensraum*. The political orientation of the male students was primarily right wing and most were organized in fraternities. The political orientation of the women was unclear and often contradictory.

1920: admission of women to habilitation[1] in the universities.

1923: the first two German women professors.

1925: twenty-five women professors in German universities.

Social origins of women students

During the Empire, women students came primarily from Protestant and Jewish backgrounds of the educated middle- and upper-middle classes (Mertens, 1991). Medicine and law were the preferred courses of study.

During the Weimar Republic, changes took place in the social origins of the women students. The teaching profession functioned as a means of social advancement for women students from families of the lower and middle officialdom (*ibid.*). The faculty of philosophy was attractive because a university degree enabled one to teach at the *Gymnasium* level, the most attractive and most secure prospect for later employment. When women teachers married they were automatically dismissed from their jobs. It was only in 1920 that the celibacy requirement for women teachers was lifted.

During the Empire, Catholic women were extremely under-represented, during the Weimar Republic, however, their participation in higher education increased (*ibid.*).

National Socialism and World War II

In general women were forced out of the universities; however, those of upper- and middle-class backgrounds were admitted on an individual basis. This era was characterized by a reversion to traditional educational and social values. Prior positive developments in the participation of women in the university were disastrously undercut. The percentage of women students was limited to 10 per cent of the student body in 1933.

Postwar period

Women had to take second place again.

1949 to mid-1960s
BRD: introduction of formal equality (1949); restoration of the universities.
DDR: founding of the Workers' and Peasants' Faculties in order to break the 'bourgeois monopoly on education'. Women enjoyed increased participation here. Legal equality; women show strong interest in employment.

Mid-1960s to mid-1970s
BRD: 'mobilization of talent'.
DDR: ratification of 'Bill for the Advancement of Women Students with Children' (1972) – specific measures for the advancement of women in the universities. End of the period of expansion in the universities. Admission to *Abitur* (academic secondary school) made harder and cutting off of new admissions to the universities.

Mid-1970s to mid-1980s
BRD: until the mid-1980s daughters of working-class families remained 'stepdaughters' in the universities and women professors were still rarities.
DDR: the former strategy of encouraging and assisting women in the university had changed to a policy of family support and population growth. This mother-oriented policy had negative effects on women's professional lives. For example, in 1985 women made up 58 per cent of workers in data processing, in 1986, 45 per cent and in 1987, 26.1 per cent (Döbbeling *et al.*, 1990).

After unification (1990–3)
Old *Bundesländer* (eleven *Länder* of the former BRD): in 1990: Bund and *Länder* legislated a *second university programme* extending to the year 2000.

Each year 700 million DM (17.5 per cent of the total budget for vocational training at the universities) were allocated to raise the percentage of women among scholars and scientists and to increase the compatibility of academic and family obligations (BMBW 12/90, 1990).

New Bundesländer (five *Länder* of the former DDR): in order to make the former DDR university system more compatible to the BRD system, the number of university teachers and scientists had to be reduced. This resulted in the reconstruction of the academic system exclusively by men for men. There was widespread expulsion of women from the middle academic levels. Two-thirds of these women were re-employed, but in other areas and at the cost of status loss.

Statistical situation of women in the universities

Girls responded to the educational propaganda of the 1960s. Through the end of the 1980s an equalization of educational opportunities between the sexes took place among *Abitur* graduates (see Table 7.1).

In the last 20 years the number of women students has nearly doubled in both Germanys (see Table 7.2).

In the BRD, female children of labourers are under-represented in schools leading to academic courses of study and in universities, in comparison to the children of members of the other groups listed in Table 7.3a. Daughters of labourers have reacted to cuts in student aid and the unfavourable job market of the 1980s by noticeably withdrawing from higher education.

The social profile of DDR students from the intelligentsia and blue-collar classes reflects the result of the 'breaking of the monopoly of the bourgeoisie' in all universities where Worker and Peasant Faculties had been established in 1949. While the percentage of children of labourers rose rapidly, the access of children of the intelligentsia was severely curtailed. After the elimination of the Worker and Peasant Faculties in 1963 the proportions were reversed (see Table 7.3b).

The choices of the major field of study of female students have expanded in the BRD in the last 30 years and have, thereby, approached the choices of the male students. During the 1960s the choices of female students had been largely concentrated in the area of languages and culture (see Table 7.4).

Table 7.1 *Percentage of 18 to under-20 year-olds qualified for university study according to sex, 1975–87 (BRD)*

		Total of those qualified to study Abitur graduates		
	Year	Female	Male	Total
old Bundesländer	1975	15.9	23.0	19.6
	1980	20.2	22.9	21.6
	1987	27.9	29.8	28.9

Source: The Bundesminister for Education and Science: *Mädchen auf dem Weg zum Abitur*, Aktuell Bildung Wissenschaft, 1990, p. 40.

Table 7.2 *Female students in the BRD and DDR in percentages, from 1960 to 1991/2*

BRD		DDR	
1960	22.5	1960	25.2
1970	25.6	1970	35.4
1980	36.7	1980	48.7
1991/2	39.1	1989	48.6

Source: Mohr, W (1987) *Frauen in der Wissenschaft*, Freiburg, 207 und Statistisches Bundesamt. Mitteilung für die Presse 49/92, 1 und Statistiche Jahrbücher der DDR.

Figure 7.1 shows first of all that the percentage of women students in 1989 was higher in the DDR than in the BRD (49 per cent to 41 per cent). Also, the percentage of women in the traditional 'male' faculties – mathematics and natural sciences, medicine, economics and engineering – was significantly higher in the DDR than in the BRD. This was a result of the special study programmes for women established in 1963 and 1972, and also of the stronger emphasis on women's employment and polytechnic education.

In the course of the last 30 years the percentage of women gaining doctorates and habilitations has steadily increased; in the DDR the increase was significantly greater, however. In previous years DDR women had gained the A-Doctorate (PhD) twice as often as men. Furthermore, for every man gaining the B-Doctorate (corresponds to habilitation in the BRD) there were six women (Döbbeling *et al.*, 1990). However, those qualifications on the part of women in the universities have not increased their representation in the academic hierarchy. On the contrary, women were noticeably seldom recommended for a professorship or assistant professorship. Only one in seven assistant professors was a woman, and only one in nineteen full professors was a woman (in 1989). However, for those women who did succeed in obtaining academic positions, guaranteed training, childcare and job security permitted uninterrupted careers, without their having to postpone childbearing.

Compared to the development of university places for students, the increase among women on the academic staff of the universities in the BRD was slight (see Table 7.6a).

In top university positions, 4 per cent were women in the DDR; however,

Table 7.3a *Social origins of female university enrolments in the BRD, per cent, 1978–87*

	Father's Profession				
	Labourer	Private Employee	Public Employee	Self-employed	Other
1978/9	11.7	37.3	22.6	23.3	5.2
1982	11.9	39.7	20.9	22.7	4.9
1986/7	8.5	37.2	21.3	19.7	13.4

Source: Mertens, L (1991) *Vernachlässigte Töchter der Alma Mater*, Berlin, pp. 130ff.

Table 7.3b *Social profile of students at university level, DDR, per cent, 1945–89*

	Intelligentsia[2]	Labourers	Employees	Members of LPG/PGH[3]	Self-employed/ other
1945/6		c.4			
1954[1]	12	48	24	6	11[1]
1958[1]	14	53	19	6	9
1960	19	39	30	3	8
1967	30	30	26	6	7
1979	59	c. 11–19[4]			
1982	69	c. 10–15[4]			
1989	78	c. 7–10[4]			

[1] Full-time study only, no correspondence courses. The percentage of labourers' children is higher and the percentage of children of the intelligentsia is lower than in all other student groups.
[2] University degree.
[3] LPG = Agricultural collective. PGH = Production collective for skilled labour.
[4] Estimations on the basis of full-time students in the year 1967. In this year 45 per cent of all students whose parents did not belong to the intelligentsia were the children of labourers

they made up about 30 per cent of the academic middle ranks. They had tenured positions and were therefore solidly and visibly represented in academia (see Table 7.6b).

The study career profiles of women in the BRD shows that although women accounted for almost half of the student body, degree obtained and faculty rank are inversely correlated with female percentage (see Table 7.7a).

The same inverse correlation between degree/rank and percentage of females is found in the DDR (see Table 7.7b).

It is clear that the current situation of women in the universities is characterized by an under-representation of women in top positions in the universities. The BRD law-makers have therefore addressed the necessity of action in this area (§2, Abs.2: the proposals made by the *Bund-Länder* Commission for Educational and Research Planning [BLK], 1990).

The implementation of the BLK proposals has been uneven, since the federal structure of the BRD makes the *Länder* autonomous in cultural matters (Grimm et al., 1992).

Table 7.4 *Female students according to faculty in the BRD, per cent, 1960–89*

	Languages and Cultures	Law, Economics and Social Sciences	Natural Sciences, Mathematics	Medicine	Engineering
1960	49	14	16	18	1.5
1975	55	24	32	35	8
1989	32	32	35	45	12

Source: BMBW 1974, 74 and Mohr, W, *op. cit.*, 230 and 232 and BMBW: Hochschulpolit. Zielsetzungen der Bundesregierung. Aktuell Bildung und Wissenschaft 14/90, 21.

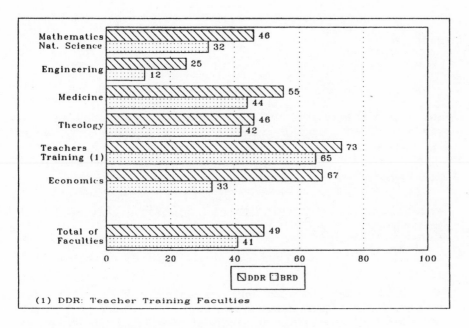

Source: Stat. Jb. BRD, 1990, p. 367; Frauenreport 1990, p. 47.

Figure 7.1 *Percentage of women in selected faculties in 1989 in both Germanys*

There are three main deficits in the current situation of women's rights in the universities. One deficit is the lack of supervision of the application of the regulations (obligatory biennial report). The majority of the old *Länder* (Baden-Württemberg, Bavaria, Bremen, Nordrhein-Westphalia and Schleswig-Holstein) have *not* legally obligated the universities to submit reports on the effectiveness of the required measures. Another serious deficit is the lack of consideration for the uniqueness of women's life situation, in that many

Table 7.5 *Percentage of women gaining doctorates and habilitations in both Germanys, selected years*

	BRD				DDR			
Degree	*1960*	*1970*	*1980*	*1989*	*1960[3]*	*1970*	*1980[4]*	*1989*
Doctorates	13.0[1]	12.3[1]	19.8[2]	26.6[2]	22.7	31.4	30.1	37.5
Habilitations			4.5[1]	9.2[1]	4.5	6.7	13.7	15.4

[1] BMBW 1991/2, p. 235.
[2] Statistiches Bundesamt 1982, 1991.
[3] Zahlen für 1960 bis 1975: vgl. Weibpfennig 1982, p. 318.
[4] Zahlen für 1980 bis 1989: vgl. Statistiche Jahrbücher der DDR 1990, p. 344.

Table 7.6a *Percentage of women among the academic personnel of the universities of the BRD according to rank*

	1960	1966	1977	1988
Teaching Assistants	8.5	10.5	11.3	20.2
Assistant Professors	4.0	3.1	6.2	14.2
Professors	1.6	2.2	3.5	5.2

See: Mohr, W, *op. cit.*, p. 210 and BMBW 1990, pp. 154ff. and 216.

wish to combine career and family. In order to make this possible, the BLK has recommended a series of measures; however, these recommendations have often been disregarded. The third major deficit is the total neglect of support for young women scholars, the correction of which is the basis for all other support measures.

Explanation for the marginality of women in highly qualified professions

The marginality of women in highly qualified professions may be explained on three levels:

- the intersection of structural and processual discrimination of women in the areas of profession and reproduction;
- the reproduction of the hierarchical structure of relations between the sexes; and
- the cultural construction of the gender differences.

An important preliminary consideration is that gender is to be regarded as a processual rather than as a structural category, as this distinction is important for current and future analysis.

The handicapping of women in the areas of professional development and family and reproduction

The structural and processual handicapping of women takes place with particular intensity because of the gender-specific division of labour, double

Table 7.6b *Percentage of women among academic personnel of the universities in the DDR, 1975–89*

Year	Total of Faculty	Untenured Teaching Assistants	Tenured Teaching Assistants	Senior Lecturers	Assistant Professors	Professors
1975	28.1	33.7	29.6	13.8	10.6	3
1980	33.5	40.5	35.5	16.6	10.1	4
1985	33.6	38.7	36.8	16.6	10.9	4
1989	35.3	37.8	40.0	17.3	12.0	4

Source: Hildebrandt, 1990, S.9.

Table 7.7a *Percentage of women (in comparison to men) among students and academic personnel of the universities in the BRD, 1988*

Enrolments	43.6[1]
Students	40.7[1]
Diplomas/masters	36.9[2]
Doctorates	26.3[2]
Habilitations	8.7[2]
Lecturers	27.0[2]
Readers, Univ. lecturer	20.2[1]
Senior lecturer, Research asst.	14.2[1]
Professors	5.2[1]

[1] BMBW 1990, pp. 154ff. and 216.
[2] Statistisches Bundesamt (hg.) 1990a, pp. 371 and 373.

load of career and family and dual socialization of women which is legitimized by means of the ideology of the 'cultural dual-gender system'. This promotes the professional careers of men and handicaps those of women.

Geißler (1992) identifies three hindrances to the professional advancement of women, which are tied up with traditional role-orientation:

- top positions are mostly jobs for 'one and one-half people';
- the central requirements for advancement to top careers are entry at the right age and 'staying on the ball'; and
- many professional careers depend on frequent change of residence.

The reproduction of the gender hierarchy

The hierarchical structure of the gender relation is reproduced through the gender-specific segregation of the labour market (ie, 'women's jobs', 'men's jobs' and processes of professionalization which are always related to gender; that is, they are processes of closing labour markets to women and of marginalizing women within them). These are processes of maintaining and increasing men's power, influence and prestige.

The cultural construction of the gender difference

Gender as a criterion for classification impacts at the individual level as well as at the cultural level. In real life the norms, values and attitudes of the

Table 7.7b *Percentage of women among academic personnel of the universities in the DDR, 1989*

Untenured Teaching Assistants	Tenured Teaching Assistants	Senior Lecturers	Assistant Professors	Professors
37.8	40.0	17.3	12.0	4.9

Source: Hildebrandt, 1990, S. 9.

culture appear in the lives of individual women as motivations, aims, hopes and responsibilities.

Strategies for change

Strategies for ending the structural and processual handicapping of women must begin on three levels, corresponding to their causes: a) the total social level; b) the institutional level, and c) the individual level.

Strategies at the level of society at large

Progress will be made towards realizing equality of opportunity between the sexes only when the preconditions of: a) labour market structure (more part-time jobs for men and women); b) family structure; and c) career structure (goals of the BLK on the compatibility of family and career), which are dependent on the economy and the state, are changed, and not before.

Women *Abitur* graduates tend – in the 1990s – less towards starting a family; they are less willing to give up their careers temporarily. Women professors are able to advance only by deviating from the 'objective family career', in that they are more often unmarried, remain childless and live alone.

Strategies on the institutional level

'Only a non-gender-specific responsibility for production and reproduction makes a non-gender-hierarchical society possible' (Maier, 1991).

Recommendations for the advancement of women in the universities

In order to raise the number of women professors the following measures are necessary:

- the preferential appointment of women with equal qualifications to university-level teaching positions until the 50 per cent quota is reached;
- the creation of funded chairs for women;
- the creation of tenured assistant professorships and lecturerships for habilitated women;
- the prohibition of in-house appointments to professorships should be set aside for a limited transitional time. Women scholars and scientists who have fulfilled professorial duties for more than ten years, but who have only enjoyed the position and status of the middle level of the academic hierarchy should be granted in-house promotions to professorships;
- a special programme for unemployed habilitated women should be created in view of the expected deficit of professors in the mid-1990s;
- half of all grants for doctorates and for habilitation should be given to women;

- social networks should be extended to women, so that they can have advocates in the external appointment committees;
- a required yearly report of the university president to the Ministry of Culture and a corresponding required report of the Ministry of Culture to the *Landtag* on the success of measures pertaining to increasing the number of women professors.

The following measures are necessary for ending the severe under-representation of women in the entire university area:

- preferential appointment of women to qualified positions until the 50 per cent quota is reached;
- women should receive half of all research assistanceships;
- encouragement of women to gain their doctorates and embark on academic careers;
- lifting of age limits for beginning studies, contracts, graduate programmes and grants, as well as recognition of childrearing years;
- creation by the universities of nearby daycare centres;
- the creation of professorships for Women's Studies by means of the reorientation of vacant positions and financial support for Women's Studies and research on and by women.

Since the advancement of women in the universities is still minimal, and since the BRD legislature has obligated the universities to end handicapping of women scholars and scientists, the funding of the universities by *Bund* and *Länder* must be tied to evidence of effective support of women.

Strategies at the individual level

At the level of the formation of identity it is necessary to:

- educate girls and women during their pre-school, school and professional socialization about the social construction of gender identity; and
- to educate them about the deconstruction of this difference and its legitimation; and about the necessity of active contribution to the deconstruction.[2]

Special strategies for change in the new Bundesländer

- The percentage of women in the committees for reconstructing the universities in the new *Bundesländer* must be increased via selective appointment;
- appointment negotiations should be clarified by means of the full disclosure of the application documents at the time of the submission of the appointments list to the Ministry of Culture;
- in the case of personnel reductions in the universities and in research institutes, a guaranteed percentage of women scholars and/or scientists must remain;
- the pensions of emerited women university professors should be

equalized to the level of the old *Bundesländer* within the context of individual evaluations;
- social security plans should be created for dismissed and older women professors; and
- a network of official equality ombudsmen should be created in the new *Bundesländer*.

Notes

1. 'Habilitation' is a second doctorate which is a precondition to achieving the rank of professor.
2. Three procedures are necessary here:
   - gaining insight into the processes by which women were and are excluded through historical research;
   - gaining insight into the (re-)construction of 'the' gender difference and into their positions with regard to it;
   - contextualizing the concrete structural integration of women and men; and
   - critique of ideology and method in order to render dual gender structures in meaning patterns transparent (Wetterer, 1992).

8. 2,500 years after Plato: Greek women in higher education

Julia Balaska

SUMMARY: In the face of a long history of patriarchy, gender-based discrimination is now illegal in Greece. However prevalent attitudes still
reflect traditional stereotypes regarding the proper role of women in the
family and in the public sphere. In higher education these are manifested
in the small proportions of women in technical subjects, in high academic
(faculty) ranks and in powerful administrative positions.

'Women qualify for equal opportunities in education, since they are
equal, by nature, to men' (Plato).

Introduction

Greece is a small southern Mediterranean country, the last eastern frontier of
the European Community. Its capital is Athens and its population totals
about 10 million. The official religion is Orthodox Christian. In 1975 Greece
became a presidential republic, but the overall policy-making authority is
vested in parliament.

Two Greek philosophers, Plato and Aristotle, have affected Greek and
Western thought throughout the centuries. Aristotle in particular was
influential regarding women and education. Reflecting his time, Aristotle
contended that in comparison to men, women were biologically defective,
and morally and spiritually inferior. Women, in his view, were not creative
and their souls were incapable of reaching the last stage of reason. History is
replete with more recent versions of this Aristotelian argument.

Greece has been characterized by a turbulent history and a special ability
to adapt to new situations (Caclamanakis, 1984). The most dramatic period
was the Ottoman rule, which lasted almost four centuries (1453–1821) and
strongly influenced all domains and structures of the modern Greek state.
Under Ottoman rule the existing segretation of males and females was
intensified. Education of the Greeks was restricted and became closely
linked with religion as the church became the focal point of Greek national
and cultural identity. This connection between religion and education continues up to the present day and has resulted in a conservative educational
system.

One foot in the West, one in the East

The situation of women has gradually improved, thanks in large measure to the struggles of women's organizations and the new feminist movement. In 1836, the newly created Greek State adopted Roman Law, which considered women as inferior human beings with limited rights. Working women at the time were poorly paid housemaids, dressmakers and confectioners. At the turn of the century, a limited number of women were employed as teachers in elementary schools (Nicolaidou, 1981).

A few enlightened women understood the prevailing oppression and inequality and established, in 1894, the Greek Association for Women's Rights and, in 1902, the Council of Greek Women. In the 1920s the women's movement was enriched by the participation of the lower social classes. The focal point of the women's movement during this decade was the demand for the emancipation of women and the right to vote.

In 1930 women were granted the right to vote in municipal elections only if they fulfilled two conditions: a) that they had reached the age of 30, and b) that they were literate. The idea was to exclude the majority of women voters, since illiteracy was predominant among women, especially in rural areas (Lazaris, 1989). Full rights to vote and to be elected were finally granted to women in 1952.

After World War II, Greece experienced rapid economic growth. Between the 1960s and 1980s, real per capita income increased by an average annual rate of 5.4 per cent, and the general standard of living improved. During the same period, 1,200,000 Greeks, mostly from rural areas, emigrated to Western Europe, the United States and Canada. This was followed by massive urbanization, which rose from 43 per cent (1961) to 58 per cent (1981). These trends affected both economic and social structures. The nuclear family replaced the extended family and the position of women gradually improved as they joined the labour force (Caragiorgas, 1990).

During the first half of the century, the participation of women in the labour market had been low, but it gradually increased from 14 per cent in 1928 to 32 per cent in 1981. In 1991, 40 per cent of employable women were in the labour force, constituting 38 per cent of the total. The contribution of women had become increasingly important during the period of the great emigration and urbanization.

Although the female working force has increased, the majority occupy lower positions. Females are also half as likely as males to work in the private sector, to employ other people, or to be self-employed (EKKE, 1988). One-third of working women are non-remunerable members of a family enterprise. In the agricultural sector, which includes 37 per cent of all working women, their proportion of the labour force reaches 73.7 per cent (*ibid.*, 1988). In the public sector, where almost 40 per cent were female employees, only 11 per cent of higher posts were occupied by women (Stratigaki, 1989); 99 per cent of computer operators were women.

With the exception of civil servants, women's wages are still almost 25 per cent lower than men's. This violates Greek law, which mandates equal rights for men and women and equal pay for work of equal value. The trend is now (especially among educated women) to work after marriage. However, the majority of women find it difficult, if not impossible, to combine employment and family. Thirty-eight per cent of married women work outside of the home, compared to 56 per cent of unmarried and 69 per cent of divorced women (EKKE, 1988). At present there are 1300 public crèches and some 1000 private ones (Balaska, 1991). This number is far from adequate to meet the demand. Educated women often choose an independent profession, such as dentistry, law or architecture in order to have enough flexibility to cope with inadequate childcare (Cacoullos, 1991).

The political and academic fields are the most resistant to the entry and full participation of women. Both areas are very competitive and male-dominated, so women entering them must be highly qualified, persistent, motivated and self-confident. In the national parliament women currently constitute about 5 per cent of the members; in local bodies 1–1.5 per cent and in trade unions 4.5 per cent (Balaska, 1991).

In 1981 the country entered a new period, when a Socialist government came into power. These years were characterized by the introduction of an extensive social welfare policy, during which the principle of equality was strongly promoted. In 1983 the General Secretariat for Equality of the Two Sexes was established with a mandate of implementing a policy of equality. This body was responsible for extensive legislation establishing and safe-guarding the rights of women in all fields. The most important achievement was the introduction of a new family law, which not only granted equal rights but also defined equal roles and protected children born both within and outside of wedlock. The signing and ratification of the United Nations' Convention on the Elimination of all Forms of Discrimination against Women on 2 March 1982, supplemented by additional constitutional provisions and a series of national laws, became the legal framework of women's rights. Nevertheless, Greek society and mentality have retained many of the old traditions. Although freedom and democracy are the main values of Greeks, deep-rooted prejudices related to the role of men and women have survived.

Although many Greek males adopt progressive and democratic attitudes in public, they still remain very traditional and often oppressive in private life. Women have been raised and educated to underestimate and devalue themselves (Lazaris, 1989). Even if they want to change their lives, women are still forced to shoulder all household responsibilities.

Women's place in the educational structure

Mandatory elementary education for boys and girls was enacted into law in 1834. After elementary education, girls continued their studies at private 'schools for girls'. Graduates of these establishments could become elementary school teachers, the only public position open to women until 1917. Since private schools for girls operated mainly in Athens, only a very limited number of girls could attend. In 1879 the rate of illiteracy among women was 93 per cent. The prevailing ideology of the time was that education must prepare virtuous girls, perfect wives and fond mothers, as women's nature and inclination dictate (Ziogou-Carastergiou, 1983).

In the 1880s enlightened women, educated in Western countries, protested against the prevailing ideology, and established additional girls' schools. The first woman was admitted to the School of Literature in the University of Athens in 1890. One year later, Angeliki Panagiotatou was admitted to the University School of Medicine and became the first woman assistant professor. Students greeted her with catcalls. Once higher education became accessible, women made rapid progress, the percentage of women students at universities increasing from 8.5 (1930) to 12 (1940) and to 24 in 1955, despite high tuition fees.

In 1963 'free education' was established in universities for all Greek citizens and, as a result, women's participation in higher education soared from 31 per cent in 1970 to 42.4 per cent in 1980 and 52.6 per cent in 1990. Since 1981, many educational reforms have been introduced. Compulsory schooling was extended to nine years, schools became coeducational, girls' schools were abolished and men were admitted to university courses in kindergarten studies and home economics. School books were revised, promoting the principle of equality and a more democratic structure was introduced at all levels of education.

A university degree: the highest value of modern Greek society

Greek universities are financed and supervised by the state and function within a specific legal framework. Greece currently has 18 universities and the duration of studies is 4–6 years, depending on the subject.

The free educational system provided opportunities for young people of lower income and social background to continue their studies in the universities. At the same time, entrance examinations have been instituted limiting the possibilities of admission. Thirty per cent of high school graduates enter the university every year and their number is increasing, making access to higher education more and more competitive.

From the 1950s to 1970s a university degree was not considered a necessary qualification for a successful career, thus neither parents nor pupils aspired to higher studies, particularly in the lower income groups. Among university students of higher social class background, 66 per cent were women and 54 per cent men, while among the students of the lower (rural and working) classes 34 per cent were women and 46 per cent, men (Lambiri-Dimaki, 1974). This indicated that poor parents were more reluctant to pay for private preparatory courses for their daughters than for their sons.

The situation changed in the 1980s, as the labour market demanded more qualified persons. A university degree acquired new prestige and became the dream of pupils and parents. This applied both to girls and boys, at least in the big cities. Parents became willing to invest in their children's higher education, even at great sacrifice. (Official statistics for 1990 show that 22 per cent of students' parents were university graduates, 37 per cent high school graduates and 41 per cent had finished elementary school; Ministry of Education and Religion, 1989–90). Cavounidis (1990) has pointed out that higher education is a family strategy for social mobility. Although a university degree does not secure a well-paid position for a young person, a high school diploma often represents an unemployment certificate.

The university staff: the female slice of the educational cake is growing

Official statistics which segregated the university teaching staff according to gender first appeared in 1962, when women were only 11.1 per cent. This percentage included Teacher Academies, which were not then regarded as true universities, although most women taking further studies preferred these institutions since they were traditionally regarded as 'proper'. In 1970, women's average participation in the total university teaching staff rose to 31.2 per cent and reached 35.3 per cent in 1980.

As Table 8.1 reveals, the female staff was not distributed equally throughout all faculty ranks, although there had been a considerable increase in all ranks between 1971 and 1990. The proportion of women is still extremely low in the three highest ranks (1990), while it exceeds 40 per cent in the lower ranks, especially when a doctor's degree is not required.

Until 1982, the main professional teaching staff was elected by a committee of full professors. The qualifications to be met included quality of postgraduate studies, publications, research, teaching experience, and personality and academic morals. The whole university system was founded on the institution of the Professorial Chair. The holder of the Chair had absolute teaching, administrative and financial power, as well as the duty to supervise all the staff associated with his Chair. In addition, he had the right to select his own teaching assistants.

This university structure favoured the full professors and had a negative impact on the rest of the teaching staff, particularly women. A full professor did not retire; he had to die in order for his Chair to be vacated. The result of these policies was that universities were often regulated by elderly men imbued with traditional and conservative attitudes towards women. Female scholars typically did not get promoted unless they had been the full professor's personal teaching assistant for years and had adopted his views. Teaching assistants had to be obedient and self-effacing, which was often difficult for male scholars.

Male university graduates often preferred to continue their studies abroad, since in practice a doctorate from abroad is counted of higher value than a Greek one. According to Cacoullos (1991, p. 61):

> Greek women have not fared well in this career area for the widely acknowledged reason that the majority of young women in Greece are inhibited, if not outrightly discouraged, by their families from studying abroad, which they would have to do in order to satisfy the qualifications for a university appointment.

A new law passed in 1982 eliminated the position of the all-powerful Chair. Since that year, all university teaching staff have been required to have a doctorate. Postgraduate students with grants are also considered teaching staff. It has been argued that current selection committees do not judge women candidates differently than men. Today there are more women who

Table 8.1 Male and female university teaching staff and the proportion of women according to faculty rank 1971–90

Rank	1971			1981			1990		
	Men	Women	%	Men	Women	%	Men	Women	%
Full Professors	444	5	1.1	689	25	3.5	1026	69	6.3
Assoc Professors	120	5	4.2	217	19	8.0	606	101	14.3
Assist Professors	15	–	0.0	24	2	7.7	1557	480	23.6
Lectors	112	13	10.4	181	18	9.0	976	550	36.0
Total Main Teach. Staff	691	23	3.2	1111	64	5.4	4165	1200	22.4
Teach. Asst. w/ PhD	453	83	15.5	1064	322	23.2	184	111	37.5
Teach. Asst. w/o PhD	1007	646	39.0	1030	750	42.1	544	453	45.5
Post-grad. students w/grant	–	–	–	–	–	–	358	211	37.0
Total Asst. Teach. Staff	1460	729	33.3	2094	1072	33.8	1086	775	41.6

Source: Ministry of Education, Bureau of Statistics (unpublished data). Higher Education Statistics (1971, 1981, 1990).

have obtained a doctorate abroad (although they are still fewer than men). However, even in the case of a Greek doctorate, statistics show that in 1989 only 32 per cent of postgraduate students were women, many of whom are expected to abandon their studies in order to have a family (Ministry of Education and Religion, 1989–90).

In Greece, university salaries are low and many academics supplement their income by doing outside research, teaching outside the university or working in an executive capacity for a public or private enterprise. All this demands time, which women usually are obliged to spend on their families.

Another adverse condition for women is the actual location of universities. Most are spread all over Greece and only a few are in Athens. That means that married women scholars often have to face the problem of leaving behind husband and children. In most cases, women accept a lector's position with limited teaching hours, so that they can commute weekly back and forth. However, despite all these obstacles more and more women scholars are determined to reach the higher ranks of the university pyramid.

Power is not shared

The university professional administrative structure consists of four bodies, considered as a pyramid; at the base there are the Chairmen of Departments, then the Deans of Faculties, then the University Senate and at the top the Rector and the Vice-Rectors. The Senate consists of the Rector and Vice-Rectors, the Deans, the Chairmen and representatives of professors, students, teaching assistants and administrative staff. In all electoral bodies, research and teaching staff and students have equal representation, roughly 50 per cent of the total membership.

Despite the democratic procedure of elections and the increased participation of women on the teaching staff, there are only two women Rectors or Deans in Greek universities. The Ionian University has a female Rector. However, in this case the Rector is not selected according to general university procedures, but appointed by the State. In addition the Harocopion University of Athens, which specializes in Home Economics, has mainly female professors and a female Rector. There is a relatively high proportion of women Chairpersons, but this post has limited power and a heavy burden of administrative tasks.

The high ranks of the administrative hierarchy are invested with power not only inside universities, but also in the political life of the country. It is not rare for a Rector to participate in national elections as a prominent member of a political party. The administrative structure of universities is intensively politicized and a high position is a good vehicle for publicity and promotion. If someone aspires to such a post, he or she has to create and use networks inside and outside the university. Women are not usually socialized to be involved in such networks and generally do not have the discretional time and money which are necessary for such enterprises.

Scientific research is still undervalued in Greece. There are no available funds in universities for research programmes. The Ministry of Education also has limited funds and as a consequence professors have to look for financing mostly from the private sector and from the European Community's programmes. This is another area where women have not done particularly well.

Female professions still exist

Horizontal segregation is also still obvious in Greek universities. As more women enter the university, social science courses are composed almost exclusively of female students. Families and schools still socialize girls to choose the so-called 'feminine' areas, such as literature, education and social sciences.

The horizontal segregation is evident in Table 8.2. Official statistics show that females have been over-represented in humanities and literature since 1937, while the proportion of women in technical and natural sciences has increased, but still remains low.

The same story is repeated in the newly developed academic field of information sciences. According to statistics provided by Cacoullos (1991), in both the universities of Patras and Crete, there was an average of 23 per cent of women students in the four-year period 1984-8. In the Economic University of Athens, where the course of study is composed of business statistics and computer science, there has been a significant increase in women students from 37 per cent in 1983-4 to 61 per cent in 1987-8.

As Table 8.3 reveals, the horizontal segregation is also remarkable among women scholars. The gender gap between social sciences and humanities, on the one hand, and natural and technical sciences, on the other, is wide and has remained constant over time. Female full professors are 30 per cent of the total in departments of education and 27 per cent in social sciences, while they are only 1.3 per cent in technical sciences and 3 per cent in natural sciences. Women lectors are 70 per cent of the total in literature, while they are 24.2 per cent in economic and political sciences and 30 per cent in technical sciences.

Table 8.2 *The proportion of female students according to field of study in universities and polytechnic schools, 1937-90*

Field of Study	1937	1960	1970	1980	1990
Univ. level					
Lit. and Humanities	51.2	52.7	68.2	76.0	84.5
Law	6.5	28.5	38.0	50.7	64.3
Soc. Eco. and Pol. Sci.	–	15.2	29.2	40.2	60.2
Medicine	7.5	23.0	28.9	34.5	45.5
Nat. Sci.	8.9	19.6	26.0	31.3	36.3
Polytech.					
Arch.	12.0	45.1	46.6	49.6	58.5
Civil Engs.	0.9	–	6.0	20.8	30.3
Elect. Engs.	–	–	–	9.2	13.0
Mech. Eng.	–	–	–	5.4	10.1

Source: Ministry of Education, Bureau of Statistics, Higher Education Statistics (1937, 1960, 1970, 1980, 1990).

Table 8.3 *The proportion of female faculty according to field in universities and polytechnic schools, 1989–90*

Field	Full Professors	Associate Professors	Assistant Professors	Lectors	Average
Literature and Humanities	20.0	33.4	45.0	70.0	54.2
Education	30.0	24.0	23.0	38.0	39.2
Law	9.4	20.0	10.0	42.0	39.0
Social Sciences	27.0	20.0	21.0	38.0	36.0
Economic and Political Sciences	6.0	0	17.5	24.2	30.0
Medicine	7.2	14.0	23.0	33.8	25.3
Natural Sciences	3.0	9.7	22.5	37.0	22.8
Polytechnic	1.3	9.8	20.4	30.0	19.7

Source: Ministry of Education, Bureau of Statistics, Higher Education Statistics (1989–90).

Although discrimination against women has been eliminated by law with regard to their access to education, employment and to power positions, statistics show that inequalities still prevail in the Greek Academy. As Eliou (1991) argues, discrimination still exists in the professional orientation of the academy, in its career perspective and in its pyramid of power.

Women's Studies: are they a hope?

Women's Studies developed in Greece very recently. The first attempt was made at the beginning of the 1980s, when the Mediterranean Women's Studies Institute (KEGME) was established in Athens. Every second year KEGME holds a summer programme on Women's Studies. It also organizes international seminars and research on women's issues. It is represented on the board of the European Network for Women's Studies (ENWS) and is a founding member of the European Network WISE.

A Women's Studies Group was also created in the University of Thessaloniki. This Group consists of women scholars who have integrated women's issues into their teaching and are also involved in feminist research. Women scholars have also introduced women's issues into the classroom in other Greek universities; however, no Women's Studies degree programmes have yet been developed.

Some concluding remarks

Despite extensive legislation to promote equality between the sexes there is still a gender gap in Greek academia. Although females often perform better than male students and there is an increasing number of women scholars in higher education, power continues to elude women. Women scholars are excluded from top positions because male academics choose to ignore or undermine women's qualifications, contributions and assets.

The main reasons seem to be: a) the still male-dominated university structure, which holds the reins of power; and b) the traditional mentality which still prevails among both Greek women and men concerning their proper roles in society.

In order to narrow the gender gap:

- the electoral bodies in universities should consist equally of men and women, so that women are given the opportunity to be judged in an unbiased spirit. Furthermore, a specific body within the university structure should be established, to which women scholars could submit their objections if they believe selection procedures dis- criminated against them;
- the state must take steps to enforce the implementation of existing legislation regarding equality. Special funds should be allocated for research on women's issues. In addition, childcare facilities, including crèches with flexible time schedules should be provided to women scholars;
- the results of Women's Studies research should be incorporated into the curriculum at all levels of the educational system in order to educate children from an early age.

If the State does not develop systematic and effective policies to promote equality in all sectors, and if society does not consider gender segregation as a common social problem, women will continue to be the 'second sex' in the academy as well as in society at large.

9. Women in higher education in Iran: tradition versus modernization

Tahereh Alavi Hojjat

SUMMARY: An era of modernization and expansion of women's rights has been followed, since 1979, by the imposition of legal disabilities and limitations. In the universities women have been barred altogether from studying certain (particularly technical) subjects and severe quotas have been placed on female enrolment in others. Although the government has attempted to maintain a sharp distinction between men's activities in the public sphere and women's within the family it has not been entirely successful because of the personnel shortages created by large-scale emigration and high casualty rates resulting from the war with Iraq.

Introduction

The origins of Persian history are shrouded in the dim past prior to the establishment of the Achaemenid dynasty in the sixth century BC. After the successors of Cyrus the Great were defeated by the Greeks (445 BC) the Persians turned their attention eastward and developed a civilization which was to dominate the region between the Central Asian steppes and the Indus Valley in the east to Anatolia and modern Iraq in the west for more than 2,000 years. In the seventh century AD the Arabs invaded Persia, bringing with them the Islamic faith which was eventually embraced by the majority of Persians, and thus replacing the indigenous Zoroastrian tradition which had prevailed since the time of Cyrus. Although there is little information about the status of women in pre-Islamic Persia, Plutarch asserts that Persian women used to fight in battle and participate in public affairs (Shaik-hulislami, 1972).

The broad panorama of Persian history is reflected in the composition of the Iranian population today. (The name of the country was changed from Persia to Iran in 1935.) Totalling over 60 million, Iran has a sparse population density of 37 per square kilometre, compared to Turkey's 76 and Great Britain's 236 (*CIA World Factbook*, 1992). Ethnically the majority of Iranians probably descend from the Aryan-speaking Persians and Medes of antiquity. However there is a sizeable Turkish minority in the north and a significant Arab minority in Khuzistan in the southwest, in addition to other ethnic groups including the Kurds, the Lur and the Baluch.

95

Influence of Islam on women

There have been two major competing arguments about the role of Islam in determining the position of women. One group has argued essentially that Islam is responsible for the low status of women in Iran and the Middle East (Kendall, 1968). In this view the Islamic tendency to assign different moral imperatives for men and women (housekeeping and childbearing for women and professional and economic activities for men) lies at the root of gender stratification in Muslim societies.

The pronouncements of various *ullama* (clerical leaders) have tended to lend credence to this point of view. For example, many clerics have asserted that it was contrary to Islamic teaching for women to learn to read and write (Sanasarian, 1982). Many also believed that women could not be educated because their brains did not have the capacity to absorb knowledge. A woman's literacy was considered such a social stigma that she often tended to hide it from others (*ibid.*). Religious leaders have traditionally encouraged veiling for women, and the conception that women are the weaker sex, in need of protection. They also advocate the exclusion of women from public and professional occupations since these would inevitably place them in direct and close contact with men (Nashat, 1983).

The second interpretation argues that no other religion has given women a higher status than Islam. This view stresses Islam's recognition of the need for women to be actively involved in social and political affairs and holds that any mistreatment of women should not be blamed on religion itself but rather on conservative and erroneous interpretations of Islam. This line of argument became popular during the peak of the anti-Shah movement in 1978. Generally, proponents of this view argue that there were explanations for the discriminatory clauses in the Koran (Sanasarian, 1982).

Women in early Iran

Toward the end of the eighteenth century women became more visible in Persian life and began to play a larger role in society (Nashat, 1983). The most important factor contributing to these changes was Persia's greater involvement with the West. In increasing numbers Persian diplomats and students travelled to Europe and Europeans came to Persia. Modern schools teaching European languages, customs and attitudes were opened.

An increased number of Persian men became advocates of modern education and began seeing to it that their daughters as well as their sons learned about the world beyond their doorsteps. However until the twentieth century there were few schools for girls in the country and the few who did receive an education had to be educated at home.

The first schools for girls were opened by American missionaries in Rizaiyeh in 1835 and in Teheran in 1895. The Persian government did not allow any Muslim girls to enter these schools so only those from Christian backgrounds were admitted. By the 1890s a handful of Muslim girls had quietly been enrolled in these schools. The first school devoted to the education of Muslim girls was opened in 1906, another was opened in 1907.

Although the founders of these schools were Muslim and the curricula included a great deal of emphasis on Islamic religious teaching, the schools and their founders were denounced by the religious authorities, who incited the populace to attack the students and teachers and to destroy the school buildings. The *ullama* regarded the schools for girls as a means of 'luring Muslim girls and leading their minds astray and turning them into unbelievers and wantons by pretending to give them lessons' (Shaikhu-lislami, 1972, p. 42).

Until the outbreak of World War II these and a handful of other schools that had been opened in Teheran, Shiraz and Isfahan were the only schools available for girls. However, the idea of modern education for girls had gradually gained acceptance and the first public school for girls was opened in 1918.

The expansion of European capitalism and the integration of Iran into the world market also affected the lives of women in Iran, particularly by increasing demand for Iranian agricultural products and handicrafts, especially rugs which traditionally were made by women. In the last decade of the nineteenth century these forces slowly gained momentum. At first only a handful of women were affected but gradually the lives of many were touched.

Women in the twentieth century

The early years of the twentieth century saw Russia and Great Britain competing for influence in Persia and by 1917 British and Russian troops had occupied almost the entire country. After the Bolshevik Revolution the Russians renounced the unequal treaties which the tsarists had imposed on Iran and cancelled Iran's debt to Russia. Britain moved into the vacuum by backing the rise to power of Reza Khan (later named Reza Shah), a semi-literate colonel of the Cossack Brigade, and encouraging him to stage a coup (Malik, 1992).

Reza Shah's tenure was a period of strong concentration of power in the central government. The power of the tribes was crushed and the foundations were laid for large-scale programmes of modernization of the army, the bureaucracy, the government and the educational system. These reforms, combined with the Shah's tyrannical method of rule, engendered fierce opposition from the clergy, who saw their traditional privileges eroded, and also from the intelligentsia whose liberalism could not countenance the Shah's tyranny (*ibid.*). However, many feminists at the time supported Reza Shah because they considered his reforms to be beneficial to women. These included changes in marriage and divorce laws, a prohibition on women wearing the veil and the expansion of education for women.

The lack of women teachers was one of the main obstacles to the expansion of educational opportunities for women. In 1934 the parliament approved laws establishing a number of women's teacher training colleges to remedy this deficiency. In 1936 the University of Teheran was opened and the first group of women entered the university along with men in that same year. Public and private schools began to mushroom in the capital and other cities. Although the increase in the number of girls' schools was impressive (from 41 in 1910 to 870 in 1933), boys' schools increased at an even faster rate, and by the 1930s they outnumbered those for girls by four to one (Woodsmall, 1983).

At the beginning of World War II the allies forced Reza Shah to abdicate because of his pro-German sympathies. His son, Mohammad Reza, assumed the title of Shah in 1941 without strong support from any of the traditional leadership groups.

In 1961 he introduced major changes in the constitution, which the clergy viewed as the initial steps towards the de-Islamization of Iran. These measures included the female franchise, the right of a non-Muslim political candidate to receive Muslim votes, and the swearing in of government officials on 'their holy book' rather than the Koran. The Shah's refusal to rescind these proposed constitutional amendments made a hitherto relatively obscure cleric named Khomeini the most vociferous critic of the Shah (Irfani, 1983; Malik, 1992).

Iran's post-World War II industrialization and urbanization did not fundamentally alter its gender-based division of labour. Only 9 per cent of all women worked for pay in 1956, and this figure had increased to only 12 per cent by 1971 (Iran Almanac, 1975). However, the female literacy rate increased from 8 per cent in 1956 (compared with 22.4 per cent for males) to 36.4 per cent in 1977 (compared to 66.7 per cent for males) (*Iran Statistical Yearbook*, 1367/1988–9).

Nashat (1983) argues that during the twentieth century, the attitude of Iranian society toward its women underwent a slow but fundamental change. This change affected women in the urban centres more than those in rural areas. Marriage was still the ultimate goal for a woman, but working outside the home and alongside men, before and after marriage, became acceptable in many families. It was increasingly recognized that women working outside of their homes could contribute to the development of the society without compromising their traditional roles as wives and mothers.

The economic and educational expansion of the 1960s and 1970s during the Shah's reign created a demand for labour which could not be satisfied with the available pool of qualified men. This increased the opportunities for women and helped to break down the remaining traditional social and psychological barriers which had been preventing women from working outside the home. As women became an important part of the labour force, they began to assume positions at all levels and in many professions, including medicine, law and the judiciary. Women even achieved high administrative posts in the government and some became members of parliament. The spread of education among girls from all social class backgrounds, including those from traditional families where women were still secluded and veiled, was another important spillover effect of the growth of employment opportunities (*ibid.*).

As a result of these changes, women's self-perceptions altered significantly. Women began to think of themselves as more than passive objects to be manipulated by men; they began to perceive themselves as active members of society who had a right to participate in government and to help shape the changes taking place in Iran. The participation of women in the massive demonstrations against the Shah's regime in 1978 and 1979 was testimony to this new consciousness.

The status of women after the revolution

As a result of the 1978 revolution in Iran and the subsequent establishment of the regime of Ayatollah Khomeini, fundamental changes occurred in society which drastically affected the lives and social position of women. One of the principal objectives of key members of the present Iranian regime has been to restore women to the positions they consider appropriate.

The view of Ayatollah Khomeini and other influential ideologues reflect long-standing traditional Iranian-Islamic attitudes about women and their proper roles in society. They generally believe that the primary division of labour in society should be based on gender. According to this view women should confine themselves to activities in the private domain and men have responsibility for the public domain (economics, politics, etc.) because the inborn physical and emotional differences between men and women dictate this dichotomy. Women are considered to be deficient in intellect and emotional stability, and thus are disqualified for careers which require cool judgement and strength of character such as the judiciary or high administrative positions. Women are considered to be particularly suited to the important tasks of motherhood; however, major decisions, both within the household and without, are to be made by men (*ibid.*).

As soon as Ayatollah Khomeini assumed power, his regime launched extensive efforts to restore women to their traditional roles. This, the clerics claimed, was in the interest of the women themselves as well as to the benefit of society. In particular, early marriage for women was advocated, birth control programmes were discontinued and young women were encouraged to devote themselves to the raising of children (and thereby become 'committed Muslims') rather than undertaking outside employment (Moghadam, 1991).

In addition, much of the legislation of the 1960s and 1970s which had favoured women was abrogated; an example was a new law barring women from acting as judges. In the early 1980s, the Islamic Republic declared certain areas of study off-limits to women. These included technology, veterinary science and agriculture. The reasons cited for the exclusion of women from these fields were the limited capacity of the university, the lack of job prospects for women in those fields, and the need for women specialists in other fields (*ibid.*).

By the 1987–8 academic year, the booklet guiding prospective university students in their choices of academic disciplines specified 65 fields out of the 108 listed in Group I (mathematics and computer science) which were closed to women. In seven other fields in this group, quotas under 50 per cent were specified for women. In Group II (experimental science), 21 out of 56 fields were open only to men, whereas two fields were open to women and men. In seven other fields in Group II, quotas under 50 per cent were specified for women. In Group III (humanities) three fields (out of 28) were closed to women and in six fields, quotas under 50 per cent were specified. In Group

IV (arts) the faculty decided to reject all female applicants at the advanced levels (*ibid.*).

Table 9.1 reflects these cultural priorities. While there are significant proportions of women at the Bachelor's level in medicine and health (61.3 per cent), social science (37.4 per cent), humanities (47.4 per cent), education (42.3 per cent) and the arts (36.7 per cent), at the PhD level there is a complete absence of women in a third of the listed areas of study and relatively small percentages of women in the others.

Table 9.1 clearly indicates the horizontal and vertical gender segregation which characterizes Iran's educational system. Traditional norms dictate a lower investment in higher education for women. For instance, some families feel that an 'enlightened woman' may have difficulty marrying, either because she may frighten off potential suitors, or because she herself may become too choosy. Furthermore, most people do not anticipate that girls would need to have an upper level position to be able to run a household financially (mainly that is the responsibility of men). Finally, only a small percentage of women have the confidence to believe that they can be successful in the stringent educational competition. All of these factors reduce the proportions of women at the higher levels of the university and also in top administrative positions in the universities and elsewhere. For instance, in 1987 only 4.5 per cent of higher administrative positions were held by women (*Iran Statistical Yearbook*, 1367/1988–9).

Both absolutely and relatively, more males than females are receiving education, at both the grade school and post-secondary levels. The gap is narrowest at the primary school level (where boys constitute 55 per cent of the student population and girls 44 per cent) and begins to widen at the intermediate school level, where the male and female shares are 60 and 40 per cent respectively. However, it is in the post-secondary student population that there is the most striking gender gap: out of 182,000 students receiving higher education in 1986, 56,000 (or 30 per cent) were female. On average, the female student population across the various levels of higher education constituted 31 per cent of the total (Moghadam, 1991).

The regime has also passed a number of laws to encourage women to return to the home and to ensure that they remain there. Various retirement programmes allow women who had worked as few as 15 years to retire with full benefits (Sanasarian, 1982). Daycare centres established during the previous regime in government agencies and factories were closed. After women were barred from the judiciary, scores of women were removed from top-level government posts; they were either forced to accept lower level jobs or to retire completely (*ibid.*). In addition to the abrupt dismissals, various psychological and verbal means were employed to facilitate and encourage the resignation of women.

The success of these policies in removing women from the work force is seen in the declining proportion of employed women (from 13.2 per cent in 1966–7 to 8.86 per cent by 1986–7). The female share of the total labour force is still small (under 10 per cent). The majority of employed women work in the public sector and as teachers and health workers; a mere 19 per cent of women in the private sector receive a wage for their work (some 42 per cent of women in the private sector are 'unpaid family workers') (*National Census*

Table 9.1 Enrolment at higher education institutes, by field of study and degree, 1988–9

Major	Professional Doctors			PhD or Specialists			Master's Degree			Bachelor's Degree			Associate Degree		
	Total	Male	Female	Total	Male	Female	Total	Male	Female	Total	Male	Female	Total	Male	Female
Medicine and Health	32037	21573 (63.4)	10464 (32.6)	1982	1462 (73.8)	520 (26.2)	1225	679 (55.4)	546 (44.6)	13519	5239 (38.7)	8280 (61.3)	16705	8676 (51.9)	8029 (48.1)
Law	0	0	0	0	0	0	168	159 (94.6)	9 (5.4)	4010	3534 (88.2)	476 (11.2)	0	0	0
Social Sciences	0	0	0	0	0	0	621	478 (76.9)	143 (23.1)	15206	9524 (62.6)	5682 (37.4)	57	57 (100)	0
Humanities	0	0	0	25	20 (80)	5 (20)	1502	1301 (86.6)	201 (13.4)	18352	9651 (52.5)	8701 (47.4)	0	0	0
Education	0	0	0	7	6 (85.7)	1 (14.2)	337	233 (69.1)	104 (30.9)	33677	19446 (57.7)	14231 (42.3)	843	543 (65.0)	300 (35)
Maths and Computer Science	0	0	0	17	14 (83.4)	3 (17.6)	204	173 (84.3)	31 (15.2)	6321	4528 (71.6)	1793 (28.4)	1432	1273 (88.6)	159 (11.4)
Engineering	0	0	0	18	17 (94.4)	1 (5.6)	1703	1656 (97.2)	47 (2.85)	36806	34623 (94.1)	2183 (5.9)	22100	21775 (98.5)	325 (1.5)
Arts	0	0	0	0	0	0	48	35 (73.9)	13 (27.1)	3341	2114 (63.3)	1227 (36.7)	67	49 (73.1)	18 (26.9)
Agriculture	1252	1238 (98.9)	14 (1.1)	17	14 (82.3)	3 (17.6)	531	495 (93.2)	36 (6.7)	8050	7525 (93.5)	525 (6.5)	4131	4131 (100)	0
Total	33289	22811	10478	2113	1575	537	8522	6944	1578	159904	110131 (68.9)	49773 (31.1)	46881	37426 (79.8)	9455

Source: Minister of Culture and Higher Education. *Iran Statistical Yearbook*, 1367/1988–9. Islamic Republic of Iran, Plan and Budget Organization, Statistical Center of Iran, Table 5–46: Teheran.

of Population and Housing, 1365/1988). This is an indication that most women are simply not being counted as part of the labour force and will therefore not be considered in any employment or income policies designed by the authorities.

Forced *hejab* is another repressive measure employed against women. Although no legislation has been enacted to make veiling compulsory, social harassment and strict office regulations have forced a majority of previously unveiled women to cover themselves. Lack of a *hejab* has been used as an excuse to remove women from their jobs. The threat of dismissal effectively silenced many women whose incomes were needed to support their families in a time of galloping inflation and worsening economic conditions.

In addition to the theological arguments which consider the veil to be the hallmark of the Muslim woman, its imposition accomplishes several stated goals of the regime. First, wearing the veil gives Iran the appearance of being Islamic. Second, wearing the veil makes it difficult for women to practice some professions (eg, surgery). Finally, it serves as a constant reminder to women of their place in society, secluded and isolated.

The post-revolution policy of gender segregation is also revamping the entire educational system. Coeducational schools have been abolished, along with all types of coeducational activities. Textbooks have been rewritten and curricula revised, stressing the different needs and natures of males and females. Moreover, all the women in textbook illustrations are veiled.

The impact of the Iran–Iraq war

On 22 September 1980 Iran was invaded by Iraq. This nine-year war brought enormous destruction to the country. Out of a population of 5.6 million in five provinces, there were 300,000 casualties, 61,000 missing in action, 50,000 disabled and 2.5 million lost their homes and/or jobs (Amirahmadi, 1990).

As the Iran–Iraq war continued, polygyny and the traditional Shi'ite custom of temporary marriage were encouraged as means of dealing with the excess of unmarried women (Moghadam, 1991). Unfavourable living conditions combined with the effects of clerical rule induced thousands of educated Iranians to leave the country. Many educated female graduates particularly resented the imposition of the *hejab*, since they perceived it as a constant reminder of their subservient place in society.

As a result of these trends, shortages occurred in the skilled labour force. With the growing demand for higher education, shortages of faculty in universities became particularly acute. This has created favourable opportunities for academic women and has led to the regime's providing more flexible conditions for female faculty as an inducement for them to remain at their posts. The relatively constant proportions of men and women students in institutes of higher education and the increase in female faculty are indicated in Table 9.2. In general, however, the government has not shown any active interest in improving the status of women or widening their career opportunities.

Notwithstanding the increased demand for skilled men and women in the

Table 9.2 *Staff and students at higher educational institutes, 1972–91*

Year	Instructional Staff*			Students		
	Total	Male	Female	Total	Male	Female
1972–3	9890	8764 88.6	1126 11.3	115311	80781 70.1	34530 29.9
1973–4	10465	9176 87.6	1289 12.4	123114	87002 70.6	36112 29.3
1974–5	12310	10628 86.3	1682 13.7	135353	96720 71.4	38634 28.5
1975–6	13492	11661 86.4	1831 13.6	151905	109116 71.8	42789 28.2
1976–7	13952	11894 85.2	2058 14.8	154215	108196 70.2	46019 29.8
1977–8	15453	13081 84.7	2372 15.3	160308	110798 69.1	49510 30.9
1978–9	16222	14008 86.3	2214 13.6	175675	121427 69.1	54248 30.9
1979–80	16877	14422 85.5	2455 14.5	174217	120646 69.2	53571 30.8
1980–83				117148	80792 68.9	36356 31.1
1981–4				121048	82405 68.1	38643 31.9
1982–3	9042	7618 84.3	1424 15.7			
1983–4	11494	9672 84.1	1822 15.8			
1984–5	13698	11557 84.4	2141 15.6			
1985–6	14690	12409 84.5	2281 15.5			
1986–7	14341	12048 84.1	2293 15.9			
1987–8	15950	13296 83.4	2654 16.6			
1988–9	17447	14500 83.1	2947 16.9			
1990–91	23376	19326 82.7	4050 17.3			

*Includes full-time, part-time and tuition earners. Figures reported for students of 1979–80 refer to graduates from October 1979 to September 1982.

Source: Ministry of Culture and Education, *A Statistical Reflection of the Islamic Republic of Iran*, 1365/March 1986.

labour market, and particularly at the university level, the gap between the professional status of men and women has increased.

The present university system and its professional structure

There are 61 state and private institutions of higher education in Iran offering 19 academic disciplines. The oldest university was founded in 1934 and the newest in 1990. State universities are subsidized by the government and the tuition fees are minimal. Entrance examinations for the state universities are highly competitive and only the top 10 per cent of applicants are successful. Among the 586,086 students who took the entrance examination for the 1986–7 academic year (383,245 males and 202,841 females), 6,100 persons were admitted (4,200 men and 1,900 women) (*Iran Statistical Yearbook*, 1367/1988–9). Admittance to private universities is less competitive. Only 1 per cent of the entire youth cohort goes on to higher education (*PC Globe*, 1992).

The present professional structure in Iranian universities follows the American pattern (see Table 9.3). Promotion from one level to another depends mainly on teaching ability, research, publication and seniority. The old system where promotion was automatic based on seniority has been replaced. Table 9.3 presents the distribution of men and women faculty in different ranks. Many of the women who have achieved the rank of full professor teach in the medical schools, reflecting the need for well-educated women to service the medical needs of the female population.

The pyramidal shape of the rank distribution among female faculty is partially explained by the discriminatory practices of the government. For instance, in order to be eligible for government scholarships to study abroad

Table 9.3 *Distribution of men and women in universities*

Rank	Men	Women	Total
Full Professor	667 94.1	42 5.9	709
Associate Professor	1,279 93.6	88 6.4	1,367
Assistant Professor	5,363 87.7	751 12.3	6,114
Instructor and Lecturer	5,803 80.7	1,392 19.3	7,195
Assistant Instructor	741 74.1	259 25.9	1,000
Total	13,853 84.5	2,532 15.5	16,385

Source: *Iran Statistical Yearbook*, Plan and Budget Organization, Teheran, Iran, 1367/1988–9, and Ministry of Culture and Higher Education, Center for Educational Planning, 1368/1990–91.

(which are often considered significant when a faculty member applies for promotion), female faculty must be married and accompanied by their husbands. A recent study (Sharfi, 1991) shows that in most cases only men are encouraged to participate in professional conferences held abroad.

Summary and conclusions

Throughout the long history of Iran the status of women has changed as their perceptions of themselves and men's attitudes towards them changed. In this century these transformations were the result partly of increased contact with the West and efforts to imitate the West, and partly of changing economic and social conditions within Iran.

After the revolution the leaders of the Islamic Republic tried to restore traditional gender roles; however, the exodus of a large part of the educated labour force combined with the massive destruction and dislocation incurred during the Iran–Iraq war had created severe labour shortages in all areas, and particularly at the university. This has encouraged the regime to adopt a more flexible attitude toward women in academia, aimed at retaining existing female faculty. In Iran today, women may be veiled, but they are to be found in schools, universities, government offices and even factories. Ideologies of gender differences and practices reflecting gender inequality may exist, but they are subject to the challenges of economic development and demographic change.

Within the university there is both horizontal and vertical gender segregation. 'Men's work' and 'women's work' are social and cultural constructs which underlie women's disadvantaged position in academia and Iranian society in general (Moghadam, 1991).

This analysis has relied heavily upon published statistics whose accuracy may rightly be questioned by those who are aware of the many possible flaws in data published in developing countries. Nevertheless, the picture that emerges is, although the authorities of the Islamic Republic view men and women as having fundamentally different natures, needs and abilities, they have not been completely successful in driving women out of public life.

10. Women academics in The Netherlands: between exclusion and positive action

Greta Noordenbos

SUMMARY: Dutch society is characterized as tolerant and caring; women are the primary caretakers at home and also in the labour market. This produces a huge vertical and horizontal sex segregation, which is clearly visible in the positions women have in the universities. Most female members of the university staff are found in the less prestigious posts in the social sciences and the humanities and typically have temporary and part-time appointments. This reduces their career mobility. Only 3 per cent of the full professors are women. Different explanations of this phenomenon are described and recommendations are given to improve this situation.

The Netherlands: a welfare state based on feminine values?

The Netherlands is a small, densely populated country with about 15 million inhabitants. Originally an agricultural and sea-faring nation, industry has transformed the economy, particularly since the Second World War. Because of its colonial past in Indonesia and Surinam, and because of the past need for unskilled labour which necessitated the import of foreign workers (for example, from Turkey and Morocco), The Netherlands is now becoming a multicultural society. At the present time, the country is a capitalist welfare state, with a relatively successful and smooth-running economic system.

Two useful stereotypes to characterize the spirit of the Dutch people are their mentalities of merchant and clergyman. The Dutch mind looks outward, driven on the one hand by its commercial spirit and on the other by its evangelizing sense of mission. This interest in other countries, and dependence upon them, is demonstrated not only in The Netherlands' membership of the European Community (EC) and the North Atlantic Treaty Organization (NATO), but also in the fact that secondary school pupils have to learn at least two foreign languages.

Equal rights before the law is a value central to the Dutch political system. Tolerance of other opinions and beliefs is reflected in the politics of most of the nearly ten political parties in The Netherlands. Hofstede (1980), in his comparison of different national cultures, argues that feminine values feature strongly in The Netherlands' scale of priorities: it is important to

106

protect (amongst others) children and old people, the handicapped and the unemployed. The result is a widespread system of social support, which has made The Netherlands the hallmark of an efficient welfare state. These social values have significant consequences for the patterns of wealth distribution: for example, the differences between rich and poor are not so marked in this country as in the United States. However, significant differences between employment patterns of men and women in the labour market and in public life remain.

Dutch women: part-time workers in a segregated labour market

The first women's movement, founded around 1900, was concerned with the struggle for granting suffrage to women, which was only realized in 1919. In the 1960s the second women's movement developed, focusing on the struggle for equal opportunities in the labour market. At that time only one-quarter of Dutch women were employed in the labour force, giving The Netherlands one of the lowest participation rates in the industrialized Western world (Oudijk, 1983).

The reason for this state of affairs is partly historical: in the first half of this century, the ruling political parties campaigned for a living wage for men which would enable them to provide for their families adequately, thus obviating the need for women to work outside the home. The primacy which Dutch society placed upon a woman's family role was indicated by a Ministerial decision in 1924 to dismiss female civil servants when they married and a law in 1935 mandating dismissal of married female schoolteachers.

These patterns were only modified in the 1960s when the demands of a now-flourishing economy could only be met by the employment of semi-skilled female workers. Women workers had become scarce, partly because young women now married at an earlier age, and partly because they were staying longer at school (Verwey-Jonker, 1981).

In 1980 the participation of women in the labour market was only 30 per cent, compared to men's 85 per cent. In 1991, however, the women's percentage reached 55 and the men's 81 (Social and Cultural Report [SCP], 1992, p. 85). This increase was due to fewer women leaving paid employment after their first child, and married women trying to get back into the labour market. At present, 50 per cent of the women who are working are married, while in 1960 this percentage was only 19 (Huisman, 1981, p. 142). Additional factors accounting for this change are the introduction of the 'pill' in 1964, the absence of financial cost for abortions since the 1970s and the legalization of abortion in 1983.

These increases in the number of women in the labour market do not imply, however, a proportionate increase in the actual hours worked by women, because most women, 54 per cent in fact, are part-time employees (Brouns and Schokker, 1990, p. 26). The Netherlands, together with the Scandinavian countries, has the highest percentage (24 per cent) of part-time workers in the European Community (SCP, 1990, p. 80). Of all part-time workers 80 per cent are women (SCP, 1990, p. 73). Basing her argument on these figures, Demenint-de Jongh (1989) concludes that Dutch women have merely distributed the available work more widely.

One of the reasons for the widespread part-time employment of women is that domestic duties are not shared equally: women spend on average nearly 30 hours each week on unpaid work in the home, while men contribute less than ten hours (Brouns and Schokker, 1990, p. 31). Moreover, childcare facilities were until recently very scarce, and most centres had long waiting lists.Yet another factor is that until 1990 only 12 weeks were allowed for full-time paid pregnancy leave (Bruyn-Hundt, 1988); in 1990 this was extended to 16 weeks. The possibility of parental, as opposed to maternal leave, has only recently been introduced.

Although more women are employed in the labour market nowadays, the horizontal sex segregation in employment has not diminished. On the contrary, most women only work in a limited range of occupations, in the so-called 'women's jobs'; they are only very slowly squeezing their way into the traditionally male occupations. Men, however, enter the higher positions in women's occupations much more easily (Mourik and Siegers, 1982; Ott, 1985).

In addition to the marked horizontal sex segregation in employment, there is also a marked vertical sex segregation. Most women work in low paid jobs which require a minimum level of schooling. Although the Netherlands has had a historical sequence of four generations of queens (Emma, Wilhelmina, Juliana and Beatrix), there were (in 1992) only three female Cabinet Ministers, and they were still consciously addressed as women rather than simply as ministers.

Notwithstanding the increasing participation of women in the labour market and in higher education, the gap between the professional status of men and women has not become smaller, it has in fact become larger. The average income of women still lags far behind that of men.

The university: the slow entry of women into a forbidden world

The university of Leiden was founded in 1575 but women had to wait three centuries before they could legally enter. In the seventeenth century a learned woman by the name of Anna Maria van Schurman was given per-mission to attend some lectures, but she had to remain invisible to the male students, and thus had to arrive at the lecture room early in the morning, sit behind a curtain during the lecture and leave the room only after all male students had gone (Baar *et al.*, 1992). It was not until 1871 that Alette Jacobs was given permission by the Minister of Education to study medicine for one probationary year. Despite difficulties, she completed her course success-fully, and shortly afterwards received her doctorate (Jacobs, 1978). Until 1900 her example inspired only a relatively small number of women, but in the early twentieth century there was a steady growth in the number of female students.

Until 1900 there was no question of participation by women in the faculties of a university even though the first women students achieved good to excellent results, and many gained their PhDs *cum laude*. It was not until 1917 that the first woman in the Netherlands was appointed as adjunct professor (Bosch, 1988). Even as recently as 1990 very few women (fewer than 3 per cent) have achieved the position of professor (Hawkins and Noordenbos, 1990).

Restructuring the university system: women as the losing party

There are 14 universities in The Netherlands at the present time, of which five are state universities, one is Protestant, two are Catholic, one is maintained by the local authorities, one is agricultural, three are technical and one is an open university.

Until recent times, Dutch universities had a system of 'automatic promotion' from one rank to the next. Financial considerations resulted in a change in this policy, so that criteria for promotion became much more stringent and automatic promotion is no longer in effect. A redefinition of ranks also took place, reducing the number of positions and creating a professional structure similar to that of American universities. In addition, when the number of tenured posts at universities was reduced for economic reasons, market related and technical disciplines were favoured at the cost of the arts and the social sciences, where most women are concentrated. Doctoral students, who formerly had been promised a tenured position after successful completion of their theses, are now generally only offered temporary contracts. It was further decided that students could no longer spend more than six years on a course which in principle should have been completed in four.

All of these changes had particularly adverse effects on women because they typically were younger than their male colleagues in a particular rank, had had fewer research experiences, and their childcare obligations tended to make them take longer to fulfil their academic requirements. For women the negative effects of the restructuring have been far more telling than the positive effects of equal rights policies (including advertisements which invite women to apply for a position at the university, affirmative action programmes, career development guidance and the introduction of childcare systems) which were introduced into the universities by Emancipation Politics (van Doorne-Huiskes, 1990).

Although between 1970 and 1980 there was a general increase in the absolute number of women academics in the universities (Hawkins and van Balen, 1984), at the same time the relative number of women in the two highest positions fell (Hawkins and Noordenbos, 1990). Table 10.1 represents the total number and percentages of academic men and women from the top three ranks in the universities in the years 1970 to 1990.

In Table 10.1 we can see that between 1970 and 1990 approximately 90 per cent of the highest ranking positions were held by men. The majority of women were to be found in the lowest rank. If we confine our attention to the two highest ranks, then we can see that the proportion of professors who were women fell from 2.7 per cent in 1970 to 2.2 per cent in 1980 and

Table 10.1 *Distribution of women by rank in 1970, 1980 and 1990*

Rank		1970 Number	%	1980 Number	%	1990 Number	%	Rank
Professor and 'lektor'	M	2,314	97.8	3,113	97.8	2,325	97.4	Prof. reader
	F	65	2.7	71	2.2	63	2.6	
WHM (associate professor)	M	2,988	90.6	5,887	91.1	2,206	93.9	UHD (assoc. prof.)
	F	312	9.4	577	8.9	144	6.1	
WM (assistant professor)	M	4,285	88.2	4,327	85.0	5,081	84.2	UD (assis. prof.)
	F	571	11.8	769	15.0	949	15.7	
Total of three highest ranks	M	9,584	91.0	13,327	90.4	9,612	89.3	
	F	948	9.0	1,417	9.6	1,156	10.7	

Source: Hawkins and van Balen (1984); Hawkins and Noordenbos (1990); WOPI (1991).

increased again to 2.6 per cent in 1990. The proportion of female associate professors, who were reorganized from *Wetenschappelijke Hoofdmedewerkers* (WHM) to University Head Docents (UHD), fell from 9.4 per cent in 1970 to 8.9 per cent in 1980 and to 6.1 per cent in 1990. Since professors are usually recruited from among those at the UHD level, this development also indicates the severity of the consequences of this reorganization for the equitable distribution of posts within the next generation of professors. Only in the lowest rank of assistant professor, which was reorganized from *Wetenschappelijk Medewerker* (WH) to University Docent (UD), do we see an increased representation of women, from 11.8 per cent in 1970, to 15 per cent in 1980 and 15.7 per cent in 1990.

Although a higher percentage (28.7) of women can be found in the position of docent or researcher (*HOOP, Facts and Numbers*, 1991), their careers are usually temporary and very restricted, because docents do not have the opportunity to apply for the post of assistant professor, which is only open to those who have completed their PhD. In 1990 female PhD students decreased to 28 per cent, so even at the entry level we can see that the position of women is deteriorating in the universities.

The present domination of the UHD and professor posts by men (more than 94 and 97 per cent respectively) will remain a permanent scenario throughout the 1990s, because professional and UHD appointments are usually long-term and there will be few increases in the scant number of UHD and professor positions in the next few years. This means that for the most part men will continue to determine the ends and the means for research and education programmes and a strong vertical sex segregation will remain in the near future. Strong horizontal sex segregation is also manifest in the university hierarchy.

Explanations for the relatively low position of women academics

The following possible reasons may explain why women are more disadvantaged by the consequences of the economies and restructuring measures than men:

- women are newcomers to the universities;
- women are a minority group and have less power and access to networks;
- women more often have part-time jobs, resulting from their upbringing and consequent double life perspective;
- women more often are appointed to short, temporary posts resulting from the policy to reduce the number of tenured posts;
- discriminatory forms of selection and self-selection;
- restrained career orientation.

Women: newcomers in academe

The majority of women in academia entered during the last few decades, a period which has been characterized by economic reductions and cutbacks.

Table 10.2 *Division of men and women by rank and field in 1990, number and percentage*

	Professor		Associate Professor (UHD)		Assistant Professor (UD)		Docent/Teacher (OVWP)		PhD Student (AIO)		Administration (OBP)	
	M	F	M	F	M	F	M	F	M	F	M	F
Agriculture	94 97.0	3 3.0	108 97.0	3 3.0	321 87.0	46 13.0	196 69.0	49 20.0	152 69.0	67 31.0	622 69.0	273 31.0
Natural Sciences	419 99.0	3 1.0	397 97.0	14 3.0	533 92.0	45 8.0	588 82.0	125 18.0	839 79.0	227 21.0	1,701 70.0	737 30.0
Technical Fields	357 99.0	4 1.0	365 99.0	5 1.0	964 96.0	40 40.0	626 89.0	79 11.0	864 89.0	106 11.0	2,077 77.0	638 23.0
Health Sciences	523 98.0	11 2.0	519 92.0	43 8.0	1,113 80.0	273 20.0	1,072 68.0	495 32.0	423 60.0	287 40.0	1,702 48.0	1,808 52.0
Economy	171 99.0	2 1.0	148 96.0	5 4.0	415 92.0	36 8.0	183 86.0	29 14.0	202 82.0	44 18.0	106 28.0	268 72.0
Law	168 98.0	4 2.0	137 91.0	14 9.0	334 67.0	162 33.0	152 53.0	133 47.0	131 57.0	97 43.0	162 36.0	322 67.0
Social Sciences	278 96.0	12 4.0	300 91.0	30 9.0	658 81.0	150 19.0	661 62.0	404 38.0	308 54.0	260 46.0	456 42.0	625 58.0
Humanities	291 93.0	23 7.0	218 88.0	30 12.0	670 88.0	190 22.0	324 54.0	278 46.0	274 57.0	204 43.0	269 41.0	391 59.0
Other	24 96.0	1 4.0	15 100.0	0 8.0	72 89.0	9 11.0	374 80.0	95 20.0	171 87.0	25 13.0	5,557 66.0	2,903 34.0
Total	2,325 97.0	63 3.0	2,206 94.0	144 6.0	5,081 84.0	949 16.0	4,175 71.0	1,687 29.0	3,365 72.0	1,318 28.0	12,652 61.0	7,964 39.0

Source: WOPI (1991).

Most new jobs are part time and short term. Women are more likely to be appointed to new posts than to take over established positions (Rendel, 1984), so women are over-represented in the most vulnerable positions – those in which whomever comes last, leaves first. Further, a PhD is now required for almost any academic career. Since many women in the 1980s were still relative newcomers, a large number of them did not have their PhDs although this was exactly the period in which that became a requirement for the attainment of high-level posts (Hawkins and Noordenbos, 1990).

Women academics: in a minority group position

According to Moss Kanter's (1977) 'token theory', the greater the extent to which women in an organization are an exception, the more likely it is that they will be kept out of informal networks, and the less likely are they to be encouraged and stimulated by their colleagues and supervisors. Indeed they will have limited access to the 'old boy' networks where important information is available and decisions are made. These are the factors which cause women, already in a minority position, to fall further and further behind men in their career development. Moreover, a large number of women on the staff does not automatically ameliorate these problems, because most women in academe have part-time and temporary posts. Promotion takes more time for part-timers and a large number of them leave academe after a few years (Beekes, 1991; Noordenbos, 1990; Portegijs, 1990).

Women academics as part-timers

Most women are still brought up with a double life perspective, and it is this which to a large extent results in their having part-time posts. Research by Demenint-de Jongh (1989) acknowledges that part-time posts have created the opportunity for women to participate in the universities even when their children are small. Noordenbos (1990) shows, in a comparison between departments with relatively few and relatively many women, that contrary to what might be expected from the theory of Moss Kanter, it is the women who are well represented in departments who have fallen behind their male colleagues after several years. It is in these very departments that women are more likely to have part-time posts. This is mainly the result of job-sharing rather than an increase in the number of hours available for women (Demenint-de Jongh, 1989). Higher-level academic posts are seldom offered to those working part time. Also, having a part-time post means that the teaching load leaves little time for research, which is the major criterion for promotion.

Women academics: the temporary workers

Of the women academics who were working in 1987, almost two-thirds had a temporary appointment, as against one-third of their male colleagues. Moreover, women academics also have a faster turnover than the men. The

Table 10.3 *Reasons given by men and women academics for leaving the universities in the year 1986–7, per cent*

Reason for leaving	Women	Men	Total
At own request	23.7	31.4	29.0
Contract terminated	64.2	46.0	51.5
Redundant	7.7	13.9	12.0
(Early) retirement	4.4	8.7	7.5

Source: Portegijs (1990).

duration of employment for temporarily appointed women academics is on average shorter than that for men (22 months as opposed to 28 months).

Table 10.3 indicates that the greatest share of women leave the university not of their own accord (as is usually suggested), but because their contracts have expired. Between 1986–8 this reason for leaving became increasingly frequent both for women (from 56 to 66 per cent) and for men (42 to 46 per cent). However, men are still much less likely than women to leave because, considering the present 'flexibility policy' whereby the percentage of women with temporary posts will further increase, it can only be expected that the turnover of women will become greater.

Forms of discrimination during recruitment and selection

From research carried out by van Vianen (1987) it appears that for higher-level posts selection boards give preference to people with 'male' char-acteristics such as competitiveness, leadership qualities, etc. Even where women considered that they possessed these 'male' characteristics, it was found that interviewers were unlikely to perceive them. Such a preferred profile may lead selection boards to favour male applicants for tenured positions and to appoint women candidates mainly for temporary posts.

In addition to these forms of discriminatory selection, there are gender-specific and power factors which play a part in the self-selection of respondents. Noordenbos (1990) shows that women on occasion fail to apply for a UHD post or a chair because they do not consider themselves (yet) qualified; more importantly, even when they consider that they are well qualified, they have the impression that:

a) the job description is already tailored to meet the profile of an existing male colleague;
b) some male colleagues who already have their doctorates have been in the department for a longer time and cannot be overtaken;
c) relationships within the department would be adversely affected if a relatively younger woman were appointed to a post where there were older male academics;
d) the social and emotional cost is too high: women who were well qualified and had applied for the higher position sometimes withdrew because the atmosphere within the department and among colleagues became unpleasant; or they withdrew their applications because of the

risk of damaging their health and the functioning of their family (Hawkins and Noordenbos, 1990).

Restrained career orientation

It is also possible that women are less inclined to apply for a higher position because they consider that their chances of obtaining it are not high. This can be a form of self-selection, which Hawkins (1990) has identified in her research comparing the different perceptions of the work situation of women and men academics. Her study shows that men are more often encouraged to attend congresses, to obtain their doctorates, etc. Women also had more restrained attitudes regarding their career development in comparison with the more aggressive approach of men. The greater initiative taken by men in the acquisition of research funds was particularly striking. Since women usually have responsibility for home and family as well as for their academic duties, they are often less career oriented than their male colleagues. The key question is, of course, to what extent free choices are available (van Doorne-Huiskes, 1990). Many women consider themselves obliged to do part-time work and not spend too long on their academic duties, because of lack of childcare facilities and parental leave and little assistance from their husbands with ordinary household chores.

Strategies to improve the position of academic women

The following recommendations are important first steps in positive action programmes to improve the position of academic women.

- Measures need to be taken to enhance the entry of academic women and reduce the turnover. Personnel policy makers and appointment boards need to be made aware of present trends.
- Positive action plans should be designed to achieve acceptable and attainable quotas for the proportional representation of women appointed at all levels.
- More attention has to be given to reducing the number of women being appointed to temporary posts and leaving academic life if it is really the intention that the appropriate quotas of representation be attained.
- Further attention needs to be given to the identification of the factors which most hinder women from obtaining higher posts.
- More information has to be obtained concerning the mechanisms which play a role in the selection procedures used in appointment to associate professor and professor.
- Women must not only be encouraged to obtain their doctorates and to publish; they must also be helped to learn how to apply for and obtain subsidies and research grants, since this is an important element in the successful attainment of high-level posts.
- Since women are so frequently appointed to part-time posts, an investigation should be conducted to determine the extent to which it

is possible to occupy a high-level position on a part-time basis. A study should also be made of the possibilities of reducing the necessity for part-time work for women through the improvement of childcare facilities and the provision of paternal leave in the very near future.

- The entrance and exit of women academics should also be carefully registered and monitored. In order to achieve this, the universities should be more carefully coordinated.
- Recruitment and selection need to remain focal points for an emancipation policy.
- Women should be encouraged to apply for higher-level posts, to form networks and to organize a lobby to press for a reversal of the deteriorating situation of academic women.

Conclusion

Although The Netherlands is often described as the model of an egalitarian welfare state, women are typically segregated in low-prestige 'women's jobs' like the caring professions, and where women are found in other occupations, very few are in higher ranks. This sex segregation, observable in employment patterns, is also observable in the participation rates of women in formal education. Not only do women spend less time than men in education, they also choose different subjects. There is a marked pattern of both horizontal and vertical sex segregation, whereby female students are typically found in subjects with low value in the labour market. Most female members of the university staff are found in the less-prestigious posts and typically have temporary and part-time appointments.

Explanations for these trends point to economic factors, which are related to fewer available positions. Since women as newcomers to the university can generally obtain only short-term, temporary appointments, they remain a minority group with respect to their male colleagues, and this compounds their difficulties in being appointed to significant positions. Pressures both inside and outside the university make it difficult for women to develop a successful academic career.

It is important to aim for an increase in the number of women at all levels via positive action programmes. Women's upward mobility may be enhanced by guiding them in their career planning; the number of women leaving the system may be reduced by improving facilities for them both inside and outside the university.

11. Higher education in Norway: a nirvana of equality for women?

Suzanne Stiver Lie and Mari Teigen

SUMMARY: Collective action on the part of the women's movement has caused a partial transformation of Norwegian society. There is now political and societal consensus regarding gender equality. Women are in the forefront of politics and are active in the agenda-setting process. Their demands have been translated into a number of national positive action measures in higher education. However, a harsh economic climate leading to sharpened competition for fewer positions and resistance from the (male) establishment to affirmative action programmes has resulted in a wide gap between the ideology of gender equality and reality in the academic world.

Introduction

A small and homogeneous nation on the periphery of Europe, Norway has a population of 4.5 million. The people of Norway traditionally wrung their living from activities connected with the sea and farming until the development of hydroelectric power at the turn of the century. Since the discovery of vast oil reserves in the North Sea in the 1970s, Norway has been among the most affluent nations in the world with a high standard of living and a well-developed and comprehensive system of public welfare.

After the Second World War, an overwhelming political consensus transformed Norway (and the rest of the Scandinavian countries) into a welfare state whose underlying ideology is based upon the ideals of justice and equality. This ideology (not only of opportunity, but of results) has found expression in three decades of expansion of the welfare state and the improvement of the status of women.

The circumstance which sets Norway apart from many countries is that the 'second wave' of the women's movement has been instrumental in affecting the national policy of equality. The purpose of this chapter is to explore the means by which the goals of the women's movement have been incorporated into the society as a whole and into higher education in particular.

The roots of Norwegian gender equality

Gender equality in Norway must be seen in connection with women's historic relatively free position (Berggreen, 1992). The geography of Norway, with its thousand mile coastline, largely accounts for the often hazy division of tasks between men and women. Traditionally Norway was a maritime nation of seafarers, traders, whalers and fishermen. From Viking times to the present, women were in charge of farming and community life when men were at sea for long periods of time. Cultural prescriptions dictated that the sea was men's domain, though women stepped aside when men were at home (*ibid.*).

Industrialization, which emerged in Norway in the last part of the nineteenth century, resulted in more rigid cultural definitions of the gender-based division of labour. In the cities, a 'housewife ideology' arose dictating that women's sphere was restricted to the home (Aasen, 1993). In the rural areas it was not until the introduction of farm machinery after the Second World War that women's activities became primarily restricted to the household (Berggreen, 1992).

The *bourgeois* ideal of the 'stay at home wife' gradually filtered down into the working classes and was ultimately incorporated into a primary goal of the welfare state – that an industrial worker's wage should be sufficient to support a 'stay at home wife' and children (Lie, 1990). This in large part accounts for Norway's having the lowest employment rate of women in Western Europe until well into the 1970s.

The Norwegian model of gender equality

Since equality is a central value in Norwegian culture, the state and political parties have been responsive to the demands of the present-day women's movement which calls for a social transformation, a new gender ordering of society – a complete redistribution of responsibilities and duties at work and within the family. This was reflected in the Equal Status Act of 1979, which had a two-fold aim: 1) equality of treatment in areas of employment, politics, etc. and 2) changing gender roles resulting in a more equitable sharing of family and labour force activities. The Equal Status Act also required that all national or municipal appointed committees should have at least 40 per cent representation of either sex. In order to achieve these goals a series of national positive action plans was introduced. The 1989 plan sets a national agenda and authorizes national, state and municipal bodies to work out their own plans to promote equality between the sexes according to national guidelines (Norge: *St meld Nr.70*, 1991–2).

With increasing numbers of women in the government and leadership posts in the public sector, a change in priorities is in the making. This gradual and unobtrusive incorporation of feminist values within the institutional structure of the state is a phenomenon which Hernes (1987) refers to as 'state feminism'. Recent examples are state programmes which include both parents, leave for parents of sick children and paternity leave (Blix *et al.*, 1993). In Norway there appears to be a stronger alliance between the state and the women's movement than in most countries.

A 'feminine political' revolution

Norwegian women's greatest success has been their integration into politics during the 1970s and 1980s. In 1986 a world record was established with a female head of state and eight (out of a total of 18) female cabinet members. Subsequent governments have followed suit, guaranteeing an almost equal representation of women in the government. Today 36 per cent of the members of the national assembly are women. Figures at the county and municipal levels are equally impressive. Although there are no formal quota requirements for elected political positions, most political parties have 40/60 internal gender quotas. The inclusion of women in politics was made possible because political parties accepted the representation of women as a group as a legitimate demand (Skjeie, 1991).

Increased equality in the labour market

By 1990 women constituted nearly 45 per cent of the labour force; more than 70 per cent of Norwegian women today have undertaken paid employment outside the home. The greatest increase has been among mothers of small children who now work full time as often as part time (Kjeldstad and Lyngstad, 1993).

In 1991 women's hourly wages were, on average, 80 per cent of men's. Wage differences are due primarily to a sex-segregated labour market. A recent study by Petersen et al. (1993) showed that wage differences in the private sector are negligible (2–6 per cent) when the position and type of occupation are held constant.

The equal rights legislation of 1987 mandates that employers make special efforts to recruit more women and promote them up the managerial ladder. Nevertheless, the proportion of women in leading positions in the private sector only increased from 16 to 19 per cent in 1983–91, in the public sector from 36 to 43 per cent. This increase has been primarily at the middle level. Among top executives there was no change in the proportion of women between 1983 and 1991. Thirteen per cent of top leaders were women in the private sector in 1991 and 20 per cent in the public sector (Kjeldstad and Lyngstad, op.cit.).

The equality myth – a barrier to equality?

In spite of many advances, equality of results in Norway is far from having been achieved. Because the welfare state is based on a model of the man as breadwinner, backed up by women's paid and unpaid work, women still face many difficulties participating in the labour market. Despite the national goal of shared family responsibilities, women still shoulder the main responsibility for home and children. A weakened economy and a wave of conservatism in the 1980s and 1990s now poses a threat to the welfare state's very existence. However, perhaps the greatest threat to gender equality is the widespread belief that equality between the sexes has already been achieved.

Alma mater's daughters: from exclusion to admittance on men's terms

The first university in Norway (the University of Oslo) was established in

1811. However, it was not until 70 years later (1882) that women were given the privilege of studying there. Women were seen as intruders, threatening the *doxa* of the male establishment (see Bourdieu [1988] cited in Chapter 1 of this volume.) The medical faculty in 1886, trying to deny women's admittance to medical school, used arguments prevalent at the time in Europe and North America. Women were not only of inferior intellectual ability, but educating them would diminish their reproductive powers and threaten the welfare of posterity. It was not until 1903 that the first Norwegian woman received a doctorate and 1912 that the first female professor came on the scene. Women did not 'storm the ivory tower' as expected by the beginning of the Second World War. Only 9 per cent of the students receiving a university diploma were women (Rørslett and Lie, 1984).

Gender equality in higher education – a national priority

The official Norwegian policy of gender equality regards education as an important (perhaps the most important) vehicle for women to achieve greater equality in central areas of society (*NOU*, 1988, p. 28; Norge: *St meld Nr. 28*, 1988–9; *St meld Nr. 36*, 1992–3). A primary national goal is to increase the proportion of women in research and in top positions within the university system. It is argued that women are an important resource because their experiences can offer new perspectives within the scientific community.

By using this rhetoric of difference imported from politics, a number of initiatives have been introduced at the national level. For example, because of the low percentage of women in top positions, the government set aside funds in 1986 for the appointment of qualified women to the position of full professor at the universities. Partly because of male protest this incentive was widened to include men who also have received full professor competence. Although universities receive funds for all advanced degree recipients, university departments receive increased funding when female students achieve higher degrees. Other national goals are made concrete in the positive action measures put forth by the Research Council of Norway, the Secretariat for Women's Research and the Equal Opportunity Council at each of the universities. Many of these initiatives have encountered considerable opposition from the male scientific community.

The Research Council of Norway

The Research Council of Norway is a national funding organization promoting research in the sciences and humanities; it has worked actively since the mid-1970s to introduce equal opportunity measures. Since 1981 a quota system has been implemented to increase the proportion of female scholarship holders (those working for their doctorates). Quotas are used to women's advantage where they are under-represented, that is, where they constitute less than 40 per cent in a discipline or within specific staff categories within each discipline. Quotas are used *only* where candidates are evaluated as approximately equally well qualified.

The Research Council's equal opportunity measures of 1989–92 and 1993–5 are extensive (NAVF, 1992). Aimed at reducing the female drop-out rate (which is higher than for males) from advanced degree programmes, these include improved counselling and equipment, and courses and research on the gender perspective. In order to increase the proportion of women on the faculty, preferential treatment is given in the form of research sabbaticals, travel grants and other types of scholarships.

The Secretariat for Women's Research

The brainchild of feminist researchers, the Secretariat for Women's Research aims to increase the number of women engaged in research and to coordinate and promote research on women. The Secretariat, which has national status, was instituted on a trial basis in 1977 and became a permanent body in 1990. The survival of the Secretariat was the result of struggle and hard-sought alliances by women both inside and outside of the university. Partly as a result of the Secretariat's initiatives there has been a blossoming of women's research (Eeg-Henriksen and Pedersen, 1991).

On the academic edge: women's research and Women's Studies

The struggle to obtain legitimacy is perhaps clearest in the reluctance of the scientific community to accept the challenge of feminist scholarship. Women's research challenges the *doxa* or established academic order. Theories, choice of research topics, concepts and methods within the various disciplines have all been criticised for making women's lives and the gendered structure of society invisible (Taksdal and Widerberg, 1992).

Women's research and Women's Studies are closely allied with the women's movement as well as with government ministries and political circles. These resources establish a demand for the results of women's research and use the results in political debates (Eeg-Henriksen and Pedersen, 1991). Women's research has had a stronger institutional base in institutions of applied research than within the universities. Centres for Women's Studies and research were initially established in the mid-1980s on a trial basis at three of the four universities; only one of these has so far been made permanent. Women's Studies programmes (run on a shoe-string) were also established around the same time by enthusiastic women researchers. Although women's research has been prolific, there has been considerable resistance to its integration into the academic curricula by male colleagues.

Changes in the university structure

At the same time (in the 1970s and 1980s) as positive action measures were being introduced, the university structure underwent a period of democratization which benefited women. Salaries have always been the same for identical ranks, and teaching loads also became the same for all faculty members. In addition, students and the administrative/technical staff gained representation on governing bodies in the early 1970s. Ironically, when the number of qualified women for faculty posts began to increase, the growth of new university positions began to slow down after a number of years of expansion in the 1960s and early 1970s.

The harsh economic climate in the current decade has once again led to radical changes in the university structure. This time the key themes are effectiveness, management by objectives, accountability, decentralization and upgrading of the university administration, the substitution of individual salary rates (within categories) for uniform, across-the-board salary scales, and increased international publications and contacts. Thus the Norwegian academic structure is beginning to imitate the American scientific centre. It is not clear how these changes will affect women.

Women in the universities

Students

In the 1960s the Norwegian student population was still largely male. (In 1960 the proportion of women was 20 per cent, in 1970, 30 per cent and in 1980, 40 per cent.) Today women constitute over half (57 per cent) of the student population. This dramatic change undoubtably reflects the emphasis on higher education within the women's movement (and the population in general) and the growing demand for women's labour in the public sector.

Despite a general policy of equality, students are primarily recruited from the upper and middle levels of society. In 1991, 40–50 per cent of the students had at least one parent who had completed a university degree. The student population will probably become even more homogeneous as entrance requirements continue to rise. In 1989, 13 per cent of the female adult population and 19 per cent of the male adult population had completed a university education. In 1970 and 1980 these figures were 5 and 9 per cent respectively for females and 9 and 14 per cent for males (*Norwegian Statistical Yearbook*, 1989).

The choice of field has also changed over time. The first women pioneers at university studied mathematics and the natural sciences, which were not, at the time, prestigious disciplines. Classical Greek and Latin were the 'in' fields then, regarded as being beyond the reach of women (Rørslett and Lie, 1984). As Figure 11.1 shows, in the past few decades women have been best represented in the humanities. Today both sexes are equally represented in the social sciences and medicine and the proportion of women in the natural sciences has been growing at a slow but constant rate. Technology seems least attractive to women. There are, however, substantial variations within each field. For example, within the natural sciences only 21 per cent of physics students and 29 per cent of mathematics students are women, compared to over half of those who study chemistry.

It appears that gendered interests lead to gender skewness. One interpretation is that women themselves take part in reproducing gender inequality.

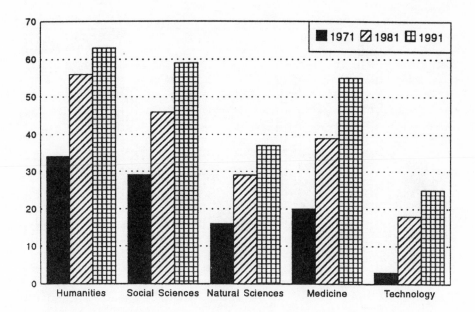

Source: Norwegian Educational Statistics, Central Bureau of Statistics, 1971, 1981, 1991.

Figure 11.1 *Proportion of female students according to field, 1971, 1981, 1991*

Female pre-doctoral scholarship holders

Scholarship holders at the pre-doctoral level are regarded as future recruits to the academic profession and as junior staff members, since they have some teaching responsibilities. As Figure 11.2 shows, the past two decades have witnessed distinct growth in the proportion of female scholarship holders. This is partly the result of the growing proportion of women with higher academic degrees and partly due to the use of the quota system.

If we compare students and scholarship holders (Figures 11.1 and 11.2), it is obvious that the increase in the proportion of women entering higher education in the last ten years has been most dramatic among scholarship holders. Increased female enrolment at the student level between the late 1970s and mid-1980s along with the institution of quotas is now resulting in greater enrolment of women at the doctoral level.

The scientific staff: still a man's world?

There has been some growth in the proportion of women on all levels within the academic hierarchy. The student and scholarship level pattern is also reflected in the distribution of women according to field. Increases in the proportion of women are most obvious on the assistant and associate pro-

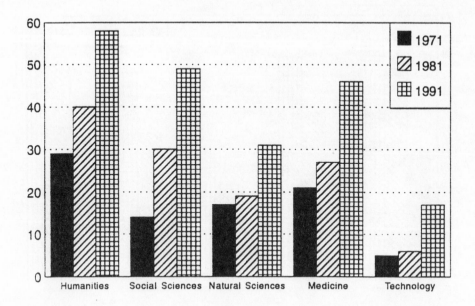

Source: Kyvik and Teigen (1993), Institute for Studies on Research and Higher Education, Oslo.

Figure 11.2 *Proportion of female pre-doctoral scholarship holders according to field, 1971, 1981, 1991*

fessor levels. However, these increases do not necessarily mean that it has become easier for women to be appointed to academic positions. Due to a policy change, all assistant professors are automatically promoted to associate professor on completion of their doctoral degree. Many more men than women obtain doctorates (78 and 22 per cent respectively in 1992). As a result of this policy change, many more men than women have been appointed to associate and full professorships during the last ten years (Kyvik and Teigen, 1993).

As Figure 11.3 shows, in 1991 more than 50 per cent of the student population were women, but only 10 per cent of the full professors. Despite the growing pool of qualified women, men statistically have better chances than women to be appointed at the full professor level (Fürst, 1988; Hansen, 1989).

The productivity gap: a barrier to women's careers?

Advancement is based on the accumulation of 'academic capital',primarily research productivity (Bourdieu, 1988). Studies in many countries have shown that men in academia are more productive than women (Davis and

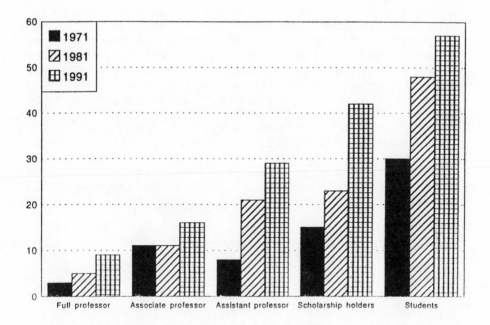

Source: Kyvik and Teigen (1993), Institute for Studies on Research and Higher Education, Oslo.

Figure 11.3 *Proportion of women on different levels in the university system, 1971, 1981, 1991*

Astin, 1990; Cole, 1987; Luukkonen-Gronow, 1987; Toren, 1990). Norway is no exception to this trend. Using a publication index which measures productivity adjusted for type of publication and multiple authorship over a three-year period (1989–91), Kyvik and Teigen (1993) find that male university teachers published an average of 6.9 article-equivalents and women 5.6. Ten years ago the corresponding figures were 5.0 and 3.5 (Kyvik, 1990).

Barriers within academia

On average, women university teachers work 48.8 hours per week and men 50.3. Both men and women spend approximately 30 per cent of their working hours on research.

There are no significant differences in obtaining external funding or supervision of students. However, it is interesting that half of the male researchers (compared with less than one-third of women) consider supervision as a part of their own research.

Several studies have shown that the most productive researchers are integrated into professional networks and collaborate extensively with colleagues (Cole, 1987; Davis and Astin, 1990; Kyvik, 1990). Women cooperate less with other researchers, both within and outside of their own institutes, than their male colleagues. In Norway more women (37 per cent) are interested in improving the psycho-social environment than men (20 per cent) within their research institutes. Women (39 per cent) also tend to place more emphasis than men (20 per cent) on cooperation among colleagues within their institutes. Forty-seven per cent of academic women in the Rørslett and Lie (1984) study maintained that they had experienced sceptical or negative attitudes from colleagues because they were women. These figures suggest that women university teachers are less integrated than their male colleagues into important collegial ('old boy') networks. This lack of 'social capital' may have a negative effect on their scientific productivity.

The gender gap in productivity is ameliorated considerably when academic rank is taken into account. Female full professors are more productive than male associate professors and female associate professors are just as productive as male associate professors; they also tend to be more productive than male assistant professors (Kyvik and Teigen, 1993).

Productivity and the gendered life course

The scholarly productivity of men peaks earlier than that of women. To a large extent responsibility for children explains these life-course differences (Kyvik, 1990; Lie, 1990). For women the age of their children has a major impact on their scientific productivity. In 1989–91, women university teachers with at least one child under 10 years published 4.1 article-equivalents, compared to 6.9 for comparable men and 6.8 for women with older children (Table 11.1). At the same time, these women worked 5.5 hours less per week on average than their colleagues. Women with children also need more time than their male colleagues to qualify for academic positions (Kyvik and Teigen, 1993).

Most literature on productivity differences has found that married women with children are more productive than single women (Cole, 1987; Davis and Astin, 1990; Luukkonen-Gronow, 1987). However, recently in Norway it was found that single women were more productive (6.1 article-equivalents) than both married women (5.4) and single men (5.1) (see Table 11.1) (Kyvik and Teigen, 1993).

The boomerang effect of the quota system

A study of the selection committees at the University of Oslo and regional colleges in 1969–79 and 1980–4 showed that female candidates for scientific positions were systematically evaluated differently and less positively than male candidates (Fürst, 1988).

The results of this study engendered a heated debate containing two questions of particular interest. First, is the number of female applicants for positions at the full professor level high enough? Second, did the introduction of a quota system, meant to favour women, in fact decrease women's chances of obtaining academic positions? Rørslett and Lie (1984) and Fürst (1988) found that women do not apply for promotion at the same rate as

Table 11.1 *Average number of article-equivalents according to family situation and age of children for university faculty, 1981 and 1991*

	Men		Women	
	1981	1991	1981	1991
Marital status				
Married	5.1	7.2	3.7	5.4
Divorced	4.8	5.8	3.7	6.3
Single	3.8	5.1	2.3	6.1
Children				
No children	4.9	5.6	2.9	4.9
1 child	4.5	6.3	2.5	6.7
2 children	4.8	7.0	4.5	5.8
3 or more children	5.4	7.8	3.5	5.1
Youngest child under 10	5.1	6.9	2.7	4.1
All children over 10	5.0	7.4	4.3	6.8

Source: Kyvik and Teigen (1993), Institute for Studies on Research and Higher Education, Oslo.

men. Fürst (*op.cit.*) shows that women's chances for promotion actually decreased after the quota system was introduced.

One explanation of this quite surprising finding may be that simultaneously with the introduction of the quota system, the 'academic freeze' (mentioned earlier) developed. This was particularly acute in disciplines where the majority of women are found – in the humanities and social sciences (Fürst, 1988). Another (but not competing) explanation focuses on the controversy within the university system which the quota system aroused. The quota system has been used extensively in politics and in the public sector and has met little opposition; however it appears to be more disturbing and perhaps threatening, within the scientific community.

It is important to note that women are not the only 'group' which is underrepresented in academe. Faculty are recruited first and foremost from the upper and middle levels of society. More than one-third of university teachers (42 per cent of females compared with 31 per cent of males) have a father with a university degree. This contrasts sharply with the general population, only 5 per cent of whom have a father with a university degree.

Women's integration into the power structure of the university: slow but sure

The gender representation in the professional hierarchy at the University of Oslo presents a typical pattern. A study by the authors shows that the power structure until the 1980s was completely dominated by men. By 1993, 18 per cent of department heads were women, as were two deans and two associate deans. Their representation on faculty councils increased from 25 per cent in 1980 to 33 per cent in 1993. The Academic Collegium, which has the final voice in policy decisions, had a female representation in 1983 of 38 per cent and in 1993 of 44 per cent.

Faculty selection committees are crucial vehicles of power since they control the reproduction of the faculty body (Bourdieu, 1988). Although national guidelines recommend that at least one woman be on these committees when there are female applicants, this recommendation has been ignored by most departments; this may cause a major obstacle to the promotion of women. Fürst's (1988) study, which provides the latest available figures, shows that in 1984, 87 per cent of these committees were composed of men only.

In the autumn of 1992, a woman was elected Rector of the University of Oslo. Not only was this the first time that a woman was elected as university Rector in Norway, but it was also the first time that a Rector had been elected by direct vote.

The change of greatest magnitude within the power structure of universities has been at the bureaucratic-managerial level, which has seen a dramatic rise of women in administrative leadership positions from 12 per cent in 1971 to 39 per cent in 1981 and 58 per cent in 1993 (NAVF: Research Personnel Register, unpublished data). In 1971 at the University of Oslo 36 per cent of departmental administrative leaders were women; in 1993 half were women. In addition, two of the six administrative faculty directors were women as were all of the associate faculty directors.

Conclusion

Although the feminist agenda has caused a partial transformation of Norwegian society, there is a wide gap between the ideology of gender equality and reality in the academic world. Equity policies have been particularly successful in increasing the proportion of women pre-doctoral scholarship holders, administrators and members of faculty governing bodies. However, changes at the higher levels of the faculty hierarchy have been small despite positive action policies and an increasing pool of qualified women. Although actively utilized in the wider society, women's research still remains on the edge of the scientific community.

12. Women in higher education in Pakistan: separate but equal?

Lynda Malik and Neelam Hussain

SUMMARY: Women in Pakistan (including university women) are currently experiencing divergent cultural influences. On one hand, during the last twenty years modernizing and liberating trends have been apparent, leading many middle- and upper-class women to discard the veil and take university degrees. On the other, an Islamization programme currently in force is perceived by many as curtailing the rights of women and forcing them out of public life. A nascent women's movement and the establishment of Women's Studies centres in two universities attest to the current interest in the problems of women.

Introduction

Pakistan was created as a national homeland for the Muslims of India when the South Asian subcontinent was partitioned in 1947. Bounded in the West by Iran and Afghanistan, in the North by the foothills of the Himalayas (across which lies Central Asia), in the East by India, and in the South by the Arabian Sea, Pakistan is the ninth most populous country in the world with an estimated population of over 112 million people and a high annual growth rate of 3.1 per cent (World Bank, 1992).

Although it is a relatively young country, many Pakistani traditions hearken back thousands of years to the Indus Valley Civilization, some of whose patterns of architecture, technology and dress may be found almost unchanged in contemporary villages. Wave upon wave of Central Asian (Aryan) invasions subsequently destroyed the Indus Valley Civilization, only to be replaced themselves by multiple Muslim invasions beginning with the Arab Muhammad bin Qasim in the seventh century AD and ending in the Mughal (Mongol/Turko/Persian) Empire which lasted until the nineteenth century. The Mughal Empire was followed by the British Empire, which lasted until the partition of India in 1947.

While the culture of Pakistan reflects its rich history, the roots of the current social structure derive from the British takeover of the Punjab after they defeated the Sikhs in 1849. The British rewarded the Muslims who collaborated with this effort with large grants of land over which they enjoyed feudal control. In return for the land the proprietors acted as

129

revenue agents for the British, collecting taxes from the peasants to be forwarded to the government. This *zamindari* system has continued into modern times with the result that almost all the mechanized farming in Pakistan is in the hands of large landowners who constitute one of the most powerful élites and have ruled the country, in concert with other influential groups, since its inception.

The second traditionally powerful group in Pakistan is composed of those who control large industrial and commercial enterprises. The majority of this group migrated to Pakistan at about the time of partition from other parts of India where they had had prior business experience. Ten years after partition they were in control of the major portion of privately owned assets in Pakistan. The control was so concentrated that one-quarter of the assets of the country were in the hands of only seven groups (Papanek, 1967). Although Pakistan experienced a rapid industrial expansion in the 1960s, a subsequent report indicated that the degree of industrial concentration had not been substantially reduced (Amjad, 1983).

The business and land-owning classes have controlled Pakistan since its creation in collaboration with the army and the civil service. The élite section of the civil service (known in Pakistan as the CSP, Central Superior Service) is the direct descendant of the Indian Civil Service developed during the days of British rule. The CSP has maintained the traditions of concentration of power, élite status and *esprit de corps* which has enabled it to hold the reins of power during periods of political instability in Pakistan.

The fourth locus of power in Pakistan has been the army, which has assumed control, in the name of order and stability, four times during the country's brief history. This tacit alliance of feudal, industrial, bureaucratic and military groups has proven to be one of the most enduring characteristics of Pakistan's social structure (Malik, 1992).

During the British rule in India a limited franchise, based primarily on income and education, had been put into effect. By 1935 the provincial franchise was still based on property, but conditions had been broadened to include 30 million voters who constituted one-sixth of the population. The standards for women were the same as those for men, but surviving property qualifications limited their numbers (Spear, 1975). When Pakistan became an independent country, all citizens were accorded equal rights, privileges and obligations (Wolpert, 1989). The 1956 Constitution of Pakistan granted the franchise to the entire adult population. Women were given two votes, one for the general seats in the legislature, and one for specific seats which were reserved for women since prevailing attitudes made it unlikely that a woman would win a general seat.

In 1971 a new type of feudal landlord took the reins of government, using the slogan of *roti, cupra* and *makan* – food, clothing and housing – and promising to dismantle the power of the traditional élites. His name was Zulfiquar Ali Bhutto, and his success at the polls 'was due in large measure to a constituency that sought a complete overhaul of the country's political, economic and social institutions' (Burki, 1980, p. 79).

Having threatened every powerful interest group in Pakistan, Bhutto was attacked as un-Islamic in his personal life and official programmes. He attempted to counter these charges by holding an Islamic summit meeting in

1976, appearing publicly at Friday prayers and changing the official weekly holiday from Sunday to Friday. Accused of drinking wine (which is contrary to the Muslim religion) he is widely known to have replied that he drank 'wine, but not the people's blood' (*Pakistan Times Overseas Weekly*, 1977).

Although many of the changes proposed by Bhutto had not been implemented (particularly those pertaining to land reform) the destabilizing forces which he had set in motion caught up with him on 4 July 1977 when General Muhammad Zia ul-Haq seized power. Ultimately Bhutto paid with his life for challenging the interests of the dominant classes.

With the rallying cry 'Islam in danger', Zia named himself the guardian of Islam in Pakistan. The interpretation of Islam which Zia chose to espouse was that advocated by a conservative Islamic political party (*Jamat-i-Islami*) which had never captured more than 10 per cent of the vote in any election. The Zia regime in Pakistan clearly stood for the interests of the dominant groups (Alavi, 1983) and attempted to legitimize its rule 'through the medium of Islam' (Ayoob, 1979, p. 535; see also Kurin, 1985 and Malik, 1982).

After Zia's demise in 1988 in a still unexplained accident, elections were held and Bhutto's party regained power, his daughter Benazir becoming prime minister. However, after a brief reign of 20 months, Benazir Bhutto's government was dismissed amidst charges of nepotism, corruption and incompetence. In October 1990 Benazir Bhutto suffered a resounding defeat at the polls with a clear victory going to the opposition Islamic Democratic Alliance headed by a well-known industrialist. In April, 1991 this government introduced legislation which would make the Koran the supreme law of Pakistan and subject all aspects of life to Islamic regulation. This program of Islamization has since been passed and implemented.

Demographic indicators

The per capita annual income of Pakistanis stands at $380 per year, placing Pakistan near the upper limit of the poorest group of nations (*World Bank*, 1992). Although the manufacturing segment of the economy is increasingly important (accounting for 19.9 per cent of GDP – Gross Domestic Product – in 1986–7 compared with 7.75 per cent in 1949–50), Pakistan's economy is still predominantly agro-based. Over half of the labour force is employed in agriculture (however, agriculture accounts for roughly one-quarter of GDP) and one-half of Pakistan's manufacturing output and four-fifths of its exports are based on agriculture.

Although during the 1980s the wages of workers employed in large industries rose, these workers account for only 2 per cent of the labour force. Slightly over one-quarter of the employed labour force in rural areas consists of unpaid family helpers; 'About 25 per cent of the urban residents reside in slums without any civic facilities' (*Government of Pakistan Economic Survey 1986–87*, p. xii). The Government of Pakistan comments that:

> there have been two direct attempts to improve income distribution, via land reforms and nationalisation of basic industries and banks and insurance. However, for various reasons their impact has only been marginal (*ibid.*, p. 3).

Clean drinking water is available to 44 per cent of the population (compared to 38 per cent in 1984–5) and over half of urban residents now have access to sewerage facilities. Since 1983 the infant mortality rate has declined from 150 to 106 per 1,000 live births (although this rate is still higher than that prevailing in 90 per cent of the countries in the world). During the same period life expectancy has increased from 45 to 55 years (*Government of Pakistan Economic Survey 1991–92*).

Literacy rates in Pakistan are among the lowest in the world, averaging 32 per cent for the total population. Literacy among males for 1991–2 is estimated at 45.5 per cent, and for females 21.3 per cent (*ibid.*). When rural and urban figures are considered separately, fewer than 10 per cent of rural women are found to be literate, as compared with over a quarter of the men. (approximately 70 per cent of Pakistanis are considered to be residents of rural areas).

Employment rates in Pakistan are also relatively low, due primarily to low female labour force participation. Male labour force participation rates average almost 75 per cent, which are comparable with other developing nations. The female percentage, however, is only 7.8 (World Bank, 1992).

The significance of gender

Although the roots of Pakistani culture may be found in a complex blend of Central Asian, Mughal, Persian, Turkish and Indian cultures, gender roles are defined primarily by two normative traditions: the Islamic codes brought to the sub-continent by the Mughals, and age-old Indian patterns retained by the indigenous population when many of them converted to Islam. Traditional South Asian patriarchal patterns are revealed in many of the customs of India and Pakistan. For example, Hindu norms forbid females to inherit their father's wealth, widows are forbidden to remarry and, until the last century, were encouraged to immolate themselves on their husbands' funeral pyres as a sign of devotion to their departed spouses. In Pakistan, Muslim women's right of inheritance was made explicit in 1962, in the West Pakistan Muslim Personal Law Application Act. However, though females may inherit, they do so at half the rate of their brothers. In a speech before the All Pakistan Woman's Association, the former Chief Justice of the Punjab High Court comments on these conditions:

> In Pakistan a woman's problems tend to increase and multiply. Her movements are restricted to the four walls of the home. She is not encouraged to receive education or seek employment ... she is often sold in marriage, or her hand is given in exchange for another woman.... It is generally expected of her that she should serve her husband and his family like an unpaid servant (Iqbal, 1988, p. 1).

Current demographic statistics give empirical support to these comments. A recent study of excess female mortality suggests that 5.6 per cent of females in India and 7.8 per cent of females in Pakistan are missing from expected population totals because of preferential treatment given to males in these societies (Coale, 1991). *Purdah* (literally meaning curtain, but referring to strict segregation of the sexes and seclusion of women) has long been observed among the middle classes. Although since the creation of Pakistan many educated Muslim women have discarded their veils, the current revival of conservative interpretations of Islamic law is reintroducing restrictions into the lives of Pakistani women.

The Islamic revival and its effect on women

The Islamization programme tentatively initiated by Zulfiqar Ali Bhutto in the 1970s and expanded and supported by all subsequent governments has had far-reaching effects on the social and legal status of women in Pakistan. During the brief tenure of Bhutto's daughter, woman activists had hoped that the anti-woman laws introduced by the Zia regime (in the name of the Islamic revival) would be abolished, but the power of the religious right proved too strong even for Pakistan's first woman prime minister (Yusuf, 1989).

The Islamizing programme affecting women can be divided into formal and informal categories. Informally women are under increasing pressure to cover their heads in public and to conform to strict Islamic standards of dress and etiquette. However, most observers consider the legal aspects of the Islamization programme to be the most damaging to attempts at equality for women.

Among these legal aspects, the law of evidence, the *qisas* and *diyat* ordinances and the *hudood* ordinances are most often cited as examples of institutionalized discrimination against women. The *qisas* and *diyat* ordinances refer to retribution and blood money, respectively. The blood money or compensation allowed for the murder or injury to a man is double that allowed for the same offence committed against a woman. The *hudood* ordinances refer to crimes relating to burglary, murder, drunkenness, adultery (which is, in practice, not differentiated from rape) and perjury. Women are excluded from giving testimony in cases involving these offences, and in certain instances the testimony of two women is considered the equivalent of the testimony of one man. Many Pakistani women activists and human rights organizations have reacted negatively to these ordinances. However, the Eighth Amendment Bill (1985) prevents the Law of Evidence and the *hudood* ordinances from being challenged in any court of law in the country.

Punishment for adultery is particularly resented by women activists in Pakistan, since the application of the law is seen to discriminate unfairly against women. The most infamous case of this type was that of a young blind woman who had been hired as a domestic servant and who became pregnant following a multiple rape. Her pregnancy was considered a self-confession and she was sentenced to 15 lashes. Upon appeal this decision was reversed, but other assaulted women continue to be punished by the courts (Weiss, 1985).

In Pakistan a man can divorce his wife at will by a simple oral pronouncement (although the Koran frowns upon men exercising this right capriciously). Women are also permitted to sue for divorce; however, this process must be undertaken in a formal judicial proceeding upon the establishment of specified grounds (for example, insanity of the husband). Widespread female illiteracy combined with traditions of seclusion often result in women being unaware of the rights that they do have, thus making these rights more theoretical than real.

Upon divorce the husband is obliged to support his former wife for three months. The wife is awarded the sum of money specified in the marriage contract, but henceforth has no further legal financial claim on her former husband. As most Pakistani women have few marketable skills, divorce often renders them homeless and without any means of financial support. Thus in the typical Pakistani family the power is skewed in favour of men. Without access to resources, the wife is heavily dependent upon the continuing goodwill and cooperation of her husband. She strives for his approval by being obedient and submissive (Malik and Pattnayak, forthcoming).

After the 1990 elections the voting rules were changed so that currently women cannot seek representation through indirect elections to the National Assembly. Women activists are proposing that either reserved seats for women be restored, or that political parties be required to allocate 10 per cent of their seats to women.

The university in Pakistan and women's place in it

Schools in Pakistan have always been segregated according to gender, with most rural girls receiving little or no education. In poor rural areas where the majority of the population lives, girls are expected to do domestic chores at an early age. Sending them to school would consequently deprive the family of their services while simultaneously forcing the expenditure of meagre resources on clothing, shoes and books. Concern about the safety and well-being of their daughters also prevents parents from sending girls to schools and strengthens many peoples' doubts about the need for females to be literate. Currently female enrolment at the primary level of education is 27 per cent of the total and declines to 12 per cent at the secondary level (World Bank, 1992).

Higher education in Pakistan is a combination of higher secondary and tertiary levels, with the former outnumbering the latter by a margin of 2:1 in student enrolments. Higher education is provided in intermediate (upper secondary) schools, colleges (grades 11 and 12), degree colleges (grades 11–14), in a few colleges that include grades 11–16, and general and professional universities (grades 13–20). At the level of the university, education has never been gender segregated. Overall resource availability is skewed in favour of university education, which enjoys near financial parity with college education despite having one-eighth of the enrolments. Universities are financed by the federal government through the University Grants Commission, and the colleges are funded by the respective provincial governments.

Universities are formally headed by a Chancellor and Pro-Chancellor who are always government officials. The highest academic officer (who is

Table 12.1 *Percentage of female enrolment in colleges and universities, 1947–89*

Year	Arts and Science Colleges	Professional Colleges	Universities
1947–8	8.1	7.5	8.7
1954–5	13.6	10.3	2.6
1961–2	19.3	16.2	18.5
1964–5	18.6	17.2	20.6
1967–8	22.4	14.0	18.8
1970–71	25.2	12.4	22.0
1973–4	27.1	16.0	22.0
1976–7	29.8	16.8	23.8
1977–80	28.0	17.0	14.0
1988–9	30.2	16.4	15.3

Source: Government of Pakistan, University Grants Commission (1989), *Statistics on Higher Education*, Islamabad.

actually in charge of the university) is the Vice-Chancellor. To date there has been only one female Vice-Chancellor of a university; this was Dr Kaneez Yusuf who headed the newly established Quaid-e-Azam University in Islamabad during the Bhutto era (1973).

Below the Vice-Chancellor are the Pro-Vice-Chancellor, the deans, directors, principals of constituent colleges, chairmen of departments and other officers. A small percentage of women are heads of departments or principals of women's colleges. Urban universities are likely to have a higher representation of women than those located in semi-rural areas. Universities in the more developed provinces (Punjab and Sind) are likely to employ more women than those in the North West Frontier Province and Baluchistan, where conservative mores are relatively more pronounced.

Although the proportion of female students enrolled in colleges and universities has dramatically increased since the creation of Pakistan in 1947, women still comprise only 30 per cent of those enrolled in arts and science colleges, and approximately half of that in professional colleges and universities (see Table 12.1).

Among the teaching staff in universities, the proportion of women is inversely related to rank and educational attainment. Table 12.2 indicates that 18.4 per cent of the lecturers are females, but this declines to only 4 per cent at the rank of full professor.

The academic fields of study available in girls' colleges have tended to be less varied than those in boys' colleges, although the situation is slowly improving (Hayes, 1987). Table 12.3 indicates that women tend to enrol mainly in arts and science disciplines.

The lack of female participation in mathematical, scientific and technological courses of study restricts their future career choices. A recent study of work options available to Pakistani women suggests that these are 'restricted' due to traditional attitudes regarding women's aptitudes and their proper role in society, negative attitudes of potential (male) colleagues, lack of opportunity to develop requisite skills, women's own negative perceptions of their own abilities and ignorance of available options (Gov-

Table 12.2 *Female teaching staff in universities by rank and qualification, 1985–6*

Rank and Qualification	All universities		General		Engineering		Agriculture	
	Female		Female		Female		Female	
	%	No.	%	No.	%	No.	%	No.
Rank								
Professor	4.0	17	6.3	17	0.0	–	0.0	–
Associate Professor	8.2	47	12.5	46	0.0	–	0.9	1
Assistant Professor	16.1	209	23.1	202	1.6	3	1.6	4
Lecturer	18.4	266	24.3	243	5.1	11	5.2	12
Qualification								
PhD	10.2	101	13.4	100	0.0	–	0.0	1
M Phil	17.1	28	22.5	27	0.0	–	4.8	1
MA/MSc	18.3	406	23.4	381	6.1	11	3.4	14
Others	1.1	4	0.0	–	1.0	3	2.1	1
Total	14.4	539	20.2	508	2.4	14	2.6	17

Source: Government of Pakistan, University Grants Commission (1987), *Statistics on Higher Education*, Islamabad.

ernment of Pakistan and UNICEF Country Program of Cooperation, 1988–9, p. 24).

Women's Studies

Although the government plans to establish Women's Studies at centres in five universities throughout Pakistan (Quaid-i-Azam University in Islamabad, Punjab University, Karachi University, Peshawar University and Baluchistan University), to date only those at Karachi and Quaid-i-Azam are functioning.

Established in 1989, these Women's Studies centres have the following objectives (Government of Pakistan, Ministry of Women's Development, 1992, pp. 10–11):

a) to introduce and promote the discipline of women's studies in Pakistan;
b) to develop introductory courses in women's studies for university students;
c) to promote both academic and action oriented research on women and development;
d) to critically examine concepts, theories, models and methodologies that have been used in scientific investigation and development;
e) to identify, replicate and translate relevant material into the national language; and
f) to redefine curricula at the university level, college level and high school level, with a view toward incorporating knowledge about women and the contribution of woman scholars.

Table 12.3 *Enrolment of women in universities by subject. Percentage of total enrolment 1985–6*

Subject	Bachelor's	Master's
Chemistry	26.0	31.0
Geology	17.0	6.9
Geography	15.0	33.0
Computer Science	–	10.0
Home Economics	100.0	100.0
Mathematics	6.9	6.3
Microbiology	54.2	55.8
Pharmacology	28.8	23.2
Physics	8.2	7.8
Physiology	60.3	50.4
Physical Education	–	11.5
Psychology	72.5	76.8
Statistics	2.7	6.0
Zoology	44.8	46.2
Commerce	6.2	6.7
Public Administration	35.6	18.4
Education	35.6	34.1
Others	–	2.0
Medical Colleges	21.0	–

Source: Government of Pakistan, University Grants Commission (1987), *Statistics on Higher Education*, Islamabad.

Islamization and higher education

A programme to Islamize the educational system was instituted by the Bhutto government and continues up to the present day. The main components of this programme consist in the teaching of the Arabic language and mandatory courses in the Muslim religion. Curricula and textbooks are also examined to ensure that material repugnant to Islam is expunged.

During the Zia era the government proposed the establishment of separate women's universities in all provinces except Baluchistan, where only a very small number of women are enrolled in higher education. According to a scheme proposed by the University Grants Commission, separate universities for women could be established by upgrading existing home economics and liberal arts colleges in major cities and by establishing additional colleges where necessary. Departments of home economics were to be upgraded into institutes of food and textile technology and arts and science colleges were to be upgraded by the establishment of Master's programmes. These upgraded colleges would be known as the Professional Colleges of the Woman's University (Government of Pakistan, University Grants Commission, 1981).

Public opinion on this issue is divided. Those of a conservative cast of mind believe that female-only universities would provide additional educational opportunities for women who are uncomfortable working and studying alongside men. However, many educated women believe that such facilities would curtail women's opportunities to be educated at the most prestigious institutions in the country and thereby further marginalize women by reducing their access to public life. The World Bank and other international agencies have in the past been critical of the disproportionate share of funding which is allocated to higher education in Pakistan. The creation of a Women's University would further skew funding patterns.

In response to the questions raised about the 1981 proposals, the Government of Pakistan established a Women's University Commission which recommended (in 1993) that in order to satisfy the Islamic requirements for separation of the sexes, a separate university for women should be established. The cost of such an undertaking was projected at 250 million rupees. The future relationship between the proposed Women's University and the existing Women's Studies centres is unclear.

Conclusion

Pakistan faces many difficulties common to developing nations; these include rapid population growth, widespread illiteracy, political instability, and a relative lack of manufacturing or technological capability. These problems are compounded for women by cultural traditions which devalue females and the recent institutionalization of gender-based inequalities.

The problems encountered by most women are, however, generally ameliorated among those in higher education (here we include students as well as administrators and teaching faculty) because most of them are drawn from the middle and upper classes. Domestic help is still widely available in Pakistan and thus academic women are, to a large extent, relieved of the burdens of the 'second shift' faced by their sisters in many other countries. Highly educated women are also much more likely than others to be cognizant of their legal rights, to be comfortable in the public (outside of the family) sphere and to have marketable skills.

Educated Pakistani women have formed associations to address women's issues and protest against the infringement of women's rights. Notable among these are the All Pakistan Women's Association and the Women's Action Forum. Currently women (including academic women) in Pakistan are faced with a new group of opportunities and a new set of restraints. Developments in the next few years will determine which prevail.

13. Women in Polish academe

Malgorzata Fuszara and Beata Grudzinska

SUMMARY: In Poland family life and the status of women were shaped by two conflicting models after the Second World War – the official model of equality between the sexes and mass employment of women as opposed to traditional family life promoted by the Catholic Church. Labour shortages caused a considerable number of women to enter higher education and the skilled labour force, but the future of women in post-Communist Poland will probably still be shaped by the two opposing models. The general trend of ousting women from the labour market may be extended to higher education. However, the high proportion of women with higher education and their ever-growing awareness of the need to defend their rights, combined with the economic necessity to provide for families, should help women counteract pressures for their return to the home.

Introduction

Poland is among those countries commonly called Eastern or Central European or post-Communist countries. Its affiliation to the Communist bloc resulted from the division of Europe into zones after the Second World War. Poland found itself in the Soviet-controlled area; the country's political system was called 'Socialist' and aimed, against the will of the Polish people, at the building of Communism. Poland was the only country in the region where private ownership of land had been preserved because all attempts at collectivization failed completely. A totalitarian regime based on Marxist-Leninist ideology was imposed on all countries within the Soviet sphere of influence, although the affected countries differed as to their histories, traditions, cultures and degree of acceptance of the Communist regime.

A specific Polish feature was the tradition of nearly two centuries of struggle for independence, starting with the partitioning of Poland by Russia, Austria and Prussia late in the eighteenth century, and continuing throughout the Second World War and during the Communist regime. During those two centuries, the only period of full Polish independence, freedom and sovereignty were the years between the two world wars (1918–39). Both the status of women and that of university staff depended largely on the external situation and the struggle for independence. During the Second World War and the struggle against Communism, the roles of men and women were similar if not identical. An important function often performed by women in those days was the preservation and transmission of cultural traditions and essential values (for a discussion of the situation of women, see Fuszara 1991a; 1991b; 1993). The educational system, including the universities, also played a key role in the struggle for independence by keeping alive Polish cultural identity.

This division into 'us' and 'them' (ie, the authorities or external enemy) was more significant than the differences between men and women. Nevertheless, women's organizations began to develop in the latter half of the nineteenth century. The efforts of these organizations led to females being granted the right to vote when Poland regained its independence in 1918. Such organizations and movements were popular between 1918 and 1939. In 1980 the first new feminist organizations emerged. Under Communist rule, all the pre-war organizations had been replaced by a single one which did not have grassroots support and was controlled by the authorities. The spontaneous formation of other groups was banned. The struggle against the totalitarian regime took precedence over the struggle for women's rights. Only today, under conditions of regained freedom and the building of a democratic state, is the situation slowly starting to change.

Another specific Polish feature was the position of the Catholic Church. Poland was the only country of the so-called Communist bloc where the totalitarian regime failed to destroy the Church. Enjoying considerable autonomy, the Church in Poland had immense social support and offered the people not only places of worship and refuge, but also centres of political and cultural life. Additionally, many Poles deeply believe in certain traditional values supported by the Church, which assigns to women mainly the roles of wife and mother.

The Poles are highly family oriented. The divorce rate in Poland is among the lowest in Europe and the birth rate is among the highest. After the war, family life and the status of women were shaped in Poland by two clearly conflicting models, each promoting different visions of women in society. The first was the official model based on equality of the sexes and mass employment of women. The other model was based on the tradition and rules of family life accepted and promoted by the Catholic Church.

The official model with its assumption of 'equality of the sexes' was enshrined in the Constitution, which guaranteed the right to work equally to men and women (the principle of 'equal pay for equal work'), the right to vacations, social security, education, and also the right to hold public office. The Constitution also guaranteed maternity and child care, protection of pregnant women and paid maternity leave.

The main avenue to equal rights for women in post-war Poland was employment. Not only was work made accessible to all; men and women alike were expected to work and women were trained for jobs which had traditionally been reserved for men. Women's unlimited access to employment was not just an attempt at implementing the ideal of equality but also – and perhaps above all – an economic necessity since reconstruction after the war seemed possible only if both men and women went to work. Admittedly these particular grounds for the mass employment of women were never quoted openly.

Demography

Since the end of the war, Poland has had a territory of 313,000 square kilometres compared with 389,000 square kilometres before the war. In 1991, the country's population exceeded 38 million, having risen from a post-war low of 24 million. Poland suffered immense population losses during the Second World War, and pre-war figures were only reached and surpassed in the 1970s. After the war there was a radical population shift from the countryside to the cities. Before the war, Poland had been largely a peasant country, with an urban population of only 30 per cent; today the rural population amounts to only 38 per cent. The proportion of women in the population is the same as before the Second World War – 51 per cent.

Polish women in the university

Early history

In the late fourteenth century, Jadwiga, the first queen of Poland, donated a portion of her private fortune to develop the first Polish university in Cracow. Although women could not enrol at Cracow nor any other university in the world of those days, during the fourteenth century a woman called Nawojka is said to have entered Cracow University in male disguise. Her true sex discovered, she was made to take the veil. Once in the convent, she was given the chance to continue her studies.

In the nineteenth century there were five universities in formerly Polish territories, but women had no access to those institutions. Offered no possibility to study at home, Polish women travelled abroad for higher education. It is difficult to precisely estimate the number of those women as they were registered as citizens of either Russia, Prussia or Austria, that is, of the partitioning states. Formally no person could be a Polish citizen as a Polish state did not exist. As shown by analyses of records at the Swiss universities, Polish female students constituted a considerable group. In Zurich, the first Polish women entered the university in the academic year 1870/71. Of the total of 237 MDs awarded to Poles at the Medical Faculty in Zurich from 1880 to 1914, 104 were awarded to women (Hulewicz, 1939). Similar data concerning female Polish students can also be found in the records of other European universities, in Switzerland and particularly in France.

Many Polish students and teachers considered Paris the best place to study. The long list of Polish names includes that of Maria Sklodowska-Curie who graduated from the Sorbonne and was to become the first woman to win the Nobel Prize. She was among the extremely small group of students who decided upon sciences. Most female students abroad applied for courses such as medicine, psychology, pedagogics and natural sciences (biology and agriculture). Finally, in 1894, two women applied for admission to Cracow University and were eventually admitted in 1897. In that same year, women were given university positions (on a temporary basis and hardly ever full time) at the universities of Poznan and Warsaw. In Poland, as elsewhere, the first fields entered by women were medicine and the humanities (Braun, 1905). Other sources indicate that Lvov University had admitted its first female students in 1896.

The re-emergence of an independent Poland in November 1918 radically changed the situation of Polish education, including the education of women. In 1919, a decree mandating coeducational, free and compulsory education was issued. The changes in secondary education were significant. Identical curricula for male and female students were introduced (Krasuski, 1985; Wroczynski, 1987). Efforts were also made to establish a new system of higher education and to remove the barriers to women's access to formal higher education. Those changes also influenced the position of women in academia. Many female researchers were given full-time positions at universities as professors and assistant professors. The actual number of women employed by universities still remains unknown, however, as many were treated as 'state officials', their wages being paid from other sources.

Contemporary developments

Further improvements in women's education were made after 1945. After the war the need for a qualified work-force gave women the opportunity to receive better education and to secure better positions. Only one-third of the pre-war academic staff survived the war. Faculty for institutions of higher education were in great demand, resulting in the unprecedented access of women to academe. The proportion of female staff and students has been on the increase from 1950 till the present day. Late in the 1970s, the proportion of female students exceeded 50 per cent in Poland (see Table 13.1).

Under Communist rule the number of persons admitted to universities was strictly limited, with the limits imposed by the state and not the educational authorities. Admission depended upon a competitive examination held by the university staff, combined with a complex system of points awarded not only for secondary school achievements but also for the so-called social background (see Chapter 4 in this volume). The official assumption was that children of workers or farmers were less likely to pass the competitive examination, and therefore deserved to be granted additional points. The system lasted until the 1980s when a Constitutional Tribunal found such preferences inconsistent with the constitutional principle of equality of citizens. Access to higher education was limited and extremely competitive due to cost; higher education was free but the state could not afford to admit all candidates. According to widespread belief, the Communist authorities were not interested in expanding access to higher education as this usually leads to non-conformist attitudes. In Poland, for example, most universities were centres of independent thought and opposition to Communist ideology and sources of dissemination of independent and illegal publications.

At present, persons with higher education constitute 7.7 per cent of the population aged 25 and over. Among men in this age cohort the proportion

Table 13.1 *Students by field of study (number of women quoted in thousands)*

Fields	1936/7		1980/81		1991/2	
	No.	%	No.	%	No.	%
Engineering and Technology	0.1	5	35.2	24	17.9	19
Agricultural Sciences	0.5	21	20.0	49	10.3	46
Economy*	1.1	31	33.7	62	27.2	54
Law	2.4	17	15.0	47	14.3	51
Humanities	6.4	53	66.2	79	83.5	76
Mathematics and Natural Sciences	no data	–	29.1	63	25.4	60
Medical Sciences	1.9	29	22.0	64	22.4	64
Sports	0.1	50	5.5	41	6.0	39
Fine and Applied Arts	0.3	43	3.9	50	3.3	51
Theology	0	0	0.8	44	3.8	43
Total	13.1	27	226.6	50	214.2	52

* Called 'commercial sciences' in the Statistical Yearbook for 1950.

Sources: Small Statistical Yearbook 1938, Warsaw, GUS 1938. Statistical Yearbook 1980/81, Warsaw, GUS 1981. Szkoly Wzeze w Roku Szkolnym 1991/1992 (Universities: Academic Year 1991/1992), Warsaw, GUS 1992.

is 8.7; among women, it amounts to 6.8. However, a closer analysis reveals that this trend concerns the older age groups only. In the youngest group (25–29 years), the proportion of women with higher education exceeds that of men (9.6 and 8.0, respectively).

Women as students

In certain years, the proportion of women students has clearly exceeded the female proportion in the population and this is still true today: the proportion of women in the population is 51 per cent, but that of female students amounts to 52 per cent. Comparisons between the faculties chosen by women in the past and today are particularly interesting (see Table 13.1). Women constitute a majority of students of the humanities, which was also the case before the Second World War (among the students of philosophy, 53 per cent were women). Some other faculties (for example, engineering and technical studies) were hardly ever chosen by women in the past and still have small proportions of female students today. These faculties had 7 per cent of female students before the war, and 19 per cent in the academic year 1991/2.

As regards the health sciences, before the war women prevailed among the students of dentistry (60 per cent) and constituted half of the students of pharmacy; they were under-represented in other related fields (21 per cent). Today, women constitute the majority (64 per cent) of all students in health and related disciplines. Before the Second World War, women constituted 18 per cent of law students; late in the 1980s, the proportion amounted to 50 per cent.

Women as faculty

Although the proportion of women students slightly exceeds the proportion of women in the population, the gender ratios of the staff of Polish institutions of higher education point in the opposite direction (see Table 13.2).

Table 13.2 indicates that the gender structure of the staff does not correspond with that prevailing among students, nor among persons with higher education, nor among the general population of Poland. As elsewhere in the world, women in Polish universities tend to hold the lower, less prestigious and lower paid positions (eg, those of lecturers and assistants with the MA degree); the lowest proportion of women can be found among full professors.

On the whole, faculties with a higher proportion of female students also have more women on the staff; however, this is not always the case. In 1990,

Table 13.2 *Number and proportion of female academics by position*

Year		Full Professor	Assoc. Professor (Docent)	Adjunct (with PhD)	Asst. (with MA)	Other (Lecturer, etc.)	Total
1955	N	84	124	528	2930	709	4375
	%	6	15	19	30	20	24
1960	N	116	210	897	3056	623	4902
	%	7	14	22	34	21	26
1965	N	131	297	1682	3044	1171	6335
	%	7	15	28	34	28	28
1970	N	159	543	2104	4552	2178	9626
	%	9	13	33	35	38	31
1975	N	211	833	3920	8402	3513	16879
	%	9	16	33	39	46	35
1980	N	330	947	5997	7762	4159	19195
	%	11	18	33	39	49	35
1985	N	431	1117	7482	6201	4002	20113
	%	13	19	33	38	51	35
1990	N	827	1078	7635	7145	5970	22655
	%	15	19	35	43	52	37
1991	N	1287	509	7755	7353	5867	22771
	%	17	17	34	41	48	36

Sources: *Roczhik Statystyczny Szkolnictwa (Annales of Educational Statistics)* (1985) GUS: Warszawa. *Szkoly Wyzsze w Roku Szkolnym 1991/1992 (High Schools 1991/1992)* GUS: Warszawa.

17 per cent of engineering and technology students were women, while females constituted 22 per cent of the staff. In naval schools, women constituted 1 per cent of students and 20 per cent of the staff. On the other hand, at faculties with a large number of female students, the proportion of female staff tends to be smaller. Thus, for example, women constitute 64 per cent of students of universities but just 42 per cent of the staff; at teachers' colleges, the proportions are 74 and 48 per cent, respectively. The discrepancy is greatest in theology, where women constitute 49 per cent of the students but just 8 per cent of the staff. (Theology was barred to women before the Second World War.)

Analysis of the PhDs awarded to women in various fields reveals that in areas where women constitute a vast majority of students, their proportion is relatively smaller among the staff and fewer of them get a PhD. Health sciences provide a good example: women constitute 64 per cent of students, 48 per cent of the staff, 49 per cent of persons awarded a PhD and just 28 per cent of persons with the title of professor. The situation is similar in fields with traditionally few women students, such as engineering and technology where women constitute 18 per cent of students, 22 per cent of the staff, and 16 per cent of PhDs, but as few as 3 per cent of professors. These comparisons show that in the faculties where women are over-represented, men find it relatively easier to become staff members upon graduation and to achieve higher academic rank (see Chapter 10 in this volume). The reverse is not true for women who are in faculties popular with men.

Among students in courses which provide additional education not leading to a PhD, women constitute the majority. In postgraduate studies that lead to a PhD, 32 per cent of the students are women. As these data indicate, the under-representation of women among recipients of degrees higher than MA is likely to persist in the future.

Postgraduate studies are, however, only one of the possible ways of obtaining a PhD in Poland, and indeed this is not a frequently chosen path. Degrees higher than MA are mainly conferred upon persons employed at universities who are obliged by the regulations to get the PhD, followed by habilitation, which qualifies them to be associate professors.

Table 13.3 *Academic titles awarded to women*

Year	Professor		Doctor hab. (Docent)		Doctor (PhD)	
	No.	%	No.	%	No.	%
1955			1	20	10	11
1960			8	23	196	20
1965			61	15	455	24
1970	16	0	100	21	627	27
1975	37	10	136	23	1003	29
1980	55	13	114	21	1188	32
1985	72	17	112	20	524	29
1991	101	22	135	23	429	29

Sources: *Roczhik Statystyczny Szkolnictwa (Annales of Educational Statistics)* (1985) GUS: Warszawa. *Szkoly Wyzsze w Roku Szkolnym 1991/1992 (High Schools 1991/1992)* GUS: Warszawa.

The data in Table 13.3 confirm the existence of trends that are disadvantageous for women. There are today fewer women among persons awarded a PhD than among those who already have a PhD and are employed in institutions of higher education. Women can thus be expected in the future to constitute an even smaller proportion of the academic staff with at least a PhD.

The power structure of the university

The supreme authority within an institute of higher education is exercised by its Rector, elected by the academic community. He is assisted by Pro-Rectors, elected on the motion of the Rector who recommends the candidates. A considerable and sometimes decisive role is played in Polish institutes by collegiate bodies, the Senate being at the highest level.

Authorities of the separate faculties have an analogous structure. A faculty is headed by a Dean who is elected by the faculty community. He is assisted by deputy Deans elected on a motion by the Dean. A considerable and sometimes decisive role is played by the Faculty Council. Faculties are divided into Institutes headed by Directors, Vice-Directors and Institute Councils.

Data concerning the participation of women in academic administration are not collected in Poland. The author's calculations are based on a single institution – the University of Warsaw. In the academic year 1992/3, the Rector and pro-Rectors of that university are men. In the Senate of the University of Warsaw 18 per cent of the members are women; the proportion of women among chairpersons of the Senate's commissions is similar (19 per cent).

Women constitute 14 per cent of the deans of faculties, and 36 per cent of deputy deans. There is a single faculty where both the Dean and all deputy Deans have traditionally been women (pedagogy). Much more often both the Dean and all deputy Deans are men; this concerns not only the faculties with a traditional prevalence of male students (mathematics), but also those where female students are in the majority (economy, modern philologies). Women constitute 30 per cent of the composition of Faculty Councils.

Seventeen per cent of directors and 35 per cent of vice-directors of Institutes are women. At the lowest administrative level (heads of departments), women constitute 24 per cent.

The general conclusions that follow from the above data are confirmed at all levels of the academic structure. Despite their rather slight predominance among students, Polish women constitute a decided minority among the staff of institutions, persons awarded degrees higher than MA, and administrators.

The future of women in post-Communist Poland and in Polish academe

The model explaining gender stratification in academe assumes that gender stratification is influenced by three groups of factors: cultural background, social system and psychological variables. Polish data seem to suggest that such a model is adequate, and supports its explanatory value. Cultural background, social system and psychological factors were largely shaped in Poland by the country's specific historical situation and the resulting status of women. History is responsible for the fact that Polish women were forced relatively early to accept as their burden the responsibility for transmission of cultural values, to take an active part in shaping history, and to enter economic life. Also quite early, in 1918 when Poland regained independence, Polish women were granted suffrage. A Communist addition was egalitarian ideology and propagation of the promotion of women as employees with value and education equal to that of men. The economic situation and the need for joint action towards the country's reconstruction included women in the labour force on a mass scale.

Women in Poland and the rest of the Communist bloc came to constitute a considerable proportion of the student population earlier than elsewhere in Europe. As early as the mid-1970s, over half of the students were women and they broke barriers as to the choice of fields. Today, 37–40 per cent of academic staff are women.

Under Communism the state had determined the number of students who could be admitted to each department and such limits could not be overridden. Currently the number of students is limited by the universities themselves due to financial constraints; as a result, the proportion of students in Poland still remains lower than in Western Europe and the USA. By contrast, the proportion of women among the intellectual élite is somewhat higher in Poland today than it is in Europe and the United States. This has probably resulted from the rapid expansion of higher education opportunities for women during the period of severe labour shortages. The equal gender ratio among students and the relatively fair one among the staff were achieved without a quota or preferential system. No preferences are applied today and none seem likely to be accepted by society in general or the academic community.

However, the future of women in post-Communist Poland and in Polish institutions of higher education will probably still be shaped by the two strongly opposed models. On the one hand, the model of an independent, educated and employed woman is increasingly popular; on the other hand, the rightist political parties now refer in their programmes to the traditional model of the family where the woman is the wife and mother above all. The latter view is unlikely to gain ascendancy because, with very few exceptions, the husband's earnings are not enough to provide for the family. However, this model poses a potential threat to the lifestyle of employed women, as it portrays them as less committed to their professional careers and working solely for financial gain.

Genuine equality of men and women was never introduced despite the official propaganda. Under Communist rule, Polish women had held as few as 35 per cent of executive posts, mostly at the lowest level. As in many other countries, women in Poland under Communism earned 35 per cent less than men. Although by the 1970s they constituted over 40 per cent of the members of Parliament, the Parliament of those days exercised no real authority. The body that actually held power – the Central Committee of the Communist Party – usually had no women at all among its members or just one token woman who symbolized the Polish woman's equal rights. Genuine equality was therefore absent, replaced by the official propaganda of equality.

The most alarming developments of today include a prevalence of women among the unemployed (women constitute 46 per cent of employees but 53 per cent of the unemployed) and segregation in the labour market, where women are wanted mainly for auxiliary jobs (young secretaries), and men for independent, responsible and well-paid positions. At the same time, the law contains no mechanisms for individual complaints of discrimination on the grounds of gender. Women are not used to struggling for equal rights: they are surprised by both the propagation of discriminating ideologies and the actual emergence of discriminating mechanisms. These factors may be conducive to discrimination against women employees, including the women employees of academe. However, the high proportion of women with secondary and higher education and their ever-growing awareness of the need to defend their rights, combined with the economic necessity to provide for their families, should help women to oppose these developments.

The general trend of ousting women from the labour market will probably be extended to higher education. However, the academic staff are extremely badly paid and this makes the profession unattractive. In many fields (eg, law, business), former researchers are now being offered positions which are much more lucrative. Thus the academic world may remain an attractive workplace for women due to irregular working hours, independence, and the relatively high prestige of research positions. These factors may in the future result in a stable or even upward trend in the proportion of women among the staff of state universities, accompanied by a persistently small proportion of women in high academic positions.

Male researchers who have been offered better paying positions often accept these while retaining their academic posts. This enables them to combine high earnings with the prestige of an academic researcher. Private schools (mainly business) are emerging in great numbers. In such schools, which charge very high tuition fees and pay very large teachers' salaries, men greatly outnumber women as students and faculty. The mechanisms of indirect discrimination thus emerge, once again based on traditional views of the roles of men and women.

14. Gender stratification in Russian higher education: the *matrioshka* image

Marina Yu Morozova

SUMMARY: The current unsettled political and economic circumstances in Russia are having an adverse effect on higher education in general, and on the position of women academics in particular. It is hoped that the official interest in Women's Studies, combined with the new development of grass roots women's organizations will help to counter these negative trends.

Introduction

Traditionally Soviet ideology presented Russian women (or, more exactly, women of the USSR) as successful members of society, having equal rights and actively participating in the political and economic life of the country – the image of the smiling Russian *matrioshka* (traditional painted doll) in her colourful dress. The failure of Socialist doctrines highlighted social inequalities (including discrimination against women) which had developed in Soviet society over many years.

Glasnost (loosening up) exposed traditional problems that had been peculiar to Soviet society, and *perestroika* (the transition to market economy) aggravated the old problems and at the same time generated some new ones. Thus the successful *matrioshka* became in reality a small unprotected doll having to deal with insurmountable difficulties.

Historically known as the Russian Empire, Russia became the largest, most populous and most economically powerful of the republics of the USSR after the October 1917 revolution. Prior to the revolution, Russia had been primarily an agricultural nation, characterized by low levels of industrialization, literacy and health care. In 1861, serfdom in Russia was formally abolished by Czar Alexander, the 'Czar Liberator', but traditional norms and values, such as patriarchy, obedience to authority and the tradition of social hierarchy, remained important guidelines, shaping the relations between men and women, nobility and peasants, and church and lay society.

The revolution and subsequent civil war (1917–20) swept away the old institutional order, but left famine and devastation in their wake, accompanied by political terror and mass repression under the rule of Joseph Stalin in the 1920s and 30s. The Second World War was followed by a period of

149

strong economic growth in the 1950s and 60s. Soviet industry was reorganized and great strides were made in the education of the populace and in
science and technology, symbolized by dramatic achievements in the space
programme.

In the mid-1980s the Soviet Union again found itself on the threshold of an
economic and political crisis. President Mikhail Gorbachev initiated the
policies of *glasnost* and *perestroika*, but without cardinal reorganization of the
power structure these did little to ameliorate the deepening economic,
political and ethnic chaos. In August 1991 pro-Communist forces led by the
military attempted to stage a coup to restore the *status quo ante* Gorbachev,
but the coup attempt failed. The leader of the anti-coup forces was Boris
Yeltsin, currently the first popularly elected President of Russia. The disintegration of central power led to the formal dissolution of the Soviet Union in
December 1991. Russia became an independent state and a member of a
commonwealth composed of sovereign republics – members of the former
USSR.

For the first time since the Second World War, Russia currently faces
severe shortages, widespread poverty, unemployment and an influx of
thousands of refugees. To deal with these problems President Yeltsin and his
advisers have instituted a programme of radical economic reforms including
privatization of key industries, the establishment of a free market economy
and the creation of joint ventures with foreign capital participation. Whether
these measures will create a viable economic basis for the new Russian state
remains to be seen. Although socioeconomic problems have always affected
Russian (Soviet) women, conditions are increasingly difficult for them now
because the support system is disintegrating.

Political system – women in politics

After the October 1917 revolution, complete equality was guaranteed to
women and the conditions for social emancipation were created. Every
citizen (18 years of age and above) was granted the right to vote and be
elected to public office, and women in the former USSR held a relatively
large number of political positions compared to those in Western countries.
In the 1970s and 80s women comprised 30 per cent of the Supreme Soviet
(supreme nation-wide governing body) and 50 per cent of the local councils
(Mashika, 1989). These seats were achieved by the use of quotas mandated
by a government affirmative action programme. Notwithstanding these
impressive figures, women were tools of state policy rather than really active
participants in political life.

In 1989 the quota system was partially abolished and in the present
Russian parliament women have about 5 per cent of the seats, only three
women having succeeded in obtaining high posts. In the local contests, the
percentage of women elected was even smaller (Zakharova and Rymashevskaya, 1990).

In spite of the small number of women holding public office, various
women's organizations including local women's councils, charitable organizations, movements of soldiers' mothers and a small number of feminist

groups which aim to improve the position of women, have flourished. These groups and movements attempt to solve various social and economic problems rather than entering directly into politics. This is a new trend because grassroot organizations were formerly forbidden.

Demographic and socioeconomic trends

According to the Russian census of 1989, the male to female ratio was 892:1,000; 53 per cent of the Russian population were female and 47 per cent were male. As a result of increases in state assistance to families with children, there was a rise in the birth rate at the beginning of the 1980s and this peaked in 1986, which witnessed the highest birth rate in 23 years. However, since 1987 this trend has been reversed and by 1989 the birth rate per thousand women had fallen 15.1 per cent (*Zhenshchiny v SSSR*, 1991).

The marriage rate is also falling, while the number of divorces is rising dramatically (the latter has been a persistent tendency during the last two decades). Currently, for every hundred marriages registered each year, there are approximately 33 divorces (*ibid.*). Quite often the break-up of the family takes place at the initiative of the woman. These trends result in an increasing number of children being born to divorced or never-married women.

The number of abortions has decreased recently, but the percentage of abortions per 100 live births is still the highest in the world (*ibid.*). Abortion is one of the primary methods of birth control used by Russian women. Current data indicate that the birth of the first child cuts the income of an average urban family by one-third, since 85 per cent of working women either take prolonged leaves of absence from their jobs, or give them up entirely (*ibid.*).

Support system

The Soviet government had implemented a widespread support system for pregnant women and women with children; this was called the Maternity and Child Protection programme. According to law, pregnant women were entitled to a leave of 70 days, plus 56 days after delivery. While on leave full wages were paid regardless of the length of service. If a woman requested it, she was also given a partly paid leave to care for a child under one and a half years of age. Additional unpaid leave was provided, at the employee's request, for care for children under three years of age (Sevost'yanov and Shtifanov, 1991).

On the whole, the support system of the former USSR was carried over to Russia, although it was improved to some extent recently in consequence of changing socioeconomic conditions. Beginning in April 1991 (when the first price escalation came into effect) special grants of 60 rubles per month were introduced for all children under 18. Quarterly grants, additional grants to single mothers, to mothers of many children and to families with children who do not attend nursery school were also introduced. In January 1992 (before the second jump in prices) on the President's order the grants for children were raised to 200 rubles per month. However, these state subsidies are only a drop in the bucket for the average Russian family since prices have risen 25 times since the beginning of 1992 (*Vetchernaya Moskva*, 22 January 1993).

Today the fees for municipal kindergartens do not cover the actual cost of caring for children, and with the low levels of state subsidies, acceptable working conditions cannot be maintained. Wages in these kindergartens are so low that employees tend to leave this occupation, and those who remain are beginning to talk about striking. A network of private nursery schools has appeared recently, but these are too expensive for the average family (*Argumenty i facty*, 19 November 1990).

The crisis in the pre-school institutions combined with difficulties in the overall system of social services are burdens which fall on the shoulders of Russian women, who have to work a double shift every day (40 hours per week for the job and approximately the same for home and family responsibilities). It is estimated that a mother has only 19–23 minutes a day for contact with her own child (*Moskovskaya Pravda*, 14 March 1992).

Women in the economic system: unemployment

The female labour force was considered essential to the development of the Soviet Union after the Second World War and for many subsequent decades women constituted half or more of the labour force. The commitment to gender equality in education and employment which had been introduced by the Soviet Union was later imposed on the Eastern bloc countries. This ideological focus was mediated by pragmatic considerations including rapid economic growth, labour shortages and a frequent shortage of males (see Chapters 4, 7, 13 and 18 in this volume).

According to official statistics, in 1989 women comprised 48 per cent of workers in the Russian economy as compared to 50 per cent in 1979 (*Zhenshchiny v SSSR*, 1991). This reduction was the consequence of changes in state policy during democratization, when President Gorbachev proclaimed that women's primary duties related to the household and upbringing of children (Pilkington, 1992). We do not have precise data for 1990–92, but it can be assumed that the proportion of women in the labour force has declined once again because of a new problem, unemployment, which disproportionately affects women.

Women of pre-pension age are much more likely than men to be dismissed on grounds of redundancy. In Moscow, 50 per cent of all those who are registered as unemployed are women above 45 years of age (the official retirement age is 55 for women and 60 for men). Those in the 'feminized' (predominantly female) professions are more likely than others to lose their jobs (*ibid.*). In addition to those dismissed on grounds of redundancy, the ranks of the unemployed are likely to be swelled by graduating students, refugees settled in Moscow and tens of thousands of housewives. Although women comprise half of the labour force, they are concentrated in certain 'feminized' occupations (education, medicine, textiles and the food industry) where the wage level is 25–30 per cent lower than average (Zakharova and Rymashevskaya, 1990). Since 1981 special labour laws have limited the amount women could be required to carry to 7 tons in one shift. Although this limit is much higher than those found in many developed countries, it is frequently exceeded. According to data from the Moscow trade unions, in 1988, 24 women were killed on the job due to unsatisfactory labour conditions (*Moskovskaya Pravda*, 5 April 1990).

In the industrial sector approximately 40 per cent of male workers have the highest professional skill rating, compared with not more than 10 per cent of the females. This means that even though theoretically there is equal pay for equal work (and thus nominally a lack of discrimination based on gender), women's wages are much lower than men's. On the whole, although most women are in the labour force, the power is concentrated in the hands of men. That was the typical situation for the former USSR, and it is true of all sectors of economic life in modern Russia. Some physicians justify such inequalities by pointing out that harsh working conditions such as constant dust, smog and heavy manual work have an adverse effect on the health of women and their future children (*Moskovskaya Pravda*, 5 April 1990).

Many women have no desire for a professional career due to the demands of their housekeeping and family responsibilities. Deeply held assumptions prevalent in the patriarchal cultural tradition engender doubt, even among women themselves, about their own abilities. Nervous diseases, lack of satisfaction, and the absence of self-fulfilment are the prices paid by women for the prevailing pattern of gender inequality (Zakharova and Rymashevskaya, 1990). Loss of an exceptional labour force is the price paid by Russian society.

Although according to official statistics there was no structural unemployment in the former Soviet Union, some forms of hidden unemployment persisted. In July 1991, for the first time since the post-World War II period, *bezrabotitsa* (structural unemployment) was officially recognized in Russia and unemployed people began to register at the Moscow labour exchange. It is estimated that by the end of the century approximately 16 million workers (13–20 per cent of the labour force) will have lost their jobs (*Vetchernaya Moskva*, 16 September 1991). The first to go will be occupations which do not require specialized education, and women occupy about half of these jobs.

Women in the educational system

History of women's place in universities

Education for females in Russia formally commenced in the 1860s and 70s, when public pressure led to the opening of girls' schools, colleges and postgraduate courses in Moscow, Petersburg, Kazan and other towns (Myzhuev, 1906). These courses were supported by tuition fees and charitable contributions. Upon graduation students had a right to teach in girls' schools and in primary schools. After 1917 separate women's higher education ceased to exist as the Soviet government guaranteed equality for men and women in higher education (*Vysshaya shkola SSSR*, 1967).

In 1918 compulsory education was introduced in Russia. As a result, the literacy rate jumped from 26.9 per cent in 1897 (44.4 per cent for males and 15.4 per cent for females) to 60.9 per cent in 1926. In 1970 the goal of universal literacy was achieved (99.7 per cent).

The proportion of the population with higher education grew tremendously in the 1960s and 70s, comprising, in 1986, 29.3 per cent among those employed in the national economy compared to 14 per cent in 1960 and 25 per cent in 1980 (*Narodnoye khozyaystvo SSSR za 70 let*, 1987). Women and men have an equal right to higher education in Russia, including enrolment in postgraduate courses and research positions, but this right has not always been implemented (see Chapter 4 in this volume).

Current university system

In Russia, as in the former USSR, university education is separated from pure scientific research and the break between them is widening. The lion's share of the state's allocation for science and education as a whole goes to pure science (under the Academy of Sciences), although the majority of Russian scientists and scholars are concentrated in the university system.

Tertiary educational institutions include universities, polytechnic institutes, branch institutes of various professions and higher military schools. Universities mainly train specialists in the humanities and natural sciences; the training of engineers is concentrated in technical institutes; and economic, scientific and cultural specialists are trained in institutes associated with these fields. The right to higher education is guaranteed to everyone who completes secondary education and passes the competitive examination. Age is the only other factor in the admissions process; the applicant must be under 35 (in night and correspondence courses the age restriction is waived). Education at all levels was formerly free of charge and fully financed by the state. Although most higher education is still free, a two-tier system of education containing non-fee-paying and fee-paying sectors is emerging at some universities. Candidates who have not passed the entrance examinations can now attend special programmes on a fee-paying basis. Private (mainly business) schools unaffiliated with universities are also springing up rapidly.

In the current economic crisis both science and education have encountered great financial difficulty. In addition, the gap between higher education and the pure sciences in widening. (Today universities receive only 2 per cent of the sum allotted to science and education.) Although fundamental science is experiencing its own financial difficulties, the situation in the university system is much more critical.

After the Second World War there was a wage cut of 20–40 per cent for university faculty. This remained unchanged for more than 30 years, resulting in a sharply declining living standard. Today the typical salary in a university is approximately 25 per cent lower than the average, often falling below the subsistence level (Aynshteyn, 1991). As this profession declines in prestige, the proportion of females may be expected to rise.

Although the separation of the university system and the scientific institutes is becoming wider, there are still some instances of cooperation. The deficit of state financing has led many universities to become involved in business and commercial activities. One of the most dangerous trends is the current tendency of many of the most brilliant and highly trained specialists to leave the university. There is a marked diminution of interest in science and university education as a whole. If radical steps are not taken by the Russian government in the very near future to maintain and preserve the university system, the scientific potential of the country will find itself on the threshold of an irreversible complete collapse.

Women as students and faculty

Women have traditionally constituted a comparatively large proportion of university students, and this has been true both in the former USSR during the past 30 years and in contemporary Russia (see Table 14.1).

Soviet ideologies have touted these figures as evidence of women's emancipation and equality, ie, 'the achievement of socialism'. There is some truth in this view; however, underlying factors such as compulsory military service for men also influence these rates. Young men often prefer highly paid jobs to existing as poor students for five years, whereas young women are more likely to be supported by parents or husbands.

Since the end of the 1980s the proportion of students who are female has been declining. Data from Moscow State University illustrate this trend (see Table 14.2).

This pattern can probably be explained by worsening economic conditions. Today the student's allowance is less than half the subsistence level, so many students are obliged to combine their study with work in the evening, a pattern considered more acceptable for male than female students.

Formally men and women have equal rights to be admitted to a university or an institute. Nevertheless, some institutes and departments have a strict quota for women, and in certain departments they are not admitted at all. These include higher military schools and various prestigious departments dealing with diplomacy, international law and journalism. Women account for approximately 10 per cent of the students in foreign area studies departments and institutes; usually they specialize in foreign trade and economics. Only a few women are allowed to receive higher military education.

Table 14.1 *The share of female students in higher educational institutions, per cent*

Specialty	1960/61	1970/71	1980/81	1985/8
Industrial and Construction	30	38	42	44
Agriculture	27	30	34	36
Economics and Law	49	60	67	71
Medicine and Sport	56	56	58	60
Education and Culture	63	66	69	74
Total	43	49	52	55

Source: Mashika, 1989, p. 242.

Table 14.2 *Moscow State University: total enrolment of undergraduate students, by sex*

Year	Total Enrolment	Female	% Female
1985	24,156	13,121	54.3
1988	23,376	12,506	53.5
1989	25,648	12,306	48.0
1990	25,961	10,882	41.9
1991	25,280	11,396	45.1

Source: Moscow State University, 1992, and Kokorev, 1992.

Of the institutes that are really available for women, those connected with education, medicine, economics and culture seem to be preferred (see Table 14.1). Some observers argue that many women apply to pedagogical or medical institutes because they think that they have a good chance of admission and not because they really prefer these professions. However, even in such 'feminized' branches as education and medicine, all things being equal, men are generally given preference over women in the admissions procedures. Such informal discrimination, together with traditional stereotypes, was typical in the Soviet Union and it continues to persist in modern 'democratic' Russia. In spite of all these difficulties, more than half of the specialists since 1970 have been women (see Table 14.3).

Since many prestigious positions are closed to her, a woman encounters obstacles even after receiving a university diploma. Many women work at a lower level than that for which they are qualified, and some remain unemployed for a long time, dependent upon parents or husbands. Family issues (for example the birth of a child) also adversely affect women's careers, especially scientific careers.

Most women marry between the ages of 20 and 24 and have their first child after they receive their university degree. Relatively few decide to continue their education at the postgraduate level and, as a result, the percentage of women shrinks from 60 per cent among undergraduate students to 33 per cent at the postgraduate level (Mashika, 1989). Many of those who do enrol in postgraduate study do not manage to complete their pro-

Table 14.3 *Educational status of women, engaged in social production in the USSR*

	1970	1980	1989
Women with higher and special technical education			
(000s)	9,900	16,956	22,191
– higher education	3,568	6,410	8,718
– special technical education	6,332	10,456	13,473
Share of women among specialists			
– higher and special technical education (%)	59	59	61

Source: *Zhenshchiny v SSSR*, 1991, p. 10.

Table 14.4 *Women in research institutions and higher educational institutions*

	Women		of whom *Dr of Science*		*Candidate*	
	Total	*%*	*No.*	*%*	*No.*	*%*
Basic Research Institutions (Acad. of Sciences)	2,271	53.1	136	6.0	974	24.9
Official Research Institutions	3,361	60.7	12	0.2	524	15.6
Higher Educational Institutions	6,261	50.6	282	4.5	3,667	58.6

Source: Leninsky District-Moscow: *Female Population of R&D Institutions and Higher Education, Special Report,* 18 January 1987.

grammes because of the demands of childbirth and childcare. Often these women find that a leave of absence puts them out of touch with contemporary research and makes it almost impossible to catch up. As a result, only 28 per cent of those achieving the status of Candidate of Science are women.

This situation is typical both of the higher education system and in the institutes of the Russian Academy of Sciences. It can be illustrated by an investigation in the Leninsky District in Moscow (see Table 14.4).

Even those women receiving the candidate degree encounter problems. If the degree was awarded after completing evening or correspondence courses, in the event that the recipient is already connected with faculty or research work, it will not help her to advance to higher professional rank. If the degree was completed at a university or in an institute, the problem of employment arises. Here, as in the industrial sphere, the higher (in salary and prestige) the rank, the lower the probability that a woman will achieve it.

The proportion of Doctors of Science who are women is only 14 per cent, half that of Candidates of Science. However, even females who become Doctors of Science are unlikely to achieve the rank of professor. Five per cent of female scientific researchers have the rank of reader and only 0.5 per cent receive professorial rank (Mashika, 1989). For example, in Moscow State University women comprise 17 per cent of professors compared to 66.9 per cent of instructors (see Table 14.5).

It is clear that in spite of the equality guaranteed by the constitution, discrimination against women still exists in the country. Socioeconomic problems are related to a general decline in the status of women and this is particularly true in the universities. For example, if a staff reduction were to occur in the near future, women would be the first to be discharged from the institutes and become unemployed. (For the time being there is no such trend in higher education but it has already occurred in the field of military economy and in some research institutes.)

There is no doubt that the political and socioeconomic changes that have

Table 14.5 *Moscow State University: full-time instructional faculty and full-time research staff, by sex and rank, 1991*

Rank	Total No.	No. of Female	% Female
Instructional Fac.			
Dept. Head	275	40	14.5
Professor	762	131	17.2
Assoc. Prof.	1356	523	38.6
Asst. Prof.	807	180	22.3
Instructor	472	316	66.9
Lecturer	468	173	37.0
Subtotal	4140	1363	32.9
Research Staff			
Director	21	1	4.8
Res. Dept. Head	33	2	6.1
Res. Div. Head	30	7	23.3
Laboratory Head	136	8	5.9
Sr. Researcher	1271	485	38.2
Reg. Researcher	1250	603	48.2
Jr. Researcher	1130	538	47.6
Leading Res. (Res. Prof.)	247	55	22.3
Principal Res. (Spec. Hon. Rank)	20	1	5.0
Subtotal	4138	1700	41.1
Total	8278	3063	37.0

Source: Moscow State University, 1992, and Kokorev, 1992.

taken place in Russia recently have complicated the position of Russian women and their status in the higher education system in particular. Many problems (unknown before *perestroika*, or existing in latent form) have become aggravated; these include the support system, unemployment, latent discrimination, etc. At the same time the democratization process provides scope for new developments.

The first is connected with a new interest in Women's Studies – a trend which is in the initial stage of development. These studies are carried out at various levels of government, up to the Supreme Soviet of Russia (where a group of gender experts was formed in January 1993). The Centre for Gender Studies of the Institute of Social and Economic Studies, Russian Academy of Sciences, is the leader in this field. Regional and international conferences devoted to the problems of women's transitions to the market economy are becoming common. More than 300 women from various women's organizations and 100 foreign guests participated in the second International Women's Forum held near Moscow in November 1992.

The second deals with the formation of a women's movement as an independent political force. In 1990–92 various independent women's organizations appeared in Russia; these included the women's centre in Moscow, 'Geya', the 'Independent Women's Democratic Initiative', and a group called 'Dignity'.

Both trends testify to the growth of a women's movement which is developing in Russia and providing some hope for positive changes in the future.

15. Higher education in Turkey: a gold bracelet for women[1]

Feride Acar

SUMMARY: The Kemalist Revolution early in the century legalized equality between men and women in Turkey. Women were encouraged to throw away their veils, become educated and participate in public life as part of the state-directed policy of Westernization. Thus, women of urban élite families who were strongly supported by familial and ideological mechanisms were able to have access to higher education and fill the positions created in modern Turkish universities with relative ease. In spite of the changing dynamics of socio-cultural forces in later eras, this has created a situation where, in a Muslim patriarchal society, the higher education gender gap is among the narrowest. Higher education in Turkey is considered a golden bracelet because it provides adornment (prestige) as well as financial security.

Some social and cultural characteristics

Located at the intersection of Europe and Asia, Turkey has been at the crossroads of civilization since prehistoric times. The roots of Turkish traditions stem from their Anatolian–Turkic origins and the Ottoman–Islamic heritage of the people. With the establishment of the Republic in 1923, the cultural alternatives of conservative–Islamic–communitarian values inherited from the past and the progressivist–Westernizing–secular worldview of Kemalism, were superimposed on the existing dichotomy. Thus religious conservatism and secular nationalism became the two main cultural axes of modern Turkey.

The cultural ethos promoted by the Kemalist élite emphasized nationhood, rationality and science, secularism, modernization and political, social and legal equality of women and differed fundamentally from the earlier cultural outlook. Although on the surface the Kemalist discourse signified a radical break with conservative–traditional values, both points of view had many underlying commonalities. Neither promoted individualism and individual rights vis-à-vis the group (an orientation that only very recently came to be overtly advocated in Turkey). On the contrary, they both emphasized communitarianism, Kemalism substituting the 'nation' for the 'community of believers' as the object of unconditional allegiance and loyalty.

Many studies of Turkish society and culture have documented this strong respect for state authority (Hyman *et al.*, 1958; Kagitcibasi, 1970). High degrees of nationalism and patriotism linked with an exaggerated sense of loyalty to the nation-state, a desire to serve it and a tendency to expect protection and security from the state (TÜSIAD, 1991), have systematically emerged as latterday reflections of the traditional in-group loyalty to the family, kinship group or community (Kagitcibasi, 1982).

A weak emphasis on individualism and strong dependence on authority have been observed, leading to a negative evaluation of competitiveness, assertiveness and open interpersonal confrontation (Kozan, 1993). In this culture, desirable conditions include interpersonal support, solidarity, loyalty, obligation and the ability to control others.[2]

The world view promoted by Kemalism did not attempt to question such key dimensions of the traditional culture as patriarchal family and gender relations (Erkut, 1982; Kandiyoti, 1982). The traditional social and political hierarchy based on age and sex was retained, particularly in the private sphere, while simultaneously an egalitarian-looking modern politico-legal order was created in the public sphere.[3] Consequently, while the reforms opened up, for women, avenues of educational attainment, economic independence, social mobility and political efficacy that were previously unthinkable, they did not effectively alter the patriarchal nature of values and relationships conditioning the day-to-day living experience of most women.

Turkey is a society with a predominantly Muslim population and a dominant patriarchal cultural heritage. However, it is also a society which has undergone a deliberate and very effective process of Westernization in the form of a 'revolution from above' pertaining specifically to women's roles and rights.[4] Turkey has a secular state and legal structure and has been oriented towards integration with the West through its military, political and economic alliances throughout Republican history.

Mainly as a result of such deliberate political choices of the state, the conditions of women in urban and educated sectors today (academia foremost among them) contrast sharply with those of others in Turkish society and sometimes even surpass the conditions of their Western counterparts (Acar, 1991a; Öncü, 1981). Approximately 20 per cent of all physicians, 25 per cent of attorneys and 20 per cent of all university full professors are women (Acar, 1991a; Öncü, 1981). The current prime minister of the country is also a woman (a former professor of economics) whose elevation to that post is due more to the combination of her gender and education attainments than to any other factors. However, these impressive figures must be considered within the context of the socio-economic realities of the country, where 31 per cent of all women are illiterate (State Institute of Statistics, 1988), the infant mortality rates are more than five times those in the West (World Bank, 1991) and 74 per cent of all economically active women are in the agricultural labour force (World Bank, 1993).

These paradoxes reflect the rather unique combination of social and political forces shaping the position of women in modern Turkey. Within this dynamic, education – particularly higher education – has played a critical role in determining the life-chances and career tracks of many Turkish women.

Educational attainment of women in Turkey

According to 1985 census figures, in Turkey 39.4 per cent of women (aged 6 and over) have elementary school education; 4.5 per cent have middle school education and 6.0 per cent of women have high school education or above. These figures are 47.6 per cent, 8.4 per cent, and 8.1 per cent, respectively, for corresponding categories of men. Similarly, 1.1 per cent of women and 3.3 per cent of men have completed university education (TUSIAD, 1990, p. 37). Particularly at the upper educational levels, the differences in proportions of men and women are unacceptably large. While women's educational attainment has been increasing over time (the illiteracy rate of women has declined from 45.3 per cent in 1980 to 28.9 per cent in 1990), the change has been slow and the inequality between sexes still increases with the level of education (Arat, 1989).

In Turkey, women's education at the secondary level reinforces women's traditional wife-mother roles and often assists their social mobility by enabling them to make more desirable marriages. Women's education at the university level and above, however, is clearly career oriented and encourages labour force participation. Professional women view their occupation as a 'career'; they exhibit strong career commitments, often defining their identities on the basis of their work (Acar, 1983). Other working women perceive their occupation as merely a 'job' and concomitantly as an additional burden on themselves (Çitçi, 1982; Ozkalp, 1990).

Women in universities

Students

Today, women constitute 25 per cent of those with higher education in Turkish society and 37 per cent of university students. Women are most numerous in language and literature (60 per cent), arts (46 per cent) and natural sciences/mathematics (46 per cent). The lowest percentages of female participation are observed in technical sciences (22 per cent) and agriculture and forestry (33 per cent) (see Table 15.1).

As can be readily observed from the distribution in Table 15.1, women students' presence in even the most unlikely branches is exceptionally large in Turkish universities. Furthermore, since the 1920s, despite some fluctuations, there has been an overall increase in the representation of women in the total student body.

While women enjoy a generally high representation in university enrolment, in some fields they are particularly numerous. These include fields that are considered to be less demanding and more suitable for women, and where women face weaker competition from men. Despite the large presence of women in unconventional areas in Turkey (Cindoglu et al., 1992) this picture suggests a gender-based differentiation that is similar to the one observed in Western societies.

Table 15.1 Number (in thousands) and per cent of women students by field, 1927–90

Field	1927–8 No.	%	1937–8 No.	%	1947–8 No.	%	1957–8 No.	%	1967–8 No.	%	1977–8 No.	%	1989–90 No.	%
Language and Literature	107	34	291	38	1506	56	1437	51	4694	42	–	–	8247	60
Educational Sciences	13	11	354	20	724	35	833	37	3012	38	29704	31	–	–
Fine and Applied Sciences	67	31	53	20	62	17	140	26	423	36	1655	40	2982	46
Social Sciences	–	–	235	24	554	21	1575	11	5146	13	16299	22	12454	37
Medicine	341	40	150	8	500	12	963	24	3728	30	8884	34	19934	39
Mathematics and Natural Sciences	107	23	393	24	512	13	976	11	1683	22	4985	32	14039	46
Law	31	7	299	13	642	11	1222	11	2614	18	2188	20	5050	35
Agriculture and Forestry	–	–	33	5	42	4	83	3	363	10	973	17	6450	33
Engineering	–	–	–	–	–	–	–	–	1840	7	7741	12	15413	22
Humanities, Theology and Religion	–	–	–	–	–	–	–	–	–	–	3819	24	–	–
Applied Social Sciences	–	–	–	–	–	–	–	–	–	–	–	–	48203	39
Women Students	–	–	–	–	–	–	–	–	–	–	–	–	–	–
Total	670	26	1609	17	4542	11	6645	16	23503	19	76248	24	345279	37

Note: The terms and classification schemes of fields have changed over the years.
Source: National Education Statistics; Higher Education Statistics.

Faculty

In Turkey, since the 1940s when large-scale recruitment of women faculty began, their numbers and proportions in all fields and ranks have generally increased. Today, female faculty constitute 32.2 per cent[5] of the total university academic staff in the country (see Table 15.2). However, if research assistants and other non-career staff are excluded from this count, the female percentage comes to 23.0.

As in the case of women students, women faculty in Turkish universities have also never been exclusively concentrated in areas designated as 'fit for women'. In fact, in the decade following their entry into the academic profession, women constituted higher proportions of the faculties in natural science and engineering departments than in social sciences, humanities and education departments. For example, Köker (1988) has noted that in 1946–7, 44 per cent of the natural sciences faculty as opposed to 22 per cent of the humanities was composed of women.

However, contemporary distribution of women faculty presents quite a different picture. While women faculty are still impressively represented in all fields, their participation rates in humanities, arts and medicine have come to exceed their overall participation rate in academe. In engineering and agriculture it falls noticeably below the average (see Table 15.2). In its rough outline this picture also resembles the typical Western model.

Over the years women faculty shares have increased in all fields except natural sciences/mathematics, but not at similar rates. For instance, in the last decade, the most noticeable gains in women's participation in academe have been in humanities and law. Against an overall increase of 6.8 percentage points in all fields, women in the humanities have increased by 23.1 per cent and in law by 14.6 per cent. In the same period, the smallest increases have been in medicine (1.2 per cent) and natural sciences/mathematics (3.1 per cent) (Acar, 1991a). Both humanities and law had contained few women academics in earlier years, in contrast to medicine and natural sciences/mathematics where women's shares had either been traditionally very high or had reached top percentages in earlier decades.

Women faculty's presence in the different academic rank categories is also illustrated in Table 15.2. Compared to most Western countries, percentages of women in all ranks of academia but particularly among the tenured faculty (assistant: 27 per cent; associate: 23 per cent; and full professors: 20 per cent) are truly impressive. Not only do women have considerable presence in Turkish academe but they are well represented in the top ranks. However, it is also clear that female faculty constitute more than half of the total only in the category of language instructors (shown as 'other'). Since this kind of personnel is by definition marginal to academia, women's majority presence here is indicative of what may be called a female 'pseudo-participation' in academia (Acar, 1991a). Women who fall into this and similar support categories (instructor, etc.) constitute 77 per cent of all female academics. The corresponding figure for men is 63 per cent. This situation undoubtedly indicates the onset of a gender-based stratification system and the feminization of lower positions in academe. In Turkish universities a pyramidal structure is evident where women are better

Table 15.2 *Number and per cent of women academics by rank and field, 1989*

	1	2	3	4	5	6	7	8	9
Teacher Training and Education	34 (3.3)	30 (2.9)	78 (7.6)	488 (47.6)	20 (2.0)	178 (17.5)	194 (19.0)	1020 (100.0)	– (32.6)
Humanities, Religion and Theology	66 (5.0)	29 (2.2)	49 (3.7)	170 (12.8)	27 (2.0)	151 (11.3)	841 (63.1)	1333 (100.0)	(43.9)
Fine and Applied Arts	13 (2.9)	31 (6.9)	45 (10.0)	233 (52.0)	3 (0.7)	78 (17.4)	45 (10.0)	448 (100.0)	– (41.7)
Law and Jurisprudence	14 (12.7)	5 (4.5)	11 (10.0)	7 (6.4)	3 (2.7)	70 (63.6)	0 (0.0)	110 (100.0)	– (30.2)
Social Science (Social, Behavioral, Commercial)	70 (8.0)	53 (6.0)	132 (15.0)	94 (10.7)	38 (4.3)	457 (51.9)	36 (4.1)	880 (100.0)	– (31.5)
Natural Sciences	100 (9.5)	60 (5.7)	158 (15.0)	64 (6.1)	51 (4.8)	617 (58.7)	2 (0.2)	1052 (100.0)	– (31.6)
Medical Sciences	456 (15.3)	195 (6.8)	277 (9.3)	131 (4.4)	114 (3.8)	1793 (60.2)	13 (0.4)	2980 (100.0)	– (34.6)
Engineering and Technology	64 (5.2)	57 (4.6)	139 (11.3)	126 (10.2)	69 (5.6)	740 (60.2)	35 (2.8)	1230 (100.0)	– (23.6)
Agricultural Sciences	34 (10.8)	10 (3.2)	30 (9.5)	7 (2.2)	17 (5.4)	210 (66.7)	7 (2.2)	315 (100.0)	– (17.4)
Other Fields	6 (1.4)	2 (0.5)	12 (2.7)	61 (13.8)	45 (10.2)	34 (7.7)	282 (83.8)	442 (100.0)	– (38.4)
Total number of women academics	857 (20.0)	473 (22.7)	931 (26.8)	1379 (30.3)	387 (43.0)	4328 (34.8)	1455 (54.4)	9810 (100.0)	(32.2)
Total number of academics	4284	2086	3480	4552	900	12521	2674	30497	–
Per cent of women academics	(20.0)	(22.7)	(26.8)	(30.3)	(43.0)	(34.8)	(54.4)	(32.2)	–

Source: Constructed from data compiled by the Student Selection and Placement Centre of Turkey.
The figures in parentheses indicate percentages ((the proportion of women in a given position compared to the total number of women academics in that field). 1=Full Professor; 2=Associate Professor; 3=Assistant Professor; 4=Instructor; 5=Specialist; 6=Research Assistant; 7=Other; 8=Total Women Academics; 9=Overall percentage of women.

represented in the lower positions; thus, despite their progress over the years, they are still disadvantaged vis-à-vis men.

The difference between the proportions of men and women increases as one moves up the hierarchy. Women professors or associate professors still constitute distinctly small percentages. For instance, although 20 per cent of all full professors are women, only 8.7 per cent of the women in academe are full professors. The figure is 16.6 per cent for male academics. Corresponding figures for female and male associate professors are 4.8 per cent and 7.8 per cent respectively. This is despite the fact that in Turkey men and women academics do not show significant time differences in obtaining degrees or promotions (Acar, 1991a). The explanation for this is that many women are stuck in the non-career track positions to start with.

So far as the distribution of senior women faculty into different areas is concerned, more than half (53.2 per cent) of the female full professors in Turkey are in medical sciences. However, these women constitute only 15.3 per cent of the full professors in this discipline, and this is where women appear to fare the best. Law, where women's share has increased significantly in the last decade, constitutes the second best alternative in terms of women's likelihood of being promoted to full professor. In this field women make up 12.7 per cent of the full professors. Humanities, education and arts are the fields where senior women faculty are relatively few. In these fields, 5.0 per cent, 3.3 per cent and 2.9 per cent respectively of the full professors are women. In fact, women even fare better in terms of being senior faculty in agriculture (10.8 per cent) where their overall share is the smallest (17.4 per cent). One could read these figures to mean that a rather negatively charged environment exists for women in those fields where their proportions show them as more than tokens.

The declining participation of women as one moves up the academic hierarchy is also supported by data on women in administrative positions (see Table 15.3).

Women in general are under-represented among administrators in Turkish universities; those who do hold administrative positions are likely to be at the lower levels. Currently 15.9 per cent of all administrative appointments are held by women. Women appointees amount to 16.7 per cent among lower level post-holders; of the higher level appointments only

Table 15.3 *Number and per cent of women academic administrators, 1989*

	Number	%
Higher level*	47	9.8
Lower level*	638	16.7
Total	685	15.9

* Lower-level administrative posts include department chairs, assistant chairs, other intra-department appointments, computer centre directors, etc. Higher-level administrative posts include university presidents and vice-presidents, deans and vice-deans of graduate and undergraduate faculties, directors and assistant directors of research institutes.

Source: Constructed from data compiled by the Student Selection and Placement Centre of Turkey.

9.8 per cent are held by women (Acar, 1991a; Günlük-Şenesen, 1992). This representation among university presidents and faculty deans indicates, once again, the presence of a gender stratification which may not be observable at first glance.

Finally, personal background data on academic women and on those holding administrative office also show that for women, combining an academic career with marriage is more problematic than it is for men. About half of all women academic personnel (48.9 per cent) in Turkey are unmarried as opposed to 38.1 per cent of men. This difference increases in higher academic positions. For instance, while 15 per cent of male assistant professors and 25.1 per cent of female assistant professors are single, among full professors 4 per cent of the men and 22 per cent of the women are single. Among all female holders of administrative office, 20.9 per cent are single and 7.7 per cent are divorced or widowed. These percentages are only 5.4 per cent and 1.6 per cent, respectively, for male administrators. Among women in high administrative office 29.8 per cent are single compared to only 3 per cent of the men (Acar, 1991a). Obviously, successful academic women find it more difficult to pursue their careers within a marriage than do their male colleagues.

Discussion

Kemalist state ideology strongly encouraged women's higher education and career orientation as part of political modernization (Tekeli, 1986). Against the background of traditional culture (whose normative framework did not include any 'proper' role for its women other than wife-mother) policies of the Republican élite in Turkey resulted in a sudden unrestricted recruitment of women into all professions. This development was possible because the (male) political authorities needed qualified personnel to fill the positions created by rapid economic and political expansion. Upper-class women rather than lower-class men were available and preferable – due to class bias – for recruitment and training for these positions (Öncü, 1981). Although the élite social background of educated women became gradually less pronounced as economic advancement and political democracy evolved in Turkish society, even as late as the 1980s professional women in public bureaucracy still tended to be primarily from middle- or upper-class backgrounds (Çitçi, 1982). Social background characteristics of female university students also remain higher than those of male students.

Systematic recruitment of women into higher education and professional careers since the early days of the Republic has produced a highly qualified female labour force and prevented the development of a tradition of sex-typing of professions (Kagitcibasi, 1990). Currently, women have an approximately 30 per cent share of the professional occupations, 38 per cent among clerical workers, 14 per cent among service workers and 10 per cent among production workers (World Bank, 1993). The participation rate of university-educated women in the urban labour force reaches 78 per cent, while it is 39 per cent for high school graduates, 16 per cent for middle school graduates and 11 per cent for those with primary education. For urban women with less than primary education this rate is 8 per cent. Mainly owing to the low labour force participation rate of urban women of the lower educational brackets, the overall labour force participation rate of women in Turkey (33 per cent) remains one of the lowest among the OECD countries (World Bank, 1993). This situation further underlines the significance of the high labour force participation rate of highly educated women in the country.

In the past, such high participation was largely facilitated by the availability of cheap household and childcare help from women of lower socioeconomic strata and support systems provided through extended families. With these support mechanisms, élite women in Turkey were able to enter demanding career tracks without upsetting family structures or threatening traditional relations between the sexes in the private sphere. In addition, through their prestigious careers they often brought social honour to their kinfolk in the modern élite subculture (Erkut, 1982; Kandiyoti, 1982). While social, structural and economic changes of more recent times render these support mechanisms less influential in the lives of career women, the cultural values and social practices that emanate from the momentum they created are still evident in Turkish society.

Universities in the early Republican era opened their doors to daughters of urban élite families who identified with Kemalist ideals. The dominant ideology of the Republic glorified 'hard' sciences; thus, women socialized in the élite subculture were expected to have careers in such fields as natural sciences and mathematics, as indeed they did.

However, in Turkey as in other developing countries, academia is marginal to the real power loci. At the time women were being encouraged to enter science fields, they were conspicuously absent among the faculty in law and political science departments – which were closely related to political power in Turkish society (Köker, 1988).

The social and political mechanisms created by the Republic (ie, political democracy, diffusion of education to the countryside, availability of education to women) facilitated the emergence of women from non-élite groups into the public domain. These new groups were essentially different from women of élite Republican backgrounds; their choices of field, as well as their career aspirations and patterns reflected such differences. These women were often motivated by traditional, conservative values of the non-élite subcultures, and economic needs.

The increased social mobility also meant more competition for élite women from upwardly-mobile men of lower socio-economic origins. The shift in the preferences of academic women from 'hard sciences' to 'soft' ones (eg, education, humanities) as well as the tendency of women to engage in 'pseudo-participation' or stay out of administrative positions in academia, can be explained largely by the change in the social class composition of those in higher education.

Other changes in Turkish society were also influential. The declining role of family support systems in the face of rapid urbanization and modernization, and the prohibitively high cost of household labour and scarcity of good childcare facilities in metropolitan centres make it more difficult for women to pursue demanding careers.

Demands of career and family roles clash more and more, and severe role conflict becomes increasingly pronounced in the lives of academic women (Acar, 1990). While early generation élite women whose identities were heavily influenced by the formal emancipatory discourse of the Republic were not altogether freed from traditional female role obligations embedded in Islamic patriarchy, later generations of educated women who come from very diverse socio-economic backgrounds are not entirely untouched by the reformist discourse of the Republic. In fact, they often feel the 'tug of war' between their public and private lives even more strongly.

Married academic women often mention the debilitating influence of role conflict in their lives and develop coping strategies. While younger Turkish academic women in metropolitan centres who have been exposed to feminist views tend to cope with imminent role conflict by actively struggling against patriarchal norms, older women and/or those with more conventional values and provincial backgrounds often prefer to compartmentalize their lives into two separate spheres and develop role-specific identities appropriate for those spheres (Acar, 1983).

Women faculty in Turkish universities generally do not report personal experiences of discrimination (Acar, 1983; Köker, 1988); these perceptions reflect the formal practices of these institutions. It could be argued, however, that acceptance of the Kemalist reforms by the educated classes in Turkish society has often meant a legalistic interpretation of social relationships alongside a denial of social realities. The Republican ideology in Turkey insisted on equality of men and women, formalizing this position into law. Even though such equality seldom went beyond legal expression or the limits of the public sphere, and rarely became characteristic of everyday existence or private lives, public recognition of women's unequal status was nevertheless inhibited, particularly among the élite. Thus, what was stated as 'should be' by the normative principles of Kemalism was often accepted as the objective reality, especially among groups where considerable real change in the status of women seemed to validate the claims of the ideology. Turkish academic women's tendency to operate with a formalistic conception of equality reflects this (Acar, 1983; 1990).

Conclusion

The 'gold bracelet' of higher education has provided many Turkish women with the ability to acquire professional careers, earn a living and participate in some decision making in a patriarchal society where traditional norms define the woman's place as in her home. At the same time, values and norms have also come to define higher education of women as a form of adornment, a prestige item that reflects on women and their families alike.

In Turkey women's higher education and its career-oriented consequences have been limited to the more modern segments of the population and, despite improvements, they remain basically a minority affair. However, women with the educational 'gold bracelet' have played a critical role in the history of this society as pioneers and precursors of change, and continue to exhibit a presence that is, by international standards, not negligible.

It is argued here that deliberate state policies and actions based on Kemalist ideals led to the wholesale advancement of women in all branches of higher education in a country where religion and culture historically have kept women secluded, segregated and confined to traditional female roles. The momentum created by such policies is the single most important force in defining the relatively advantageous position of women with the 'gold bracelet' in contemporary Turkish society.

However, it is also possible to delineate negative trends. Among these are the appearance of a Western type of gender stratification where women are concentrated in lower-status positions and/or so-called conventionally 'feminine' disciplines as well as the tendency of women to exhibit 'pseudo-participation' in academia.

Also, at the personal level it is possible to talk of an increasing role conflict in educated women's lives. The co-existence of emancipation and equality in the public domain with relative inequality and patriarchal oppression in the private sphere has perhaps always been characteristic of the world of educated women in this country. Yet economic advancement, political democracy and social mobility have, paradoxically, brought these incongruous worlds closer together for women with the 'gold bracelet'. It is perhaps incongruities of this nature that lie behind the emergence of a feminist movement, among the most active members of which are academic women (Tekeli, 1986), almost simultaneously with the development of conservative religious movements which promise women escape from role conflict and a respected identity via the glorification of the wife-mother role. Conservative Islamic groups also find receptive audiences among some young university women in contemporary Turkish society (Acar, 1991b; Göle, 1991). It prompts one to ask whether the 'gold bracelet' is getting heavier and less affordable in our day.

Notes

1. Anatolian traditions define gold bracelets not only as items of adornment, but also as sources of financial security for women to fall back upon in times of need. As such the gold bracelet has both symbolic and practical functions. In Turkish, the term is also used with reference to education, particularly job- or career-orientated education, to which prestige and security functions are also commonly attributed.
2. For a concise overview of this literature see Kagitcibasi, 1982.
3. It is noteworthy in this respect that while the civil code of the Republic bestowed equal citizenship status to women in all aspects of public life, it retained the husband as the 'head of the family'; bestowed on him final decision-making power with regard to children in case of disagreement between the spouses; and made the wife's right to be employed subject to the husband's formal approval. The latter limitation has recently been revoked the others remain.
4. Following the disintegration of the Ottoman Empire after World War I, the new Republic under the leadership of Mustafa Kemal Atatürk enacted a series of reforms among which changes made to give women equal status with men were of paramount importance. With the establishment of the Republic as a secular state, replacement of the Islamic code (*Sharia*) with the civil code, and other constitutional and legal changes, women were granted equal citizenship rights. With respect to their status in law, they were granted equal rights of inheritance, divorce, ownership of property, custody of children, etc.; polygamy was outlawed; dress codes for men and women were changed, discouraging veiling, seclusion and segregation of women in public life; women were provided with the right to elect and be elected to all political offices.
5. This includes instructors, research assistants and others not included in Table 19.1.

16. Two steps forward and one step back: women in higher education in the United Kingdom

Margaret B Sutherland

SUMMARY: This chapter discusses the gradual increase in women students' access to higher education in the United Kingdom during the twentieth century, indicating reasons for slow growth during earlier decades and the factors still complicating women's progress. It notes the as yet unsatisfactory position of women at postgraduate level and continuing gender bias in the choice of subjects studied. Among university teachers women are shown to be still in a minority and clustered at the lower levels of employment; the consequences of this situation are outlined, yet the innovatory development of women's studies is recognized. In general, while various developments helpful to women's progress are shown, the continuing influence of factors inhibiting the achievement of equality in study and authority is also acknowledged.

Introduction

The United Kingdom is composed of England, Wales, Scotland and Northern Ireland. Each country has its own unique local traditions and its own educational system (at the primary and secondary levels). Although there are some distinctive differences in school education in the three countries, the provision of university education has not been differentiated. Until 1990, conditions for universities throughout the United Kingdom were determined by the University Grants Committee (though it had only an indirect influence in Northern Ireland).

The low percentage of the population who are active members of Christian churches (less than 20 per cent) has contrasted in recent decades with the growing number of citizens who are adherents of Muslim or Hindu faiths. Different regions also vary, as do different ethnic groups, in the importance they attach to the education of girls and women. Social class, traditionally, has affected access to education in England though class barriers have been less important in Scotland. In the United Kingdom during this century legislation has allowed no discrimination on the grounds of gender, race or religion. Nevertheless, the introduction of the Sex Discrimination Act in 1975 (incorporating the 1970 Equal Pay Act) was necessary to ensure that gender discrimination did not prejudice women's chances at some levels and in some types of education and employment.

In general, women's paid work outside the home has been accepted for many years. Women were 37 per cent of the labour force in 1971 and 42 per cent in 1987 (EOC, 1988); they are expected to reach 45 per cent by the end of the century (*Social Trends*, 1992). In 1990, more than four women in ten were part-time workers as compared with one man in ten. A rise in the numbers of women employed outside the home is likely as demographic statistics predict a reduction in the number of young people leaving school during the 1990s; yet a continuing economic recession could adversely affect women's employment.

Some employers seeking to recruit more women workers have tried to do so by providing additional facilities for childcare and for career breaks. Women's pay has remained consistently less than that of men: in 1990, the average weekly pay of manual workers was £237.20 for men, £148.00 for women; the average pay of non-manual workers was £354.90 for men and £215.50 for women. The greater number of hours worked by men (including overtime) admittedly distorts such figures slightly (*Social Trends*, 1992).

Women enter a more restricted range of occupations than men and within occupations they are likely to be numerous at lower levels but become a small minority at top levels, eg, 7.8 per cent of women at the top grades of the Civil Service and 74.7 in its lowest grades (EOC, 1988).

There have been various attempts to improve the situation of women at work by better provision of maternity leave and other welfare benefits and by legislation intended to remove disadvantages for females in education and employment. The Equal Opportunities Commission, established by the 1975 Act, has given important support to women (and men) in legal actions against discriminatory practices.

Further, although they have equal political rights, women still play a minor role in the political affairs of the country. The proportion of women Members of Parliament has remained deplorably low. It was only 6 per cent in the parliament of 1987–92, and, with the exception of the Prime Minister for some years, Mrs Thatcher, the Cabinet then included no women. At the 1992 general election the number of women MPs increased but remained under 10 per cent, though two women were appointed to the new Cabinet.

Women have made advances in education and in access to professional employment, yet in various ways these advances have been restricted or cancelled out. A review of what has been happening in the higher education of women may cast light on why they do not exercise greater authority in the political and social life of the United Kingdom. There is evidence of progress, but also evidence of continuing impediments to that progress.

The Higher Education Acts of 1991–2 led to dramatic changes in the names of some institutions of higher education though not immediately to corresponding changes in their activities and prestige. The Higher Education Funding Council replaced the former University Grants Committee and the Polytechnic Funding Council. To the existing 52 universities were added 37 'new' universities which had formerly been colleges or (in England and Wales) polytechnics or (in Scotland) Central Institutions. Mergers between colleges of education and universities or polytechnics also confused former classifications. It is not yet possible to judge which distinctions between institutions will disappear. Prior to the new system, older universities enjoyed higher prestige, engaging in higher levels of teaching and research; polytechnics were considered more practically oriented, principally teaching at undergraduate level. Statistics in this chapter have been provided in respect of the old structures: to avoid confusion, the familiar nomenclature for institutions of higher education has been used.

Women as students in higher education

Changes for the better

Approximately a century has gone by since women were first admitted as students in most universities of the country. The end of the nineteenth century was a time of rejoicing among those who had struggled for women's rights to higher education – even if dire predictions of appalling results for women and society were still widely heard. Enthusiasts then could scarcely have foreseen that in Britain over a hundred years would pass before women student numbers approached those of men and that even then women would still be a minority among teachers and leading administrators in higher education.

The success of the campaign for access to universities was in fact, as in some other countries, followed by a long period of quasi-stagnation. As Table 16.1 shows, women remained only about 25 per cent of university students until the mid-1960s; it was not until 1991 that they were 45.1 per cent of all UK university students and 48.5 per cent of those beginning first degree courses (UCCA, 1992). In polytechnics and colleges women were, by 1988, 49.6 per cent of the UK student population (DES, 1990).

In colleges of education, admittedly, women students had long been in the majority, but the status of teacher education as higher education was anomalous and in the 1980s mergers of colleges with other institutions and diversification of college courses complicated the situation. A major development of the late twentieth century has certainly been women's increasing presence as university or polytechnic students in programmes other than those preparing for school teaching.

Why was a balance of male and female students in higher education so slow in developing? University women student numbers of course depend on the numbers of girls taking full secondary education leading to entrance qualifications for higher education; only in the post-war decades did these numbers increase. Yet these increases did not lead directly to increased entry of women students to universities. For many years young women with

Table 16.1 *Percentage of women among full-time university students*

1938	23.3	1965	27.7
1954	25.0	1975	36.2
1959	24.0	1980	39.8
1961	25.4	1991	45.1

Sources: Robbins Committee, 1963a; DES Statistics of Education, various years; *Universities' Statistical Record*, 1992.

entrance qualifications for higher education chose rather to enter colleges of education. Oddly enough, the government-imposed reduction in the numbers of teacher-training places in these colleges in the 1980s possibly served to encourage women to enter universities and so increase their range of vocational options.

Girls' preference for teacher-training courses was associated with social attitudes which held marriage to be the only important career for women and esteemed school teaching as an eminently suitable occupation for them. Changes in these attitudes also are recent and to some extent incomplete though they have been helped by the efforts of feminist organizations, by some teachers' organizations and of course by the European Community. Along with changes in the work and career patterns of women, social attitudes seem the major factor in recent advances in women's higher education.

Some new developments also favour continuing progress by women. In different parts of the country 'access' schemes offered by universities or further education colleges assist adults who lack formal qualifications to acquire these and enter higher education. Women are certainly benefiting by such schemes, even if, from the government's point of view, the objective is not simply to allow full development of individual potentialities but to create a more highly skilled work-force. Mature women still tend to opt for traditionally female studies, of lesser vocational value, though various authorities try to convince them of the charms of computing and science studies. In any case, women are certainly more often found as mature students in higher education. Among full-time mature students in 1979, women were 41 per cent; by 1988, 48 per cent. Among part-time students in higher education, women were 27 per cent in 1979, and 42 per cent in 1988 (DES, 1991).

Women's studies may be interrupted by family commitments, so recent changes in the structure of many university and polytechnic programmes can help them. Where formerly year-long courses over a continuous period were required, students can now gain degrees by accumulating credits in a number of shorter courses immediately assessed. The growth of the Open University has similarly enabled women to gain degrees.

Remaining problems

What kind of qualifications do women gain by higher education? Table 16.2 shows continuing gender differentiation in choice of subjects – with obvious consequences for careers.

Within these subject groups, women have moved towards law, business studies and accountancy; but despite admirable efforts by engineering departments, professional organizations and specific educational projects, gender bias remains strong in science and technology. Similarly, although women's entry to courses in medicine in universities has strengthened since quotas were eliminated in the 1970s, differentiation remains within medical specialities and in allied subjects, eg, nursing and pharmacy.

The significance of subject bias is that it produces gender segregation in the labour market where 'women's occupations' are likely to be less well paid and often less prestigious. Naturally there would be little point in

Table 16.2 *Percentage of women students (UK domicile) among university undergraduates, 1972 and 1992*

	1972	1992
Medicine and Dentistry	29.0	47.8
Studies allied to Medicine	61.6	69.5
Biological Sciences	42.9	57.7
Vet., Agric. and related studies	24.2	50.1
Physical Science	14.7	30.4
Maths	27.5	25.3
Engineering and Technology	2.9	14.2
Architecture, Building, Planning	21.3	26.1
Social Studies		48.3
Business and Admin. Studies	34.7*	41.7
Communication and Documentary		62.5
Language, Literature, Area Studies	59.9*	
Languages		70.0
Other Art subjects	51.4	
Humanities		48.1
Creative Arts*		61.2
Education	67.0	78.7

Sources: Education Statistics for the UK, 1972 and the *Universities Statistical Record*, 1992. As asterisks indicate, slightly different subject groupings were used at different times: 'other Arts subjects' in 1972 included history, archaeology, philology, theology, art and design, drama, music. Where possible, equivalents have been calculated.

urging women into studies which they did not like or which would not lead to any subsequent vocational outlet. However, much research (see, for example, Arnot and Weiner, 1987) has indicated that other factors contribute to maintaining the usual separation between female studies (and occupations) and male studies, notably, the attitudes of teachers, tutors, parents and peer groups, combined with inadequate educational guidance in schools and incomplete career guidance. Moreover, the continuing popularity of school teaching as an occupation for women may mean, as in other countries, that scientific studies lead to a smaller range of careers for women than for men – women scientists entering teaching rather than research or industry.

A gender difference is also seen in access to postgraduate studies. Full-time postgraduate study has suffered from reductions in the availability of financial support and the arts, where women are likely to be candidates, tend to receive less funding than the sciences. Among postgraduate students (full time and part time) in universities in 1991–2 women were 38.7 per cent of Master's degree candidates and 31.5 per cent of PhD candidates (*Universities Statistical Record*, 1992). Considerable subject differentiation remains at the PhD level, the women's percentage ranging from 13.7 in engineering and technology, and 15.9 per cent in maths, to 49.1 per cent in education and 52.1 per cent in studies allied to medicine. (Total numbers here are relevant: engineering and technology had 1426, maths 843, while allied medical had 543 and education, 55.)

Women as teachers in higher education

In British universities and polytechnics at present, women students will find a scarcity of women to serve as role models in some subjects and at the top levels of teaching and administration.

The entry of women to teaching in higher education has been even slower than their entry as students. Though the University Grants Committee report of 1921 recognized that some university teachers were women – who might serve usefully on student welfare committees – the UGC clearly thought of the profession as mainly for men and opined (1953) that salary levels should enable a professional man to support a family. Various publications on higher education in the decades following the Second World War similarly ignored the existence of women as university teachers.

Such lack of interest was probably associated with the expectation that a women would retire from university teaching – as from school teaching in the period between the wars – on marriage. The 'conflict' between home-making and professional activity is still widely found, as various researches (Council of Europe, 1990; Lie, 1990; Sutherland, 1985a) have shown.

From the 1950s onwards, UNESCO charted increasing numbers of women students in higher education worldwide, yet this did not *immediately* attract attention to the status of women as teachers at this level. Thus, the Robbins Committee (1963b, p. 18) contented itself with remarking that:

> University teaching is predominantly a male profession. Only 10 per cent of the teachers are women, although 25 per cent of the university students who graduated in 1962 are women. 34 per cent of the women teachers are married and 21 per cent have children. The percentage of teachers who are women is highest among the junior grades (16 per cent of assistant lecturers are women) and lowest among professors (2 per cent).

In 1966 one researcher (Sommerkorn, 1966) did draw attention to the situation of women university teachers, especially in Oxford and Cambridge, discussing their conditions of work and the interaction of marriage and career. But in times when increases in women student numbers were evident, it was perhaps optimistically assumed that these increases would automatically improve numbers and promotion prospects of women teachers in higher education. For a variety of reasons, including gender-biased expectations, this has obviously not happened in the United Kingdom.

What is the present proportion of women teachers in universities and polytechnics in Britain today? At what levels of seniority are they? As Table 16.3 shows, the pyramid structure remains: the minority at lower levels becomes a still smaller minority at higher levels.

Subject differentiation also continues for teachers in both universities and polytechnics: women are often employed in education (25.3 and 33.0 per cent), in language, literature and area studies (universities 22.5 and, in polytechnics, a remarkable 43.1 per cent). They achieve the astonishing percentage of 57.1 among polytechnic teachers of medicine, dentistry and health studies, presumably because of the inclusion of nursing and para-medical courses: in universities women are only 17 per cent of this category.

Table 16.3 *Percentage of women among full-time academic staff in universities, 1992, and polytechnics, 1989, all subjects*

Universities
Teaching & research, and research only

Professors	4.9
Readers and senior lecturers	10.2
Lecturers and assistant lecturers	25.2
Others	41.8

Polytechnics

Professors, heads of department	6.7
Principal lecturers	18.7
Lecturers	22.9
Research workers	28.6

Source: *Universities Statistical Record*, 1992 and Halsey, 1990.

In engineering and technology, not surprisingly perhaps, women's representation falls to 2.0 (universities) and 3.3 per cent (polytechnics) (Halsey, 1990).

Since equal pay has long been official policy in the UK, it might be expected that female and male teachers in higher education would be equally well paid, but individual universities have discretion as to the scale-point at which appointments are made and as to merit awards. An AUT (Association of University Teachers) investigation in 1991 into the salaries received by senior people in UK universities showed inequalities. Returns of the AUT questionnaires were not complete (the overall response rate was 41 per cent of all senior staff) and they varied from one category of teacher to another, but the proportions of women respondents corresponded to the national averages at these levels. Analysis showed that for all subject categories the average salary of women was less than that of men. Salaries were higher in some subject areas than in others, the highest paid being agriculture, medicine, engineering and technology, and architecture and planning (in ascending order) while the lowest pay went to 'other arts', languages and literature and education. (It was also noted that in various science departments no comparison could be made because there were no women professors.) This means that women's salary prospects at top level are also likely to be affected by their subject choice. It remains true, nevertheless, that within subject areas women professors were still paid less than their male peers. The discrepancy in pay was less at lower age levels than at higher but it was present at all age levels (AUT, 1991).

One of the questions raised in such discussions of women's relatively disadvantaged position in academic careers is whether women are as productive as men in research and publication. For university promotion, the research and publication record is often the major – sometimes the only – criterion for advancement. In general, for various reasons, women have been found to be less 'productive' in this sense than men. Halsey (1990) cited some remaining differences in women's and men's publication records in both universities and polytechnics. Women, as he put it, tend to be more frequently 'non-producers' and less frequently 'high producers' (defined in this context as having published more than three books) (see Chapter 17 in this volume for reasons for women's lower productivity).

What difference does it make if women generally receive less advancement in academic institutions? One major effect is that women play less part in determining academic policy. Decision-making committees tend still to be predominantly composed of those at professorial or equivalent levels. Similarly, on research councils, women members are still in a minority – which is to be expected if nominations to such bodies are made on the basis of academic position.

Women as administrators in higher education

Not only in teaching and research in higher education but in formal appointments to administrative posts there is a paucity of women at top levels. In the mid-1980s the appointment of a woman as a London Polytechnic Director made educational history in the United Kingdom, but few such appointments followed. In the old universities there were in 1992 no women as full-time vice-chancellors or principals. In teacher-training institutions, the move towards coeducation had in fact reduced the number of women at head-of-college level (Sutherland, 1985b). The familiar pyramid structure thus reappears in educational administration.

Admittedly it is uncertain whether women and men have distinctively different styles of management, just as the extent of difference in their research interests is uncertain. Considerable overlap is probable. In any case, to argue that there is an absolute difference between men and women in management styles would be to fall into precisely the error which has hampered women's progress in education and in society, namely that there is an absolute dichotomy between males and females in abilities and interests. Much also depends on the nature of the institution in which management roles are assumed. One observer (David, 1989) has suggested possible differences in management styles between universities and polytechnics. But new governmental pressures may also be changing management styles throughout higher education. In any case, no justification for women's under-representation at top administrative levels can be found.

Women and the content of higher education

One of the major controversies of the nineteenth century was whether girls' secondary education, and the higher education of women, should be the same as that of their male peers. There were enough criticisms of existing education for boys and men to support the view that it would be better to create a new and distinctive curriculum for girls and women – not a domestically oriented curriculum, as many would have been ready to argue, but one which would dispense with the pedantry, bias and academic lumber found in existing secondary and higher education. Yet there was the danger that separate provision for females would automatically be judged inferior, and, of course, there was also among women a great deal of enthusiasm for some of the studies and teaching which men were already receiving in universities. For whatever reasons, until the late twentieth century university studies remained largely unchanged by the advent of women students.

The causes of the upsurge of Women's Studies in the 1970s and 80s are hard to evaluate – possibly they lay in the new awareness developed by feminist movements in different countries, possibly in the reaching of a 'critical mass' of numbers of women students and teachers. Certainly the development of Women's Studies has been one of the most remarkable innovations in the curriculum of higher education in our time.

After developing in the United States in the late 1960s, Women's Studies had by 1975 been introduced in the United Kingdom in 25 courses in 19 universities and in various courses in polytechnics and other educational establishments (Rendel and Hartnett, 1975). Since then many other diplomas, degrees or short courses in this new area of learning have been developed. Unfortunately, confusion sometimes arises in the definition of Women's Studies. Some interpretations indicate simply research on matters of women's education, employment, social welfare, while others emphasize the teaching of such research results and/or new interpretations and contents in traditional academic disciplines like literature, history, philosophy.

In the United Kingdom there has sometimes been reluctance to accept Women's Studies as normal undergraduate fare though they can be combined with more traditional subjects to obtain Bachelor's degrees in a number of institutions of higher education. In the earlier stages of development, postgraduate diplomas or degrees were most commonly offered. This provision was designed to ensure that those entering this new field had the usual kind of prior qualifications as evidence of academic respectability.

The future of women in higher education

There is some irony in the fact that when women at last seem to have secured equal access to higher education in the UK and have even made some progress as teachers at this level, higher education itself is currently in a state of flux and possible degeneration. This combines with other factors to suggest continuation of the pattern of advance and retreat in women's progress in higher education.

While women are benefiting by Open University and other opportunities for part-time or home studies, women's participation as full-time day students is much affected by the provision of childcare facilities in places of higher education. Here the situation is very uneven. Some institutions have made crèche or nursery school provisions, sometimes on student initiatives, but others remain inactive (traditional funding of universities did not provide for such expenditure). Facilities for school-age children outside school hours are also urgently needed, but inertia about childcare is fostered by arguments as to which authority (higher education or local communities) should make provision.

Similarly, for women teachers in higher education, improvements in maternity leave arrangements or in job-sharing have been uneven. The level of awareness of possible discrimination against women in universities has risen and this should indeed improve their future progress. Yet agreement among institutions of higher education as to a common code of practice in these respects had not been achieved by the beginning of the 1990s. As Bacock and Temple (1990) pointed out, an institution's statement of policy in such matters does not always relate to the actual situation of women on its staff.

More general attitudes and factors continue to be influential in determining women's education. Although the social class structure of the country has changed, the reduced working class now forming less than 40 per cent of the population, social class continues to affect access to higher education. Gains have been made by middle-class women but working-class women – and men – remain insufficiently represented (Sanders, 1992b). The introduction in the UK of student loans to replace or largely to supplement student grants is likely to be prejudicial, especially to women from unskilled manual families. Lingering prejudices in favour of supporting sons rather than daughters may indeed still affect more than one social class. Moreover, psychological traits or employment prospects may make men more willing than women to accept incurring large debts as the price of higher education.

Ethnic differences, which are entwined with social class differences, are even more difficult to analyse since official statistics are not available. Official 'colour blind' policies are not always helpful to enthusiastic researchers. There is, observably, only a very small minority of women from minority ethnic groups teaching in institutions of higher education. Part of the reason for this may be that not all ethnic groups regard higher academic education as appropriate to their daughters – or indeed, to their sons. Researches at school level have begun to show the complex interplay of factors in the educational progress of different ethnic groups: such work certainly needs to be extended. In 1992 a survey did indicate that women of minority ethnic groups are less likely than their male peers to enter higher education (Sanders, 1992a).

Within higher education establishments, numbers of women students and women teachers have increased. However, reduction of subject differentiation is slow and will continue to be strongly affected by employment prospects. Much of the increase in numbers of women teachers in higher education has been due to appointment on short-term contracts. Women's improved access to the top levels of teaching and administration must depend at least partly on whether changes in social attitudes continue.

If governmental pressure indeed reclassifies universities (including the 'new' universities) into higher and lower institutions – the elect being recognized as having research competence, the third rank being mainly teaching institutions – evidence from other countries (the United States and Japan, for instance) would suggest that women will be more often appointed in the low-ranking teaching institutions.

Perhaps higher education of the usual kind will prove increasingly less attractive to men. Statistics of recent years suggest a decline in male applications for places. Women then might be increasingly admitted to higher education *faute de mieux*. Similarly, institutions anxious to build up student numbers will look favourably on more applications from mature students, including an increasingly large proportion of women. But as we have noted, large numbers of women at the student level do not necessarily lead to women's promotion at higher levels. While of some benefit to students, such developments would scarcely constitute ideal progress for women.

It would be good to think that there are already enough women in positions of authority in the UK to counteract the implementation of undesirable policies in education and to improve the policy for higher education in general. Increasing numbers of women students and women teaching and researching in the lower ranks of academic institutions can certainly give support and understanding to such leadership. Such development seems essential if higher education in the UK is to continue to benefit society by fostering individual talents and interests and if it is to be accepted as worthy of women's – and men's – attention and commitment.

17. Academic women in the United States: problems and prospects

Helen S Astin and Lynda Malik

SUMMARY: Although higher education became available for women more than 100 years ago, significant numbers did not participate in the university until after World War II. Currently women account for half of all students enrolled in higher education and over a quarter of all university faculty. Although overt gender-based discrimination is no longer widely reported, many university women feel that they are victimized by subtle biases. When these are combined with the stiff job competition in the current economic environment, the progress of women in higher education is jeopardized.

Introduction

The United States developed as a nation of immigrants seeking freedom from religious and political persecution, greater economic opportunity and relief from rigid and unforgiving systems of social inequality. The emphasis on freedom and equality appears early in the history of the country (for example in the works of Thomas Paine, the pamphleteer of the American revolution, such as *Common Sense* and *The Rights of Man*) and is enshrined in the Constitution and the Bill of Rights. The endurance and continuity of this cultural focus is evident in many contemporary sources, including that insightful study of current America done by Robert Bellah and his associates, *Habits of the Heart* (1985).

Like all normative systems, this one must be considered ideal in the Platonic sense, in that it has not been equally applicable to all segments of American society throughout the history of the nation. The most obvious examples concern minorities, particularly African Americans, who were involuntary immigrants and continue to suffer under the burden of various inequalities; persons who were not property owners; and women.

Gender inequalities in the United States have been considered in detail by many, including Friedan (1963), Bernard (1981; 1987), Weitzman (1985) and Davis (1991). Evidence presented in these studies indicates that gender inequality is endemic in all American institutions, and in almost every informal area of American life. The disparity between average earnings of men and women, the small percentage of female members of Congress (even in 1993, the year of the woman!), the glass ceiling which effectively bars women from top positions in most companies, and the disastrous economic consequences of the no-fault divorce revolution, are all powerful testimony to patterns of gender-based inequality which have deep roots and are ubiquitous in American culture and society.

Historically, role obligations of American women have centred on family duties. Although a majority are now in the labour force, in most cases women retain primary responsibility for family chores (Hochschild, 1989); therefore, women's participation in other activities such as professional development, politics or business remains contingent upon the ability to make satisfactory substitute arrangements for family and childcare. The difficulties faced even by the most capable and highly motivated women were dramatically illustrated in 1993 by Zoe Baird and Kimba Wood, who were both considered for the position of Attorney General of the United States and who both had to withdraw from the competition because of irregularities in their childcare arrangements.

Such differential expectations for men and women ultimately result in unequal distribution of autonomy, power, prestige and financial rewards. A cursory glance at important American institutions highlights this trend.

Occupational structure

In 1990, 58 per cent of all American women were in the labour force. More than half of all women with young children worked outside the home and it is projected that, by the year 2000, 63 per cent of all women will be so employed. These rates represent dramatic changes since 1950 when only 34 per cent of all women were employed outside the home.

Although the percentage of the labour force who are women is approaching 50, males and females are not equally distributed along the occupational spectrum. Women are concentrated in a pink-collar ghetto of low pay, low power, low prestige occupations and are under-represented in executive and managerial positions and in upper-level blue-collar jobs (US Department of Labor, 1988). In 1990 more than two-thirds of employed women worked in services (45 per cent) and retail trade (22 per cent). Full-time female workers in the United States earn approximately 70 per cent of the salaries of their male colleagues, making the earnings gap one of the highest among industrialized nations (Renzetti and Curran, 1992).

Politics

Since 1980 many observers have commented on the 'gender gap' in American politics, which manifests itself in differing views of men and women on key political issues and in a greater proportion of men than women voting for Republican rather than Democratic candidates. During the presidential elections of 1992, the women's vote was mobilized around the issues of sexual harassment and the right to abortion, and the proportion of women elected to national and state offices rose dramatically. In the lower house of the United States Congress the number of women elected rose from 28 in the 101st Congress to 47 (out of a total of 435) in the 102nd; in the upper chamber, the number of female senators rose from two to six (out of a total of 100).

Families

The traditional American family consisting of a husband in the labour force, a wife who is a full-time homemaker and their children living all together in one household is no longer the typical American family. More people are remaining single, those who do marry are marrying later, approximately half of all marriages end in divorce, the proportion of single-parent households has increased significantly, cohabitation rates have increased and, in the majority of families (including those with young children), both parents are in the labour force (Renzetti and Curran, 1992; Richmond-Abbott, 1992). Although the employment of women probably has increased their power within the family, the unforeseen consequences of the no-fault divorce revolution have proved to be disastrous for women and children and have contributed substantially to the feminization of poverty in the United States. Women and children make up 77 per cent of those living in poverty (Thurow, 1987; Weitzman, 1985).

Although many Americans would argue that the family is the most cherished of American institutions (and this point of view has been evident in the emphasis on 'family values' in the political campaigns of the 1980s), the high divorce rate, the increasing proportion of single-parent households and the large numbers of divorced fathers who fail to support their children financially, offer mute testimony to the force of competing values within the framework of American culture. These competing values emphasize hedonism and the obligation to 'put number one (oneself) first', which some consider to be the dark side of the American overemphasis on individual freedom.

Education

From earliest times, education in the United States has been structured according to social class and gender. During the colonial period the few towns that had schools typically excluded girls (Woody, 1966), whose education consisted largely of learning domestic responsibilities at home. As public education expanded in the nineteenth century, opportunities arose for women to become elementary school teachers. Training for this position was carried out at 'normal schools' (precursors to teachers' colleges), as institutions of higher learning were closed to women. In 1833 the first woman was admitted to Oberlin College in Ohio, and in 1837 women began to be accepted on a regular basis, thus making Oberlin the first formerly male college to admit women.

During the latter part of the nineteenth century the first women's colleges were established (Vassar in 1865, Smith and Wellesley in 1875, Bryn Mawr in 1885 and Mt Holyoke in 1888), offering higher education comparable to that offered to men in the most prestigious men's colleges. At this stage higher education for women still consisted of preparation for the traditional female roles of wife and mother. A few élite colleges including Harvard, Columbia and Brown permitted the formation of affiliated women's colleges, but most prestigious private colleges remained closed to women.

At the turn of the century fewer than 4 per cent of the entire college-age population were enrolled in institutions of higher education, which had been established primarily to train those entering the ministry, law and medicine. Women entered higher education mainly to prepare for teaching, which was seen as 'a natural extension of the mothering role' (Chamberlain, 1988, p. 4).

During the early twentieth century the proportion of women earning bachelor's degrees increased dramatically (from 19 per cent of all bachelor's recipients in 1900 to 40 per cent in 1930; *ibid.*). This proportion fluctuated during the depression, war and post-war years, returning to the 1930 level only in 1970. The proportion of master's degree recipients who were female increased from 30 to 40 per cent between 1920 and 1970; the proportion awarded doctorates reached 15 per cent in 1920 and, after 50 years of considerable fluctuation, again achieved this level in 1972 (*ibid.*).

Using 1989 census data, we observe that women's level of education has also increased quite dramatically. For example, in 1970, among white women, only 8.4 per cent had completed four or more years of college; by 1989 this percentage had climbed to 18.5. None the less, comparing women to men with respect to higher education, women lag behind. In 1989, 18 per cent of women, compared to 24.5 per cent of men, reported having completed four or more years of college (Ries and Stone, 1992). However, women's college participation continues to increase and currently women constitute the majority of college students (54 per cent).

The fields of study chosen by women have tended to differ from those chosen by men. Traditionally, women have been much more likely than men to concentrate in the humanities and arts and were under-represented in mathematics, engineering and the sciences. These differences in educational foci ultimately found expression in varying career patterns, with most women concentrated in education, home economics, library science and teaching. Recently, women have made great inroads into traditionally male fields, including engineering, science and business. Mariam Chamberlain, the chairperson of the 1980s Task Force on Women in Higher Education, has observed that 'One of the most fundamental changes in women's higher education since 1970 is the shift away from conventional "women's fields" ...' (*ibid.*, p. 193). This view is borne out by the data presented in Table 17.1.

In the 1970s, numerous federal laws and regulations were enacted, aimed at equalizing opportunities for women in higher education. These regulations, together with the activism from the second wave of the women's movement, have resulted in changes in the structure of opportunity for women, which accounts to a great extent for the changes described thus far in women's participation in higher education and employment. We have

Table 17.1 *Women's undergraduate degree attainment in selected fields**

	1979–80	1988–9
Business	33.7	46.7
Engineering	9.3	15.2
Biological Sciences	42.1	50.2
Physical Sciences	23.7	29.7

Source: These data are abstracted from Table 5–6 of Ries and Stone, 1992.

* These percentages represent the proportion of women within each pool of BA recipients in each of the four major fields.

also witnessed a great growth in women's participation in graduate education and doctoral attainment (see Table 17.2) – the preparation for entry into academic careers.

Not only has the total proportion of women as recipients of PhDs increased dramatically (more than doubling between 1972 and 1990; see Table 17.3); their participation in some traditionally male fields has also changed.

While women are still under-represented in the sciences and proportionally not equal to men in graduate and professional education, the trends appear to suggest that educational equality may be achieved sooner than equality in academic employment with respect to position and rewards.

Academic women: a recent profile (1989–90)

The profile reported here is based on data collected by a survey administered by the Higher Education Research Institute at UCLA to the teaching faculty at 392 institutions during academic year 1989–90. There were a total of 35,478 respondents (55 per cent response rate) of whom 10,476 (29.5 per cent) were women. The data are weighted to represent the universe (2,528 institutions) and 401,431 teaching faculty.

Trends in overall participation

Overall, the proportion of women in academe has increased from 22 per cent in 1972–3 to 29 per cent in 1989–90. Likewise, the proportion of women within each rank has also increased, from 9.8 per cent women at the full professor rank in 1972–3 to 14 per cent in 1989–90. Among assistant professors the percentage changed from 23.8 in 1972–3 to 38 in 1989–90, and

Table 17.2 *Doctoral degree attainment, 1972–90*

	1972	1980	1986	1988	1990
Total number of doctorates	33,001	30,982	31,770	33,456	36,027
Percentage of women	16.0	30.3	35.4	35.2	36.3

Table 17.3 *Changes in the proportion of women doctorates in selected fields, 1972–90*

	1972	1990
Physical Sciences	6.6	18.2
Engineering	0.6	8.5
Life Sciences	6.7	37.4

among associate professors from 16.3 per cent (1972–3) to 26 per cent (1989–90) (see Table 17.4).

While there has been a more dramatic change in the potential pool of academics, as indicated by the change in doctoral completion rates (from 16 per cent women in 1972 to about 36 per cent by 1990, see Table 17.2), there has been a smaller increase of women employed by academe: 6.5 percentage points of change overall between 1972 and 1989–90.

Women's participation differs by institutional type (see Table 17.5). While women constitute 26.0 per cent of the faculty at all institutions, they are only 21.3 per cent of faculty at public universities; at public two-year institutions, however, they are 39.2 per cent. While across all types of institutions 53 per cent of women are tenured compared to 73 per cent of the men, at private universities only 44 per cent of the women are tenured compared to 71 per cent of the men (see Table 17.6).

There are also gender differences by rank. Comparing the rank distribution of women to men across all institutions (see Table 17.7), 14 per cent of women are full professors compared to 41 per cent of men. Twenty-three per cent of women list their rank as instructor compared to 9 per cent of men. Looking at private universities, the differences are even greater: 14 per cent of women are full professors compared to 48 per cent of men and 13 per cent of women indicate lecturer as their rank compared to 1 per cent of men.

Academic women also report that opportunities to be promoted to senior administrative posts are rather limited. In the United States women represent only 10 per cent of all chief executives of colleges and universities. While there has been a change since 1975 when women were less than 5 per cent of all college and university presidents, growth in these ranks has been rather slow (Chamberlain, 1988).

Salaries

Salary differentials also continue to persist (see Table 17.8): 41 per cent of the women (compared to 18 per cent of the men) earn less than $40,000 per year.

Table 17.4 *Trends in distribution of women in academic ranks, in per cent*

	All ranks	Professor	Assoc. Professor	Asst. Professor
1972–3	22.3	9.8	16.3	23.8
1982–3	27.1	10.7	22.0	36.1
1989–90	26.0	14.0	26.0	38.1

Table 17.5 *Distribution of women by type of institution, 1989–90, in per cent*

	Women
All institutions	26.0
Public university	21.3
Public 4-year college	28.1
Public 2-year college	39.2
Private university	20.3
Private 4-year college	31.4
Private 2-year college	47.7

At the high end, 3.5 per cent of women earn $70,000 or more, compared to 17 per cent of men. Within public universities women's salaries are 76 per cent of men's, and within private universities women earn 74 per cent of what men earn.

Using these data we can conclude that changes in women's participation in academic employment have been occurring at a rather slow pace, and the differences in terms of academic rank and salary continue to favour men quite extensively.

Also, women's lower participation at the country's most élite institutions, such as research universities, contributes to their disadvantaged status. Faculty at research universities have more opportunities for research and publication which, in turn, present further opportunities for public recognition, consulting, and overall greater occupational mobility.

Teaching, service and research activities

Examining the time spent on various activities, we find that women continue to spend more time in teaching and advising students and less time on research (see Table 17.9). Time spent on committee work is similar between women and men. While one might expect women to be teaching more and doing less research since they are less likely to be employed at research universities, even the women at research universities tend to teach more than men and to spend fewer hours in research.

Background characteristics

In part, some of the differences reported earlier with respect to rank and salary can be explained by the fact that fewer women hold a doctorate (see Table 17.10). Across all institutions 45 per cent of women compared to 68 per

Table 17.6 *Trends in tenure, in per cent*

	Women	Men
1975–6	46	64
1977–8	45	66
1981–2	48	70
1985–6	47	69
1989–90	53	73

Table 17.7 *Rank by type of institution, in per cent*

	All Institutions		Public University		Private University	
	Women	Men	Women	Men	Women	Men
Professor	14	41	15	47	14	48
Associate	23	25	28	28	28	26
Assistant	31	20	34	21	40	23
Lecturer	3	1	7	2	13	1
Instructor	23	9	9	2	5	1
Other	4	2	7	–	1	2

cent of men report the doctorate to be their highest degree. These percentages change considerably when we look at faculty at private universities, where 78 per cent of women and 89 per cent of men hold the doctorate. Women also continue to indicate less interest in research. Across all institutions 20 per cent of women compared to 31 per cent of men indicate that their interests either lean toward research or that they have a strong interest in research. The differential between women and men with respect to research interests is somewhat smaller for faculty at private universities: 54 per cent of women and 58 per cent of men indicate greater interest in research activities than in teaching.

The differences between men and women are partially a function of the time of entry into academe. Examining the age distribution we observe that 51 per cent of women compared to 37 per cent of men are 44 years of age or younger. Thus, in part the rank and salary differentials can be explained by the fact that women lag behind because of their shorter time on the professorial ladder.

Fields

Similarly, the distribution of disciplines continues to differentiate faculty according to gender: 12 per cent of the women compared to 33 per cent of the

Table 17.8 *Salary, in thousands, of US faculty members by type of institution*

	All Institutions		Public University		Private University	
$	Women	Men	Women	Men	Women	Men
Less than 20	1	0.4	0.2	0	0.1	0.1
20–29	13	5	8	2	9	2
30–39	27	13	25	8	19	6
40–49	32	26	32	21	33	17
50–59	15	21	16	21	16	20
60–69	9	18	12	21	13	22
70–79	2	8	3	11	5	10
80–89	1	5	2	10	1	12
90–98	0.3	2	1	3	2	5
99+	0.2	2	1	5	2	7
median	12.4	17.3	44.8	59.0	46.3	62.2

Table 17.9 *Activities in hours per week, 1989–90*

	Teaching 13+		Service 5+		Advising students 5+		Research 13+	
	Women	Men	Women	Men	Women	Men	Women	Men
All Institutions	41.2	31.5	27.6	26.1	45.1	39.1	22.7	26.9
Public Universities	16.4	13.3	31.1	31.1	43.2	35.8	26.4	45.6
Private Universities	7.5	5.4	19.4	24.2	34.7	36.5	40.4	50.7

men are in science and engineering; 14 per cent of women and 21 per cent of men are in social science; 18 per cent of women and 14 per cent of men are in humanities, and 24 per cent of women and 11 per cent of men are in education. More than half of faculty women are in the humanities, education and health-related fields (nursing); on the other hand, one-third of men are in science, maths and engineering.

Research and publications

In the aggregate, women report fewer publications than do men (see Table 17.11). Over the career life-span, 23 per cent of men and 43 per cent of women report not having published any articles. However, these percentages are much smaller for faculty at universities: 8 and 21 per cent, respectively, report no publications, and in private universities 5 per cent of men and 19 per cent of women report no publications. While differences between men and women are in part a function of years in academe, the differentials persist even when we control for time period. For example, during the last two years, 41 per cent of men and 56 per cent of women report not having published anything. Mean publication rate during the last two years was 1.48 for women and 2.58 for men. While there is some decline in number of publications over time in career, the differentials between men and women continue to be evident.

While research publications are considered essential for one's progress up the academic ladder, when faculty were asked how important or essential they considered certain professional goals, only half of the women and 61 per cent of the men indicated doing research as an important goal, compared

Table 17.10 *Highest degree earned by faculty members, in per cent*

	All Institutions		Public University		Private University	
	Women	Men	Women	Men	Women	Men
BA or less	7.3	4.4	2.7	1.6	2.0	1.2
MA	42.0	22.5	24.1	9.5	16.1	6.1
Professional degree	1.5	1.7	1.5	1.9	0.6	1.1
Doctorate	44.9	67.5	68.4	83.9	78.0	89.3
Other	4.3	3.9	3.4	3.0	2.6	2.2

Table 17.11 *Publications in the last two years, by age*

	All Institutions		Public Universities		Private Universities	
	Women	Men	Women	Men	Women	Men
Under 35	1.48	2.77	2.17	4.36	2.61	3.70
35–44	1.72	3.01	3.39	4.44	3.44	5.58
45–54	1.36	2.49	2.93	4.14	3.34	4.84
55–64	1.15	2.18	2.28	3.70	2.65	3.80
65+	1.60	2.12	1.57	3.11	2.59	3.41

to 98 per cent of each group who indicated 'being a good teacher'. Being a good colleague also gets high endorsements (86 per cent of women and 77 per cent of men indicated this as a very important or essential goal). Committee work gets the lowest endorsement (38 and 26 per cent, respectively).

Marital status and family life

With respect to marital status, smaller proportions of women than men are currently married (60 per cent of women compared to 82 per cent of men). Proportionately, almost twice as many women as men report being divorced (13 per cent versus 7 per cent). Among all academic women, about one-third report that their spouse/partner is also an academic. Similar proportions of men report having an academic spouse. However, correcting for the fact that only 60 per cent of women report that they are currently married, the proportion with academic spouses or partners among women is almost half. Less than half of the women and about 58 per cent of the men report having dependent children. Again, this differential is the result of differences in marital status. A quarter of the women but only 4 per cent of the men report having interrupted their careers for at least one year for family or health reasons. Indeed, marriage and childbearing or caring responsibilities continue to present barriers for women and to slow their progress in academe.

Stress and satisfaction

While both women and men academics admit to feeling quite stressed about time pressures and the lack of personal time, they still tend to be quite satisfied with their lives as academics, about 80 per cent indicating that they would choose the same profession again. However, when we examine the sources of stress more closely, we find that almost half of the women but less than one-fifth of the men report a feeling of 'subtle discrimination' (see Table 17.12). Also, the review and promotion process is perceived as a source of stress by a higher proportion of women than men (51 per cent versus 41 per cent), and the differential is greater for those teaching in universities. For example, 63 per cent of women compared to 49 per cent of men in public universities indicate this is as a great source of stress.

With respect to job satisfaction, what is interesting is that while on overall satisfaction women seem to be as satisfied as men, they differ regarding their level of satisfaction with the various aspects of the job. For example, commenting on opportunities for scholarly pursuits, 30 per cent of women compared to 48 per cent of men indicate satisfaction. Likewise, with respect to job security, 67 per cent of women compared to 78 per cent of men say that they are satisfied.

Table 17.12 *Satisfaction and stress factors in an academic career, in per cent*

	All Institutions		Public Universities		Private Universities	
	Women	Men	Women	Men	Women	Men
Sources of stress						
Household responsibility	73	60	77	58	71	60
Physical health	43	36	45	34	41	35
Review/promotion	51	44	63	49	51	42
Subtle discrimination	48	22	55	21	59	17
Colleague	57	53	63	57	54	50
Students	56	48	56	46	49	44
Research/ publishing demands	48	51	77	72	78	70
Fundraising expectations	18	22	25	32	18	27
Job satisfaction						
Salary and benefits	45	44	41	45	50	52
Opportunities for scholarly pursuits	38	48	40	57	51	66
Relationships with other faculty	77	75	67	69	71	75
Job security	67	78	57	78	57	78
Grad. course assignment	66	74	71	76	73	79
Overall satisfaction	70	69	62	67	73	75

Summary and conclusion

In summary we conclude that although significant gains have been made, American academic women continue to lag behind men with respect to their overall participation, status and rewards. Moreover, while overt discrimination no longer exists, subtler forms of discrimination continue to affect the lives of academic women. This subtle discrimination manifests itself as a feeling of benign neglect and in the tension that continues to exist between managing family concerns and the demands of an academic career.

We believe that the second wave of the women's movement (known as 'second wave' to distinguish it from the efforts centring on the female franchise in the early decades of this century) is primarily responsible for most of the gains made by women in economics, law and education. In her encyclopaedic history of the women's movement, Flora Davis comments that:

> between 1960 and 1990 feminists achieved half a revolution. ... Probably the movement's single greatest achievement was that it transformed most people's assumptions about what women were capable of and had a right to expect from life (Davis, 1991, p. 16).

Thus, although academic women continue to report unpunished sexism and sexual harassment and women continue to be under-represented in higher academic and administrative positions, there is no doubt that in the past three decades the position of women in the American system of higher education has improved. The proliferation of Women's Studies programmes (now established at half of American colleges and universities) which highlight gender inequalities and question traditional patriarchal cultural assumptions, are testimony to this positive trend.

Currently, demographic and economic trends are producing a mixed message about the future of academic women. On the one hand, the growing number of faculty reaching retirement age should increase the number of positions available. On the other hand, economic difficulties and budgetary constraints faced by many institutions of higher education may portend a decline in academic employment. The heightened competition for those positions which do become available will provide an opportunity to test the strength and depth of the commitment to gender equality in higher education.

18. Gender stratification in Uzbek higher education: old traditions and new reality

Railiya Mukhsinovna Muqeemjanova and
Gulnara Tukhlibaevna Quzibaeva

SUMMARY: This chapter describes the changes which have taken place in Uzbek society during this century, with a special focus on life in the universities. Since 1918 Uzbek women have had full legal equality with men in all areas of life and, since the end of the 1950s, have achieved universal literacy. However, patriarchal traditions continue to co-exist alongside of formal egalitarian norms, marginalizing the position of women in politics, education, economics and other important sectors of Uzbek life. The quota-based affirmative action programme which had formerly prevailed has now been abolished and the current privatization, with its accompanying high unemployment rates, has had a particularly adverse impact on women. The true position of women in Uzbekistan does not correspond to the stereotyped image of the flourishing Central Asian woman who has severed the chains of inequality. The activity of nascent women's organizations provides hope for the future.

Introduction

The Republic of Uzbekistan, lying in the heart of former Soviet Central Asia, is one of the sovereign states which arose from the collapse of the Soviet Union. Its population numbers 21 millon, 84 per cent of whom are ethnic Uzbeks; 60 per cent of the people reside in rural areas. Tashkent, the capital, has a population exceeding two million. Although it is the most advanced region in Central Asia (having a relatively well-developed industrial sector) Uzbekistan's economy is still based on agriculture, cotton being the most important crop. The standard of living of most people is lower than that prevailing in the European part of the former Soviet Union. In 1990 the per capita income was only 52 per cent of the USSR average. In 1989, 45 per cent of the population of Uzbekistan lived below the poverty line (*Zvezda Vostoka*, 1990) and since then the situation has deteriorated.

Currently the young state is going through an extremely difficult time. The economic crisis of the former Soviet Union continues to affect Uzbekistan, which has been plagued by a sustained rise in prices and a shortage of essential consumer goods, including food. The leadership of Uzbekistan is planning radical reforms to improve the economic condition of the country. These include a gradual transition to a market economy, privatization (denationalization) of public sector enterprises and encouragement of foreign investment and expertise. The initial steps of this plan have already been implemented.

Demographic, economic and cultural trends

Like many developing countries, Uzbekistan is experiencing rapid population growth. The population has doubled in the past 23 years (1970–92) and is now increasing at the rate of 3–3.5 per cent every year (*Respublika Uzbekistan: Spravochnik*, 1992). The high proportion of people in the younger age groups, when combined with the negligible participation of Uzbek women in the paid labour force, places a heavy burden on the economically active sector of the population and on the country in general.

The high birth rate is a result of several factors. The status of women in traditional families depends on the number of sons they have. The high fertility rate is also tied to the comparatively early age of marriage (17–24 years). There have been no effective family planning programmes and the majority of women are ignorant of birth-control facilities. The birth rates are inversely related to the social and educational level of the mothers; the average number of children in families where the mother has had higher education is 2.3, compared with 5.1 in families where the mothers are uneducated (Burieva, 1991).

Seventy years ago maternal mortality was the leading cause of death among Uzbek women. Public health programmes substantially reduced maternal mortality rates and contributed to the high rate of population growth. However, since the end of the 1980s poverty and rising prices have made it difficult to provide a healthy diet for many mothers and children. This is particularly true in the lower strata of society. Nationally, the output and consumption of meat and dairy products has been found to be insufficient. A large proportion of the population does not have access to safe drinking water or sanitary facilities: 70 to 80 per cent of all diseases and at least one-third of the deaths in the country have been linked to the consumption of contaminated water. Infant mortality rates in Uzbekistan have been twice the average of the former Soviet Union as a whole.

The present government of Uzbekistan has retained and expanded all the entitlements awarded to women and children by the former USSR. These include pregnancy leave, monetary grants awarded upon the birth of each child, partially paid leave for mothers with small children and special grants for children under 18 years of age. During the first quarter of 1993, the wages (and pensions) of many state employees were substantially raised to compensate for sharp price increases. More than 300,000 hectares of arable land have been distributed among one million peasant families and the President of Uzbekistan has decided to increase the minimum peasant holdings (Karimov, 1992) thus providing substantial assistance to rural families with many children.

By the end of the 1980s Uzbekistan had more than 9,000 kindergartens, with enrolments of nearly 1.3 million children. Fifty-two per cent of pre-school children in urban areas were enrolled in these kindergartens, com-pared with 33 per cent of those in rural areas (*Uzbekskaya SSR v Tsifrah v 1988 godu*, 1989). Most (93 per cent) of the kindergarten costs used to be sub-sidized by municipalities or the parents' places of employment but sharp price increases combined with a general decline in living standards have reversed this trend. Many young mothers are now forced to rely either on older relatives to care for their children, or to give up their jobs or studies.

Women in Uzbekistan account for nearly half of the agricultural labour force and some 43 per cent of employees in other fields. However, compared with other countries, female labour force participation is relatively low. In 1989, 35 per cent of the female population was in the labour force (compared with 33.5 per cent in 1970). In the same year, 47 per cent of the female population were dependent on their relatives and 18 per cent had other sources of income such as pensions and scholarships.

A quarter of all working women are in the teaching and medical profes-sions. Women may also be found disproportionately in the service occu-pations, in culture and the arts, in science and in managerial and clerical positions (see Table 18.1).

Some women also are employed in technical fields such as geology and mine engineering; however, these tend to be from Russian and other Eur-opean ethnic backgrounds. (Russian and other European Russian-speaking peoples comprise nearly 10 per cent of Uzbekistan's population.) Indigenous Uzbek women tend to shy away from technical specialties.

In the majority of rural and urban families, domestic chores remain the sole responsibility of women even if they are employed outside the home. (This is especially true among Uzbek families.) Domestic work is not counted as productive labour but still takes up a significant amount of time and energy. This is one of the reasons why, barring a few exceptions, women still have not attained decision-making positions.

Unemployment is one of the most acute social problems in the country. Although the official number of unemployed is only 150,000 (beginning of

Table 18.1 *Number of women engaged in selected areas of the state sector,* 1980 and 1990, in thousands*

	1980	1990
Wholesale and Retail Trade, Restaurants, Hotels, etc.	181.9	203.9
Medicine and Sport	209.5	354.3
Education	313.1	469.6
Culture and Arts	30.1	41.6
Science	45.3	35.8
Finance and Insurance	12.2	14.9
Public Administration (Management)	50.7	30.3
Total	1784.2	2418.3

* With the exception of those engaged in collective farming (*kolkhozs*).

Source: *Narodnoe Khozyaystvo Uzbekskoy, SSR v 1990 Godu*, Tashkent, 1991, p. 26.

1992) reliable sources estimate that the true figure is at least 2 million and that it may exceed 3 million by the year 2000. Uzbekistan has a huge labour surplus in rural areas and a shortage of skilled industrial workers. Most of the unemployed are young people who have left school without continuing their education in technical or other professional schools or institutes of higher education. These restless young people comprise a potentially explosive population who may be exploited by antisocial elements for their own vested interests. Unemployed young women are in an especially difficult position; they have limited opportunities to find a job, yet are usually ashamed (particularly Uzbek women) to register as unemployed. Most unemployed indigenous women, therefore, are not even included in official statistics. The government is attempting to reduce unemployment but does not have sufficient resources to create the necessary number of jobs.

In the political sphere, the quota-based affirmative action system for women which prevailed in the former Soviet Union has been abolished. Under the old system women comprised a third of the members of the Supreme Soviet (the highest elected body) in Uzbekistan and nearly half of the membership of various local councils (*Zhenschiny Sovietskogo Uzbekistana*, 1984; *Zhenschiny Respubliki Uzbekistan*, 1991). Currently, although women are theoretically entitled to an equal role in the political process by virtue of a universal adult franchise, few women are able to win a political contest against a male opponent.

The women of pre-Soviet Central Asia had few civil rights and often did not even enjoy the most basic of human rights. In 1918 the official policy of the state guaranteed full equality for males and females in all spheres of life. However, the indigenous traditions were based upon a patriarchal value system, in which a woman's proper place was considered to be in the home rather than in the public sphere. For many years a woman who worked outside of the home was stigmatized. Thus, although the law placed women on an equal footing with men, in reality the vast majority of Uzbek women were excluded from social and political life. Although today a great number of Uzbek women take an active part in the cultural, political and economic life of the country, progress has been slow and intermittent. In spite of official prouncements and persistent efforts by governmental and private (mainly women's) groups, there is no reason to suppose that Uzbek women have yet achieved full equality.

Women in the educational system

Until the end of the last century, census data (1897) indicated that almost all females in the territory now comprising Uzbekistan (then called Turkistan) were illiterate. The urban rate of female illiteracy was 98.9 per cent and the rural rate was 99.8 per cent. In 1918 the new (Soviet) authorities of Turkistan introduced universal free education. However, this policy was difficult to implement, particularly in the case of indigenous girls. Many parents, under the influence of feudal and Islamic traditions, refused to send their daughters to secular schools. Only in the 1930s after education had been made compulsory, did literacy rates begin to rise. A crash programme of adult literacy classes and groups was also established and by the end of the 1950s virtual universal literacy was achieved in Uzbekistan (*Zhenschiny Sovetskogo Uzbekistana*, 1984).

Currently education is coeducational and free of charge at all levels. However, it must be pointed out that severe shortcomings in the education system impair its quality and efficiency. Many schools, particularly in the rural areas, are substandard.

Many students, especially girls, drop out of the educational system before the fifth class of primary school; many also are lost in middle (secondary) school. The belief that women do not need to be educated is still alive. Uzbek families often have five to seven children (and sometimes more), so elder daughters are expected to help their mothers raise younger sisters and brothers. In adulthood those women who had dropped out of the educational system early often lose their literacy. In spite of these difficulties, Table 18.2 indicates that the government's policy of promoting education, particularly among women, has been quite successful.

Most of the teachers in schools are women, but most of the directors and deputy directors are men; the percentage of female top administrators does not exceed 25 (*Zhenschiny Respubliki Uzbekistan*, 1991).

Women's place in the university

The first institution of higher education in Central Asia was the Turkistan State University established in Tashkent in 1920. This university has played an important role in the development of higher education in Uzbekistan, its subdivisions becoming bases during the 1920s and 30s for newly established medical, agricultural, pedagogical, polytechnical and other institutes. In the 1960–61 academic year, Uzbekistan had 30 institutions of higher education, with a total enrolment of 101,300. These numbers rose to 38 and 232,900 in 1970–71, and 43 and 278,100 in 1980–81. Currently there are 52 institutions of higher education in Uzbekistan, where more than 300,000 students are enrolled (*Uzbekskaya SSR v Tsifrah v 1988 godu*, 1989; *Respublika Uzbekistan: Spravochnik*, 1992). In 1992 several leading institutions of higher education (including, for example, Tashkent Polytechnical Institute) were upgraded to university status; also the new University of World Economy and Diplo-

Table 18.2 *Women with varying types of education, in per cent*

	1979	1989
Women with Higher Education	9.2	12.8
Women with Vocational Education	11.5	20.4
Women with Secondary Education	40.0	48.6
Other	39.3	18.2
Total	100	100

Source: *Zhenschiny Respubliki Uzbekistan*, Tashkent, 1991, p. 4.

macy was established. The quality of instruction in these institutions is uneven, with the highest level generally found in the capital.

As in other former Soviet republics, the systems of higher education and research are independent of one another (see Chapter 14 in this volume). Scientific research is generally conducted in research institutes, the most important of which is the Academy of Sciences of Uzbekistan founded in 1943.

Operating under the auspices of the Ministry of Higher and Vocational Education, the universities and institutes are financed by the state budget. Increasingly, additional funding may also come from various enterprises which pay the expenses of their future specialists. The universities and institutes have two primary functions: the most important of these is to produce highly qualified graduates; the second is to carry out important scientific research in various fields. Athough universities and research institutes are nominally independent, they often cooperate and form elaborate networks of teams to work on important projects.

The right to higher education is guaranteed to everyone who completes secondary school and passes the entrance examinations. However, there are usually several applicants for every vacancy and admissions are decided on the basis of merit. As a rule it takes five years to complete tertiary education.

Until the mid-1930s there were comparatively few women enrolled at universities; this was particularly true of Uzbek women. Although the authorities have established an affirmative action programme for Uzbek and other indigenous women (especially those who live in remote rural areas), many circumstances prevent them from taking advantage of these benefits. These obstacles include a lack of adequate preparation in local secondary schools, traditions of early marriage for girls and economic difficulties. Nevertheless, women now constitute approximately 40 per cent of the higher education student body in Uzbekistan. Unfortunately, the enrolments of females training for positions in industry, construction and agriculture are currently declining. The fields which attract most female students include pedagogy, philology, foreign languages and medicine and biology (see Table 18.3).

These trends can be illustrated by comparing student enrolments at two institutions of higher education in Tashkent. In the Tashkent Medical Pediatrics Institute, during the 1991–2 academic year 61.4 per cent of the

Table 18.3 *Female enrolment in higher education, in per cent*

	1980/81 academic year	1990/91 academic year
Industry and Construction	29	20
Agriculture	15	10
Economics and Law	39	29
Medicine and Sport	55	52
Education and Culture	57	60
Total	43	41

Source: *Narodnoe Khozyaystvo Uzbekskoy, SSR v 1990 Godu*, Tashkent, 1991, p. 122.

entire student body was female. Uzbek women comprised 42 per cent of the total enrolment. Almost 55 per cent of the female students came to Tashkent from other regions of the country. (These figures are derived from an unpublished study conducted by one of the authors.) By contrast, female students were only 35 per cent of the total student body in the Faculty of Geography at Tashkent State University; 27 per cent of the enrolments were Uzbek women, the majority of whom were inhabitants of Tashkent. These figures indicate that parents (even in traditional families) may permit their daughters to go to the capital to study medicine because medical education is considered suitable for women. However, training in fields which require working in inconvenient conditions (often in remote locations) is not looked on favourably by the parents of girls, who are consequently not encouraged to pursue these occupations.

Most students at institutions of higher education receive stipends, which were increased during 1992 and 1993 because of the inflation prevalent in the economy, particularly in the price of food. However, even with the increases, the stipends are not sufficient for the students, who must depend on part-time jobs or their families to supplement their incomes. This problem becomes particularly acute for those from poor and even middle-class families which cannot contribute to their support. University dormitories tend to be overcrowded and characterized by unsanitary conditions. New dormitories are not being built and other student needs cannot be met because of a shortage of funds.

Obtaining a university diploma does not necessarily protect a woman against unemployment. Girls are often subject to much family pressure and pushed into professions without consideration of their abilities or wishes. Uzbek (and other indigenous) women often marry and have one or two children before receiving their university diplomas. Twenty-six per cent of the women with higher education in urban areas are married when they are 18 or 19 years old; almost all of the rest (66.7 per cent) marry between the ages of 20 and 24 (Burieva, 1991). The graduation and employment of these women then becomes dependent on the wishes of their husbands.

Educated urban women often have difficulty finding appropriate employment in urban areas. Although there is a lack of doctors, teachers and other qualified specialists in rural areas, young women born in urban regions are generally reluctant to work in villages where the standard of living may be relatively low.

After receiving a university diploma, talented male and female graduates may continue their education at the postgraduate level. Successful post-graduate students are awarded the status of Candidate of Science (approximately equivalent to the US PhD) and may then apply for a pro-gramme leading to the Doctor of Science degree (approximately equivalent to the German Habilitation); see Table 18.4.

Officially the only criteria for admission to the programmes leading to Candidate (or Doctor) of Science status relate to the qualifications of the applicant. However, the imperatives of gender become so strong at this point in the life of the Uzbek woman that very few are able to participate in these programmes, and they thereby forgo careers in science or academe. The burden of family responsibilities combined with worsening living

Table 18.4 *Qualifications of women engaged in scientific research as of 1 January 1991, number of persons*

Fields of Science	Total Female Specialists	Doctors of Science	Candidates of Science
Physics and Mathematics	1168	7	278
Chemistry	801	15	290
Biology	918	22	361
Geology and Mineralogy	539	8	58
Technology	8413	2	284
History	268	8	123
Economics	1148	1	277
Philosophy	229	3	106
Philology	1071	7	345
Geography	207	–	18
Jurisprudence	66	1	27
Pedagogy	312	1	74
Medicine	1426	53	601
Pharmacology	7	–	–
Vet. science	30	–	–
Study of Art	23	1	3
Architecture	404	–	11
Psychology	13	–	7
Sociology	2	–	1
Agriculture	1155	5	165
Total	18200	134	3029

Source: *Zhenschiny Respubliki Uzbekistan*, Tashkent, 1991, p. 5.

conditions makes postgraduate education an impossibilty for many talented female university graduates. As a result only 20 per cent of the Candidates of Science and not quite 10 per cent of those admitted to Doctor of Science programmes are women. At the beginning of 1991 more than 18,000 women were engaged in scientific work in Uzbekistan, but only 17 per cent of these women (3,029) advanced to Candidate of Science status and fewer than one per cent (134) became Doctors of Science (*Zhenschiny Respubliki Uzbekistan*, 1991).

In traditional women's fields the proportions are higher. For example, in 1991–2, 44.5 per cent (299 of a total of 672) of the faculty of Tashkent Medical Pediatric University were women. Forty-five per cent (140) of the 308 Candidates of Science teaching there were female, and 17.5 per cent (10) of the Doctors of Science were women. The Vice-rector of the Institute is female and several women of standing and experience have applied for the posts of dean and heads of department (author's unpublished study).

These figures are not typical of most institutions of higher learning in Uzbekistan; Tashkent State University presents a more representative picture. Since its foundation more than 70 years ago, not a single woman has occupied the position of Rector and only two women have been appointed to the post of Rector's deputy. In 1990–91 two (out of a total of 16) deans were women. Of the 20 leading scholars at the university who were either full or corresponding members of the Uzbek Academy of Sciences none were women (*Tashkentakiy Gosudarstvenniy Universitet Bibgraphicheskie*, 1990).

In Uzbekistan the prestige of teaching in a tertiary institution is high. This profession is also one of the most convenient for women because it allows more discretional time than other occupations (in spite of the 450 to 900 hours per academic year teaching schedules) and includes an eight-week summer vacation. Until recently those teaching in the tertiary educational system were among the highest paid groups of intellectuals; however, inflation has eroded the standard of living of many occupational groups, including the higher education faculty. Although after independence the salaries of intellectuals were raised (including higher education faculty) and they have a right to free housing and other benefits, their rates of compensation are barely above the subsistence level. This is very dangerous for the future of Uzbekistan because it will inevitably result in a brain drain of many of the most talented young members of the faculty.

Conclusion

Although the level of female education is high, especially in comparison with other developing countries, the proportion of females in the academic hierarchy declines as rank increases. In Uzbek academe, as everywhere else in the former Soviet Union, there is latent discrimination against women which is a reflection of general gender inequality. The real position of women, particularly in Uzbekistan, does not correspond to the stereotyped image of flourishing women of the Soviet East who severed the chains of inequality. The preservation of female inequality in various spheres of life, including the university system, is closely connected with the severe socioeconomic crisis which prevails in the country. The few examples of Uzbek women who have achieved high positions indicate the potential of the rest. The realization of this potential will depend upon the policies of the government and the increasing activity of non-governmental women's organizations.

Part 3: Conclusion

19. Trends in the gender gap in higher education

Suzanne Stiver Lie and Lynda Malik[1]

Women's early struggle as intellectuals

During its early history, the university was a forbidden world for women; those who attempted to enter experienced a wide variety of discriminatory practices. Graphic examples are Nawojka of Poland (Chapter 13) who had to disguise herself as a man when attending Cracow University in the fourteenth century and Anna Maria van Schurman from The Netherlands (Chapter 10) who was made to conceal herself behind a curtain in order to follow university lectures at the University of Leiden in the seventeenth century. Evidence from the seventeenth and eighteenth centuries suggests that, although not in the mainstream of scientific and intellectual activity, women (particularly from the aristocracy and the artisan classes) were interested in the sciences – in princely courts, informal salons, the artisan workshop and king's academies. However, as scientific endeavours began to be concentrated in established academies and universities and science itself became a legitimate profession, women were increasingly excluded from scientific activity (Schiebinger, 1989).

In the late nineteenth or even in the twentieth century, women as a group began to pressure for admission to higher education in many countries around the world. The industrial revolution enabled those from the upper and middle classes to have more leisure time and a surplus of single women from the middle classes led to pressure on the universities to provide an education which would prepare them to earn a livelihood. Arguments used to exclude women from universities were reminiscent of Aristotelian and Confucian views of women's intelligence, and at this time emphasized the adverse effects of education on women's health.

In 1833, Oberlin College in the United States was the first university to officially admit women to higher education. Subsequently in many countries university barriers came tumbling down (Table 4, Statistical Appendix).

The gender gap: current trends

Unequal distribution of wealth, rank and power are found currently in all higher education systems. Although the *doxa* theoretically requires that the distribution be based on achieved criteria (such as theoretical innovation or contribution to knowledge) ascribed characteristics everywhere play a critical role. Among the ascribed characteristics which are related to an individual's position on the hierarchy, none is more important than gender.

In this volume the gender gap in higher education among students, faculty and administration in 17 countries has been documented and analysed. In each country women have been found to be under-represented in positions of prestige and power. However, when the gender gap is considered in terms of size, history, current trends and ideological and contextual underpinnings, it is far from uniform. In certain countries, including Poland, Bulgaria, France, the United States and Turkey, the relative position of university women has improved dramatically in this century. However, in many others opportunities appear to be narrowing as a consequence of political and cultural developments.

Even in those countries where the position of university women has improved, it would be a mistake to conclude that this improvement has been linear; rather it has generally been, as described by Margaret Sutherland (Chapter 16 in this volume), one step backwards for each two steps forward. In the United States there has been a marked rise in the number of women receiving master's degrees and doctorates; however, in the immediate post-World War II period these figures dipped sharply, and only in 1972 did they regain the rate prevalent in the 1930s. In China the rate of women's relative enrolment in higher education has remained stable during the past 20 years after a substantial spurt 40 years ago. In Russia at Moscow State University the percentage of female students fell from 54 in 1985 to 45 in 1991.

The same trends may be observed among the faculty in many countries, where after relatively good years in the late 1960s and 70s the percentage of women in top faculty positions is now decreasing. The poor economic environment has led to a university restructuring in The Netherlands, United Kingdom and Norway, among others. These restructuring plans emphasize a cost-benefit approach and fiscal efficiency which often directly conflict with the positive action programmes introduced earlier. In the United Kingdom women now fill fewer senior university posts than they did a decade ago and the current trend is to increase the number of short-term appointments. In Norway and The Netherlands this restructuring of academic ranks has led to increased competition for fewer positions. In many countries, therefore, it can be seen that women are running fast to stay put.

Vertical gender stratification

It might be expected that as the pool of women who are enrolled in higher education increases, the proportion who receive first level and higher degrees would correspondingly increase, and that this growth would be reflected in the percentages of women in various ranks in the university hierarchy. The female proportions of students enrolled in higher education has increased in most countries under consideration, and in the majority is approaching or has exceeded 50 per cent (Table 5, Statistical Appendix). These impressive figures are related, in some countries, to even greater proportions of the total number of (first degree) university graduates who are female.

However, in most countries the female proportions of those who receive higher degrees drops sharply. Outstanding exceptions to this trend are Australia, Poland and Turkey. Other countries which have relatively uniform percentages of female student enrolment and degree attainment are France, the United Kingdom and the United States. Since advanced degrees are necessary for a career in higher education, it is clear that the low proportions of women on university faculties is determined, to a large extent, by the low proportions of female advanced-degree recepients.

In this regard, a number of questions need to be addressed. These include an examination of the conditions which lead high proportions of women students in some countries, but not others, to pursue advanced study. In countries where women constitute a large proportion of those receiving advanced degrees, are they also a significant proportion of the faculty? What is the distribution of ranks in countries where women do constitute a significant portion of academic personnel?

Of the 17 countries included in this volume, only in Australia, Poland and Turkey were the female proportions of those who took higher degrees approximately the same as the female proportion of first-degree recipients. At first glance few countries would seem to be more disparate than Australia, Poland and Turkey. Although the latter two have approximately the same per capita GNP, the religious traditions of all three countries differ, as do their political and cultural history in this century. The infant mortality rate per 1,000 live births of Australia is 7.2 (one of the world's lowest), while Poland's is double that (16.3) and Turkey's (59.5) is more than three times as high as the one in Poland (Table 1 in the Statistical Appendix).

In Turkey, higher education was restricted to a small élite. Women from this group were encouraged to pursue advanced studies, both as a source of prestige and as a means of achieving financial security – the golden bracelet. Upon completion of advanced studies, their social class position provided them with an advantage in the competition for university positions. In Poland two circumstances combined to encourage women to attain advanced degrees and secure university positions: the great demand for faculty to fill vacant academic positions (as a result of the death, during World War II, of two-thirds of the academic staff), and the stress placed on employment as a means of achieving equality for women. In Australia the stable proportion of undergraduates, bachelors and higher-degree recipients appears to be related to the change from an élite to a mass system of tertiary education in which Colleges of Advanced Education (traditionally popular among women) were combined with universities in a unified system.

Proportions of women on the faculties in the countries we studied range from a high of 37.1 (for Poland) to a low of 11.0 (in Iran). Stability in student enrolment and degree attainment is generally positively related to female share of faculty positions (although this is not true in all countries, particularly Bulgaria and Australia).

The proportion of female faculty in most countries is also positively related to the proportion of women having high rank. Those countries with the highest percentages of women on the faculty are also, in general, those in

Table 19.1 *Relative position of women in higher education*

	% of Faculty who are Female	% of Full Professors who are Female
Poland	31.7	16.9
Bulgaria	30.8	12.0
France	27.1	11.4
USA	26.0	14.0
Turkey	25.0	20.0
Russia	24.3	11.3
Norway	24.2	9.3
China	23.8	11.0
Greece	20.5	6.3
UK	20.5	4.9
Australia	18.6	7.4
E Germany	18.6	4.9
W Germany	16.6	5.2
Botswana	13.9	–
Netherlands	13.2	2.3
Pakistan	11.8	4.2
Iran	11.0	5.9

Source: Based on figures in Table 6 in the Statistical Appendix.

which a women is most likely to have achieved the rank of full professor. For example, in Poland and Bulgaria, which have the highest proportions of women faculty (31.7 and 30.75, respectively), women are most likely to have achieved the rank of full professor. In Iran and Pakistan, where women do not constitute a high proportion of the faculty, they are also among the least likely to be full professors.

Female proportions of total higher education faculty and full professors can be considered indicators of the extent of gender stratification. Table 19.1 makes it clear that this is not exclusively determined by any single factor. Countries with small academic gender gaps are found in the East and the West, in societies which have experienced structural upheavals and in those which have not.

Horizontal gender stratification: subjects 'fit for women'

Regarding the horizontal aspects of gender stratification, culturally derived notions of appropriate male and female behaviour strongly affect choices of fields of study and careers. The overall tendency in most countries is for women to predominate both as students and faculty, in social science, humanities and education. However, history shows that subjects 'fit for women' have changed over the decades. In Norway, mathematics and natural sciences were the choices of the women pioneers in universities in the late 1800s. Classical Greek and Latin were the disciplines with most prestige and were regarded as beyond the abilities of women. In Turkey, in the decade following their entry into academe, women were more strongly represented in the faculties of natural sciences (44 per cent) than in the humanities (22 per cent). At this time the Turkish alphabet was Latinized and the government was attempting to modernize the country. The fields of law, economics and business, where the men were concentrated, were considered more critical to Turkey's development than the natural sciences. The natural sciences, including chemistry, physiology, zoology and micro-biology, which were then regarded as unusual choices by many women, were typical in Iran, Turkey and Pakistan, as they prepared women to serve the women of their countries as physicians.

In the former Soviet Union and Eastern Europe after World War II, acute shortages of skilled labour facilitated many women's entry into non-traditional studies and careers. The percentages of women in traditional 'male' disciplines (engineering, economics, medicine, mathematics and the natural sciences) are high. For example, in Poland, 60 per cent of mathematics and natural science students were women in 1991–2 and in the former German Democratic Republic (in 1987) 46 per cent.

Although in many Western countries there has been a significant shift away from conventional 'women's' fields, the presence of women in natural science and technical disciplines is still considerably lower than in Eastern Europe. For example, in Greece 26 per cent of the students in the natural sciences in 1970 were women; in 1990 this figure reached 36.3 per cent. In the United States a similar shift has been noted, which although it is small on a percentage basis, is impressive numerically: in 1989, women constituted 29.7 per cent of undergraduate students in the physical sciences; in 1979–80 this was 23.7 per cent (Chamberlain, 1988).

Women administrators: room at the top?

There are two types of policy-making structures in most universities: the professional and the bureaucratic. The professional structure consists of university presidents (rectors), department heads, deans and collegiate bodies such as faculty councils and committees. The bureaucratic-manage-rial structure controls the operational and support aspects of the institution. The autonomy of these structures is limited to a greater or lesser degree by the state. For example, in Chapter 4 Nicolina Sretenova outlines the limited autonomy which had prevailed under the Communists in Bulgaria, the government's conception of 'political correctness' having become a major consideration in the selection of students and faculty. In Norway, national priorities regarding gender equality have had considerable impact at the administrative level, but continue to meet considerable resistance among the (mostly male) faculty.

There has been little systematic study of either the professional or the bureaucratic structure of universities (Moore, 1987). In this volume, only three countries – France, Turkey and Norway – examined both of these and they all found similar trends: most of the bureaucratic staff are women and their presence is inversely related to rank. In Norway, however, women have made dramatic gains in their share of administrative leadership positions in the last three decades (from 21 to 58 per cent).

Women's leadership positions on the professional level are generally even lower than that at the bureaucratic level. For instance, in Botswana women are completely absent from the university council and among the deans, and only 15 per cent of the department heads are women. In Turkey the percentage of women among presidents and deans is 9.8. In the United States the proportion of heads of colleges and universities has risen from 5 per cent, during the 1970s, to 10 per cent currently.

If a woman does achieve a top position, she appears as a 'miraculous exception'. Moi (1992) argues that members of minority groups who do succeed in a system are at least as likely to identify with it as to turn against its unjust distribution of symbolic capital. Women also seldom figure on powerful selection committees which decide faculty appointments. For instance, in Norway almost 90 per cent of these committees were male-only in 1984.

Summary

History and culture set the stage for contemporary developments. In societies with backgrounds of relative gender equality (such as that prevailing among the peasants of Bulgaria and the fishermen/farmers of Norway), the groundwork was laid for egalitarian ideology and practice. In those in which gender roles have been highly differentiated and stratified, acceptance of egalitarian codes is more problematical.

The tenacity of traditional values is apparent in many countries, including Turkey and China. In Turkey the Kemalist reforms were superimposed on a conservative and highly stratified society. The new norms were coopted by the upper classes, including particularly those who supported the regime, but encountered resistance from others in the population, especially from those in rural areas. The effect of this duality was that within the university, class became more salient than gender in the processes of recruitment and promotion. Thus, a society which has remained traditional in many ways has developed a university system with one of the smallest gender gaps in the world. In China, in spite of the revolution and institutionalization of egalitarian gender codes, entrenched views remain influential. Within the university, as elsewhere in society, formal and informal mechanisms operate to keep most women out of positions of power.

Although traditions importantly influence modern life, they do not entirely determine the course of events. Norms and values change as a consequence of altered circumstances and diffusion. Interesting examples of normative change are provided by France and the United States, where the development of egalitarian programmes has led to (relatively) small academic gender gaps.

The case of Germany is particularly instructive in this context, in light of the contrasting developments in the eastern and western sectors during the post-World War II period. In the East, the commitment to equality brought about a change in the composition of the student body (which began to include large numbers of students from working-class families) and in the female proportion of those who were awarded the two highest degrees. It is interesting to note, however, that, as in Norway, the ideological and political changes were not strongly reflected in the academic ranking; the proportion of female academics in East Germany in the top two grades remained lower than the corresponding proportions in West Germany.

The interaction of structural, cultural (ideological) and economic factors may be observed in Poland and Iran. In Iran, when the Western-looking regime of the Shah was replaced by the inward-focused government of Ayatollah Khomeini, a fundamental structural upheaval occurred. Traditional élites were replaced by a coalition of clerics who articulated the grievances of the urban shopkeepers and others who felt shut out and alienated from the wave of prosperity which the Shah's regime had brought to the upper classes. This structural realignment was accompanied by a dramatic cultural shift which centred around the revival of traditional norms and values. However, the limitations which the latter imposed on the participation of women in public life, and in the university in particular, were mitigated by the need to fill positions left vacant in the wake of Iran's war with Iraq.

In Poland the circumstances were analogous. The fall of Communism brought about massive structural change which was accompanied by a sharp cultural shift in the direction of capitalism, Catholicism and other traditional patterns. As in Iran, the negative impact of these changes on academic women is mitigated by economic factors.

If structural factors are defined as characteristics of a society's state and class structure (Skocpol, 1979) it is clear that dramatic structural changes have less effect on the gender gap than do cultural patterns. In some of the most egalitarian societies, revolutions have not occurred, whereas in many societies where the state and class structure have undergone basic transformation, the gender gap remains pervasive.

One generally assumes that as egalitarian norms become widely accepted, the position of disadvantaged groups (including women) improves. However, we have found that while generally true, this is not always the case. In Turkey the Kemalist de-emphasis on Islam was related to a decline in the relevance of gender as a criterion of social differentiation. As less importance was placed on gender, increased attention was focused on class. The relatively large proportion of university women selected on this basis were able to maximize their opportunities because of the availability of domestic help. Thus, sharp differentiation between classes helps to explain the small size of the higher education gender gap in Turkey. In egalitarian societies where household servants have disappeared, academic (and other professional) women argue that their household responsibilities impede their careers.

Nevertheless, in general, an egalitarian normative system does seem to reduce the gender gap in higher education. In fact this effect is so powerful that it appears in some countries to override the adverse effects of poor economic conditions. Significant exceptions to this trend are Norway and the Netherlands where formal commitments to equality co-exist with high levels of economic development, and yet the higher education gender gaps are still relatively great.

It is also important to note that gender stratification is not monolithic. Factors related to the ranking of students, faculty and administration appear to differ. While the proportion of women students in higher education is nearing or has achieved parity in many countries, this is not true of faculty (particularly at the upper ranks) or of administration. Although it has been argued that as the pool of qualified academic women grows their proportions in the academic and administrative hierarchies will automatically increase, so far this has not occurred. A key question in this regard concerns the choices made by individual women. Having internalized potentially conflicting sets of norms regarding family and career, in most countries female university students decide not to obtain advanced degrees. This choice is related primarily to conceptions of the 'proper' role of women in society, and economic factors. Thus, the stage is set for the under-representation of women at high levels of the university. Throughout her career the university woman is confronted by this conflicting set of goals, and this uneasy situation occurs within a social/cultural context which impedes her access to high positions.

Lie (1978) has argued that the value system and work structure of science is an exaggeration of so-called 'masculine' characteristics. Some feminist scholars have challenged the scientific canon, showing women have been excluded from the priorities of science and questioning the central values of the scientific ethos and methods. There has been a proliferation of women's research over the past two decades which Professor Emeritus Jessie Bernard (1989) has provocatively labelled the 'feminist enlightenment'.

Through their own networks and alliances, women have developed Women's Studies courses and programmes and research centres both within and outside of the university system. Although these incentives have met with considerable resistance from the (male) establishment (see Chapter 11 in this volume), Margaret Sutherland (Chapter 16 of this volume) rightly points out that the development of Women's Studies has been one of the most remarkable innovations in the curriculum of higher education in our time. We might add it is also one of the greatest successes of the women's movement. Although the relationship between the existence of a higher education gender gap and a women's movement is equivocal, Women's Studies document gender inequalities and question traditional patriarchal assumptions. From their beginning in the United States in the late 1960s, they have spread like a chain reaction throughout the academic world. Table 7 in the Statistical Appendix shows that all the countries in this volume, with the exception of Uzbekistan and Bulgaria, have started either Women's Studies courses, programmes or research centres within the context of their university structures.

Concluding thoughts

In each country most indicators show an improvement in the life of women during this century. Everywhere we find an increase in life expectancy and literacy rates. Institutionalized discrimination against women appears to be on the wane and this is symbolized by the ubiquity of female suffrage.

Nevertheless, nowhere do women and men share power and privilege equally, and this is illustrated very clearly in the academic world. Considering students, faculty and administrators separately, it is clear that the greatest gains (numerically) have been made among the students. However, although the proportions of male and female university students are approximately equal in many countries, women tend to specialize in fields which do not prepare them for future positions of prestige and power.

Women faculty are concentrated in the lower academic ranks; most investigators report that this is due to lower research and publication rates which are the main avenues of academic advancement. Although some studies have not found marital status to be a good predictor of publication rates, when age and number of children are taken into account, the relationship between gender and publication rates is clarified. Academic women report, and the data confirm, that the presence of young children hinders publication (see Chapters 11 and 17).

High-level administrators in most countries are unlikely to be women, although in a few countries great strides have been made with the implementation of affirmative action programmes.

Although in most countries in this volume gender-based discrimination has been legally abolished, substantial numbers of university women report instances where they have been victimized by latent or informal forms of discrimination.

The smallest academic gender gaps have been found in countries where egalitarian traditions are combined with economic opportunities. In the face of adverse economic circumstances, even a powerful feminist movement and a strong governmental emphasis on equality do not appear to appreciably reduce the size of the gender gap. This means that there is no universal solution to the question of the gender gap in higher education. Each country operates within its own historical and cultural context and must work out its own unique solutions.

Note

1. No order of seniority is implied.

Statistical appendix

Unni Hagen in cooperation with the editors

Explanatory notes

Figures in the tables may vary from the text because of recent availability of new information.

The following symbols are used in the tables:

NA   Not Applicable
NI   No Information Available
*   See note
**   See source

Table 1 Demographic indicators

Country	Population[a] 1990 (millions) (year)	Per cent female[b] (year)	Life expectancy at birth[c] (overall/female) (1992)	Infant mortality rate[c] (per 1,000 live births)	Legalization of contraception[d] (yes/no – year)	Contraceptive prevalence[e] (per cent of women 15–49) (1985)	Legalization of abortion[f] (year)	Paid maternity leave[g] – year, first provision (year)	– weeks, current length (weeks)
Australia	17.0	50.6 (1990)	76.7/80.0	7.2	Yes*	76	1958*	1979	12
Botswana	1.3	52.0** (1990)	67.4/69.4	37.7	NI	33	No	NI	12
Bulgaria	9.0	50.9** (1992)	72.7/75.6	13.1	NI	21	1990**	1924**	17*/** (1992)
China	1,139.0	49.0 (1987)	70.2/71.3	28.9	Yes	74	1955**	NI	NI
France	56.7	51.3 (1991)	76.8/81.1	7.1	1967	80	1975	1910*	16*/**
Germany Fed. Rep.	61.5** (1988)	51.9 (1988)	76.2/79.8	7.5	1961	78	No*/**	NI	14** (1989–90)
Germany Dem. Rep.	16.6** (1989)	52.1	NI	NI	Yes	NI	1972**	NI	26** (1988–9)
Greece	10.1	50.8 (1989)	77.1/80.1	11.3	Yes*/**	57** (1990)	1987*/**	NI	16**
Iran	54.6	48.9 (1986)	62.9/62.8	88.3	NI	17 (1970)	No	NI	10**
Netherlands	14.9	50.5** (1988)	77.1/80.2	7.1	1964*/**	76	1984**	1919	16
Norway	4.2	50.5** (1990)	77.3/80.7	8.1	Yes*	84	1978**	1936	42*/** (1993)
Pakistan	112.0	48.2 (1991–2)	55.8/55.3	102.9	Yes	12	No/1984*	1958	12**
Poland	38.1	51.2** (1988)	71.3/75.4	16.3	NI	11	1956*/**	NI	NI
Russia	148.2	53.3 (1989)	NI	NI	Yes	NI	1920	1936	18
USSR	288.5** (1989)	NI	70.7/75.6	27.5	Yes*/**	NI	1920	1936	18
Turkey	56.0	49.7** (1991)	66.6/69.2	59.5	Yes*	63	1983**	1930	9/12*/**
UK	57.4	51.2 (1990)	75.6/78.4	8.4	Yes	81	1967*/**	NI	NI
USA	250.0	51.2 (1991)	76.0/79.6	9.5	Yes	74	1973*/**	NI	NI
Uzbekistan	20.7** (1991)	50.7** (1991)	NI	NI	Yes	NI	1920	1936	18

Sources and notes

a. 1990 estimates. Unesco (1992) *Statistical Yearbook*, United Nations Educational, Scientific and Cultural Organization, France.
Germany: Fed. Rep. and Dem. Rep.: United Nations (1990) *Demographic Yearbook*.
USSR: The World Bank (1992) *Social Indicators of Development 1991–92*, The Johns Hopkins University Press, Baltimore and London.
Uzbekistan: Unpublished data provided by the contributors.

b. International Labour Office (1992). *Yearbook of Labour Statistics*, 51st Issue, Geneva, Table 1.
Bulgaria: National Institute of Statistics (1993) *Census of Population taken on 4 December, 1992*, *Demographic Characteristics of Bulgaria*, Sofia.
Botswana, Netherlands, Norway and Poland: United Nations (UN) (1990) *Demographic Yearbook*.
Turkey: State Institute of Statistics (1991) *Statistical Yearbook of Turkey 1991*, Prime Ministry, Ankara.
Uzbekistan: See a.

c. Most recent estimate. The World Bank (1992) *Social Indicators of Development 1991–92*, The Johns Hopkins University Press, Baltimore and London.

d. Information provided by the contributors if not otherwise indicated.
Australia: It has never been illegal but advertisement was briefly illegal in the 1930s.
Greece: It was never forbidden. Margaritidou, V and Mestheyeau, L (1991) *Evaluation and Family Planning Services in Greece*, Family Planning Society, Athens.
Netherlands: Introduction of 'the pill'. Vrouwenlexicon (1989) *Twenhonderd jaar emancipatie van A tot Z*, Scala, Het Spectrum, Utrecht.
Norway: No legal provision is necessary because contraception has never been prohibited.
USSR: The primary form of contraception was abortion, due to the total lack of information and qualified personnel, and the unavailability of modern contraceptives. Popov, A A (1991) 'Family planning and induced abortion in the USSR: basic health and demographihc characteristics', *Studies in Family Planning*, **2**, 6, November/December 1991, pp. 368–77.
Turkey: Contraception has never been illegal.

e. Most recent estimate. The World Bank (1992) *Social Indicators of Development 1991–92*, The Johns Hopkins University Press, Baltimore and London.
Greece: See d.

f. Information provided by contributors if not otherwise indicated.
Australia: Menhenit ruling 1958 allowed abortion to preserve a woman's life or health.
Bulgaria: Dimitrina Petrova, The Center for the Study of Democracy, Sofia in *Reproductive Rights in East and Central Europe*, HCA Women's Commission, Helsinki Citizens' Assembly Publication Series, 3, June 1992, pp. 15–17.
China: 'China' (1984), in Morgan, R (ed) *Sisterhood is Global*, Anchor, New York, p. 145.
Germany: The former Republic of Germany legalized abortion in 1970, but in 1976 abortion was declared unconstitutional by the Supreme Court. Kerstin Koanbek and Christiana Schubert, Independent Women's Association (UFV), Weimar and Berlin (1992) in *Reproductive Rights in East and Central Europe*. HCA Women's Commission, Helsinki Citizens' Assembly Publication Series, 3, pp. 21–23.
Greece: Since 1978 abortion was legal only for health reasons. See d.
Netherlands: See d.
Norway: Falkinger, A (1983) *Jente med argumenter*, Grøndahl & Søn forlag A.S., Oslo.
Pakistan: The law does not permit abortion under any circumstances, not even for rape victims.
Poland: Fusgara, M (1991) 'Will abortion issues give birth to feminism in Poland?', in Maclean, M and Goves, D (eds) *Women's Issues in Social Policy*, Routledge, London. In 1988 an informal group of Catholic deputies (PAX) began work on a draft of an anti-abortion law. This proposed law completely outlawed abortion and did not allow for any exceptions. Women who had abortions were to be imprisoned for 5 years. Slawka Walczewska (1992) Polish Feminist Association, Krakow in *East and Central Europe*, HCA Women's Commission, Helsinki Citizens' Assembly Publication Series, 3, pp. 27–30.
Turkey: *Law of Population Planning* (1983), Articles 5 and 6, Turkey.
UK: Not applicable to Northern Ireland, Great Britain only. *Abortion Law Reform Act* (1967), Great Britain.
USA: United States Supreme Court. Abortion was legalized in Roe vs. Wade, 1973.

g. Information provided by contributors if not otherwise indicated.
Bulgaria: Gazette (1924) *Act on Social Security (Royal) decree N7 of 25 March, 1924*, N289, Article 21, Sofia. According to the Bulgarian *Code of Labour* (1992), Article 163, 164 and 165, pp. 34–36, Sofia, the woman is paid maternity leave as follows: 1st child – 120 days; 2nd – 150; 3rd – 180; for every following – 120 days. On mother's consent her paid maternity leave could be used by her husband or parents.
France: Dhavernas, O (1978) *Droit des Femmes, Pouvoir des Hommes*, Le Seuil, Paris; McBride Stetson, D (1987) *Women's Rights in France*, Greenwood Press, London. A statute in 1909 required 8-weeks leave, unpaid. Public employees received paid leave from 1910. In 1966 all workers received 14-weeks paid leave.
Germany: Queitsch, M and Zich, B (1992) 'Frauen leben in Ost und West: The situation of women in East and West Germany in the last 40 years – Challenge for a common future, paper presented to the 24th IFUW Conference, Standford University, Palo Alto, USA, 13–23 August 1992.
Iran: 'Iran' (1984), in Morgan, R (ed) *Sisterhood is Global*, Anchor, New York, p. 326.
Norway: From 1993 the fathers must take 4 of the 42 weeks. Barne- og familiedepartementet (1993) *Tiltak for barn og ungdom*, St.prp.nr.1, 1992–93, Oslo, 6.; NOU 1993 no. 12 *Tid for barnet*, Oslo.
Pakistan: Klein and Nestvogel (1986). *Women in Pakistan: General conditions, approaches and project proposals for development and vocational qualification of women*, Eschborn, Federal Republic of Germany, pp. 148–9.
Turkey: 9 weeks for workers and 12 weeks for civil servants. *Labour Law* (1971), Article 70; *Civil Servant's Law* (1965), Article 104; and *General Health Law* (1930), Article 155.

Table 2 *Economic, political and cultural indicators*

Country	GNP[a] per capita (US $) 1990	Women in labour force[b] (per cent)	Women in parliament[c] 1985–87 (per cent)	Religion[d] Predominant	Largest minority
Australia	16680	36.3	10.9	Protestantism	Roman Catholicism
Botswana	2040	22.7	5.4	Animism	Christianity
Bulgaria	2250	44.6	21.0	Greek Orthodox **	Islam **
China	370	53.9	21.2	Confucianism	Islam
France	19490	36.0	6.4	Roman Catholicism	Islam
Germany*	22360	37.8	15.4*	Protestantism	Roman Catholicism
Greece	5990	20.0	4.5**	Greek Orthodox	Roman Catholicism
Iran	2490	10.9	1.5	Islam	–
Netherlands	17320	25.6	20.0	Roman Catholicism	Protestantism
Norway	23120	41.4	35.7 (1989–93) **	Protestantism	–
Pakistan	380	7.8	8.9	Islam	Christianity
Poland	1690	45.6	20.2	Roman Catholicism	–
Russia*	4200 (1985)	46.1	34.5	Russian Orthodox	Islam
Turkey	1640	30.0	1.8 (1993) **	Islam	–
UK	16156	37.4	6.3	Protestantism	Roman Catholicism
USA	21790	39.7	5.3	Protestantism	Roman Catholicism
Uzbekistan **	NI	45.0 (1990)	35.0	Islam	Orthodox

Sources and notes
Germany: Data refer to the former Federal Republic of Germany only.
Russia: Data refer to the former USSR.
Uzbekistan: Unpublished data provided by the contributors.

a. GNP = gross national product, US$ 1990 – most recent estimate. The World Bank (1992) *Social Indicators of Development 1991–92*, The Johns Hopkins University Press, Baltimore and London.

b. Most recent estimate. The World Bank (1992) *Social Indicators of Development 1991–92*, The Johns Hopkins University Press, Baltimore and London.

c. United Nations (UN) (1990) 'The situation of women in 1990' (Poster). Statistics from UN women indicators and statistic data base for computers (Wistat), Statistical Office, Department of International Economic and Social Affairs, UN Secretariat.
Germany: The figure for the former German Democratic Republic is 32.2 per cent.
Greece: National Election of 1985, information provided by the contributor.
Norway: The Equal Status Council (1991) *Minifacts on Equal Rights*, Oslo.
Turkey: Information provided by the contributor.

d. *The World's Religions* (1982) Lion Publishing, England; Derbyshire, J D and Derbyshire, I (1989) *Political Systems of the World*, Chambers, Edinburgh. Bulgaria: National Institute of Statistics (1993) *Census of population taken on 4 December 1992, Demographic Characteristics of Bulgaria* (2 per cent representative sample), Sofia, p. 57.

Table 3 Legalization of equality

Country	Universal male suffrage[a] (year)	Universal female suffrage[b] (year)	Right for women to practise a profession[c]	Pay equity act[d] (year)	Equal opportunity act[e]	Equal male–female inheritance[f]	Legality of women's testimony[g]	Polygamy[h]	Divorce[h]/different rules for male–female
Australia	1901	1902	1885	1972	1975	1788*	1788	No	No (since 1975)
Botswana	1966	1966	Yes	NI	NI	NI	NI	NI	NI
Bulgaria	1879*/**	1937**	Yes**	1944**	1944**	1890**	1879	No	1879/No
China	1949	1949	Yes	1949**	1952**	Yes	Yes	No	No
France**	1848	1944	Yes*	1972	1975	1791	1938	No	No
Germany*	1867	1918*	1977	NI	1949	NI	NI	No	No
Greece**	1867**	1952	1836	1975	1984	1836	1836	No	No
Iran	1903	1963**	Yes	No	No	No*	*	Yes	Yes
Netherlands	1887**	1919*/**	Yes	1975**	1980**	1838	Yes	No	No
Norway**	1814	1913	1858*	1959	1979	1854	Yes	No	1927/No
Pakistan	1947	1947*	Yes	NI	No	No*	*	Yes	1947/Yes
Poland	1907	1919	Yes	1953**	No	Yes	Yes	No	No
Russia*/**	1917	1917	1917	1918	1918	1925	Yes	No	1925/No
Turkey	1876	1934	Yes	1950**	No	1926**	1927**	No**	1926/No**
UK	1689**	1928	Yes	1970	1975	Yes	Yes	No	No
USA	NI*	1920*	Yes	1963	No	Yes	Yes	No	No
Uzbekistan*	1918	1918	1918	1918	1918	1925	Yes	No	1925/No

Sources and notes

Information provided by the contributors if not specified otherwise.

France: (For all categories) Dhavernas, O (1978) *Droit des femmes, pouvoir des hommes*, Le Seuil, Paris; McBride Stetson, D (1987) *Women's Rights in France*. Greenwood Press, London.

Germany: Data for all categories, except b., refer to the former Federal Republic of Germany only.

Greece: (For all categories, except a.) Nicolaidou, M (1981) *Women and Emancipation: Women in Greece*, Castanictis, Athens.

Norway: (For all categories, except a.) Likestillingsrådet (1989) *Milestones in 150 years' history of Norwegian women (Minifacts)*, Oslo.

Pakistan: (For all categories) *Percival Spear, A History of India* (1975), Penguin Books, England, pp. 188, 189, 208; Wolpert, S (1989) *Jinnah of Pakistan*, Oxford University Press, Delhi, p. 337.

Russia: All data refer to the former USSR. *The Fundamental Law of the USSR* (1980). Progress Publishers, USSR.

Uzbekistan: See Russia.

a. Bulgaria: *Constitution of the Bulgarian State* (1879), Reprinted, Sofia, 1980.
Greece: *First Constitution Act*, Greece.
Netherlands: Jacobs, A (1978) *Memories*, SUN-Reprint, Nijmegen.
Poland: Universal male suffrage was introduced in 1907 under Austrian rule.
UK: Derbyshire J D and Derbyshire, I (1991) *World Political Systems: An Introduction to Comparative Government*, Chambers, Edinburgh, Table 11.
USA: Male and female suffrage were qualified by property and literacy restrictions in many states until the 1960s.

b. Derbyshire, J D and Derbyshire, I (1989) *Political Systems of the World*, Chambers, Edinburgh, if not otherwise specified.
Bulgaria: It affected only women who were single mothers of children or had been married, divorced or widowed. Full electoral rights for women were guaranteed by law in 1944. *Decree on Election of Members of Parliament for National Assembly* (1937), (Royal decree N264 of 21 October 1937), N234, Article 8, Sofia.
China: 'China' (1984) in Morgan, R (ed) *Sisterhood is Global*, Anchor, New York, p. 142.
Germany: Data refer to Germany before the split into the Federal Republic of Germany and the Democratic Republic of Germany in 1946.
Iran: The Women's Organization of Iran (1975) *The Iranian Women Past and Present*, Offset Press, Teheran.
Netherlands: 1917 passive and 1919 active. Jacobs, A (1978) *Memories*, SUN-Reprint, Nijmegen.
Pakistan: In 1956 women got two votes, one for the general seats, and one for specific women's seat.
USA: See a.

c. Australia: Varied by profession: doctors 1985; lawyers 1919.
Bulgaria: Gazette (1897) *Trade Law* (Royal decree N93), N114, Article 9, Sofia.
France: Women got the right to dispose of their own wages in 1907 and to work without their husband's consent in 1938.
Norway: In 1858 women had access to the public sector, and in 1866 they were given the same right as men to carry on a trade.

d. Bulgaria: *Act on Equality of Rights between Sexes* (1944) (Decree N30 of 12 October 1944), Ministry of Justice, N227, Sofia.
China: See b., p. 143.
Netherlands: Vrouwenlexicon (1989) *Tweehonderd jaar emancipatie van A tot Z*, Scala, Het Spectrum, Utrecht.
Poland: 'Poland' (1984) in Morger, R (ed) *Sisterhood is Global*, Anchor, New York, p. 556.
Turkey: Süral, N. (*et al.*) (1993) Working Women, Right of Protection in Turkey, in Gülmea, M (ed) *Proceedings of the Collaquim on European Social Charter and Turkey*, Todie Pub., Ankara.

e. Bulgaria and Netherlands: See d.
China: See b.

f. Australia: Exact rights vary by state.
Bulgaria: Gazette (1890) *Act on Inheritance* (Royal decree, N484 of 25 January 1890), N20, Article 21, Sofia.
Iran and Pakistan: Women inherit their parents property at half the rate of their brothers.
Turkey: *Civil Law* (1926), Article 439–580.

g. Iran and Pakistan: In certain cases, women may not testify; in others, the testimony of two women is equal to that of one man. In some cases a woman is a fully competent witness (eds' comment).
Turkey: *Civil Procedural Law* (1927), Article 245–274.

h. Turkey: *Civil Law* (1926), Article 129–150.

Table 4 Educational indicators

| Country | Illiteracy rate[a] age 15+ (overall/female) | Enrolment – 1988[b] Females per 100 males | | University first established[c] (year) | Women first admitted to university[a] (year) |
		Primary	Secondary		
Australia	+	95	99	1851*	1881
Botswana	26.4/34.9	107	103	1982	1982*
Bulgaria	NI	94	180	1888**	1901**
China	26.1/38.2	84	69	1895	1905/1920*/**
France	+	94	108	1257**	1862**
Germany*	+	96	97	1348	1908
Greece	6.8/10.9	94	101	1837**	1890**
Iran	46.0/56.7	80	64	1934	1938**
Netherlands	+	117*/**	111	1575**	1871**
Norway	+	95	103	1813	1882**
Pakistan	65.2/78.9	49	39	1882*	1920
Poland	NI	95	262	1364*/**	1897*/**
Russia	NI	105*/**	NI	1755**	1917**
Turkey	19.3/28.9	89	60	1870**	1915**
UK	+	107	96	12th century	1876*
USA	+	94	99*/**	1636	1833
Uzbekistan	NI	NI	NI	1920	1921

Sources and notes

Germany: Data a. and b. refer to the former Federal Republic of Germany only, c. and d. refer to Germany before it was divided in 1946.

a. Most recent estimate. + = illiteracy >5 per cent according to UNESCO. The World Bank (1992) *Social Indicators of Development 1991–92*, The Johns Hopkins University Press, Baltimore and London.

b. UNESCO (1991) *Statistical Yearbook*, United Nations Educational, Scientific and Cultural Organization, Paris, if not otherwise indicated.
Netherlands: Percentage of female age group enrolled in primary education. The World Bank (1991) *World Development Report 1991, The Challenge of Development, World Development Indicators*, Oxford University Press, Washington, Table 29.
Russia: Data refer to the former USSR, and shows gross enrolment ratios, most recent estimate. The World Bank (1992) *Social Indicators of Development, 1991–92*, The Johns Hopkins University Press, Baltimore and London.
USA: See b. The Netherlands.

c. Information provided by the contributors if not otherwise indicated.
Australia: University of Sydney.
Bulgaria: Arnaoudov, M (1939) *History of Sofia University during the first half century (1888–1938)*, Court Publishing House, Sofia, p. 171.
China: The People's Republic of China (1989) State Education Commission, p. 72. China had established institutions of higher education as early as 500BC. However, modern higher education was first established in 1895.
France: Verger, J (ed) (1986) *Historie des universités en France*, Toulouse, Private.
Greece: Kintis, A (1980) *Higher Education in Greece: thoughts on its restructuring*, Gutenberg, Athens.
Netherlands: Jacobs, A (1979) *Memories*, SUN-Reprint, Nijmegen.
Pakistan: Panjab University was established in undivided India (Lahore). This area became part of Pakistan after the partition of the subcontinent in 1947.
Poland: Krakov University. Kurkiewicz, W, Tatomir, A and Żurawski, W (1962) *A Thousand Years of Polish History*, LSW, Warsaw (in Polish).
Russia: Billington, J H (1970) *The Icon and the Axe: an interpretive history of Russian culture*, Vintage Books Edition, New York, pp. 208, 450.
Turkey: Tekeli, I (1983) 'The development of educational institutions from the Ottoman Empire to contemporary times', in *Encyclopedia of Turkey Republican Period*, Vol. 3, Iletisim pub., Istanbul, p. 657.

d. Information provided by the contributors if not otherwise indicated.
Botswana: As an independent country, Botswana never prohibited women from enrolling in higher education.
Bulgaria: See c.
China: 1905 – private college; 1920 – government university. Research Centre for Women's Movement, All-China Women's Federation (1986) *Zhongguo funu yundongshi* (History of Women's Movement in China), All-China Women's Federation, Beijing, pp. 49–51; Cheng Zhefan (1936) *Zhongguo xiandai nuzi jiaoyushi* (History of Women's Education in Modern China), *Zhonghua Shuju*, Shanghai, p. 169.
France: See c.
Greece: Ziougou-Carastergiou, S (1985) (see text for full citation).
Iran: The Women's Organization of Iran (1975) *The Iranian Women Past and Present*, Offset Press, Tehran.
Netherlands: See c.
Norway: Norske Kvinnelige Akademikeres Landsforbund (1932) *Kvinnelige studenter 1882–1932*, Gyldendal Norsk Forlag, Oslo, p. 64.
Poland: Krakow University. Hulewicz, J (1939) *Women in Higher Education in Poland in the XIXth Century*, PAU, Krakow.
Russia: See c.
Turkey: Lie, S S and O'Leary, V (eds) (1990) *Storming the Tower: women in the academic world*, Kogan Page, London.
UK: Different English universities admitted women at different dates; Scottish universities from 1876.

Table 5 Female academic attainment, per cent

Country	Year	Female enrolment at university level[a]	Degree earned[b]		Doctoral degree[c]	
			BA (or equivalent)	Post-graduate (incl. MA, PhD, Dr Habil.)	Lower (eg, PhD)	Higher (eg, Habilitation)
Australia	1990	50.6	53.5	52.4	NI*/**	NA
Botswana	1991	49.0*	NI	NI	NI	NA
Bulgaria	1990	48.4*	51.7	32.8*	NI*	NI
China**	1991	33.4	NI	12.0*	7.0 (1985)	NA
France**	1990	53.9	53.6	47.8	30.8	NA
Germany						
Fed. Rep.	1988–89	38.2*	37.1	NI	26.6*/**	9.2**
Dem. Rep.	1987–88	57.5*	72.8	47.1	37.5*/**	15.4**
Greece**	1990	52.6	53.2	32.4	32.0	NA
Iran	1987–88	30.6	35.7	25.9	NI*/**	NI*/**
Netherlands	1990	45.0	41.0*/**	NA	10.0**	NI
Norway	1990	53.8	64.6	35.9	24.8	NA
Pakistan	1986	18.3*	33.0	15.3	12.5**	NA
Poland	1990	50.9*	54.0	50.1	33.0**	NI
Russia*	1990	49.3*	36.0*	NA	28.0*	14.0*
Turkey	1990	34.0	35.7	34.8	38.1**	NA
UK	1989	45.8	46.5	40.4	25.2 (1987/88)*/**	NA
USA	1985	51.0	50.7	45.3	36.3 (1990)**	NA
Uzbekistan**	1989	42.0	46.0	NI	18.0	9.0

Notes

Russia: All data refers to the former USSR only.

a. 'University level' refers to level 6 and 7 as defined by the International Classification of Education (ISCED). UNESCO (1992) *Statistical Yearbook* has the following note (quoted from table 3.14):

Level 6: First university degree or equivalent qualification. These represent higher studies of normal duration (generally three to five years and, in certain cases, seven years). These are the most numerous. They include typical first degrees such as the Bachelor's degree, the *Licence*, etc., as well as in certain countries first professional degrees such as *Doctorates* awarded after completion of studies in medicine, engineering, law, etc.

Level 7: Post-graduate university degrees or equivalent qualifications. These are qualifications which persons who already possess a first university degree (or equivalent qualification) can obtain by continuing their studies. For example, the various diplomas obtained after completion of a first university degree (post-graduate diploma), the Master's degree, the various types of Doctorates, etc.

The classification according to level is intended to establish a distinction between the different degrees and diplomas and to facilitate international comparability on third-level qualifications. It should be noted that the classification by ISCED level category in no way implies an equivalence of the degrees and diplomas either within a country or between countries and that any comparative studies should be made with caution.

Botswana: Includes students only at the University of Botswana.
Bulgaria: Including evening and correspondence courses.
Germany: Fed. Rep.: Level 6 includes level 7. Dem. Rep.: Including evening and correspondence courses (see text).
Pakistan: Data do not include arts and sciences colleges and open admission universities.
Poland: Including evening and correspondence courses.
Russia: These figures were provided by the USSR, according to their own system of classification.

b. *BA or equivalent* (first university degree such as *Licence*) refers to ISCED's level 6 (see note a). *Master's and postgraduate university degrees* (which generally require a first university degree), refer to ISCED's level 7 (see note a.).
Bulgaria: A specific type of postgraduate studies (1–2 years), which is not equivalent to *Master's degree*.
China: Data provided by contributor; see text.
Netherlands: Level 6 includes level 7.
Russia: See note a.

c. The *higher level doctorate (habilitation)* is not applicable to most countries, which only award one type of doctorate.
Australia: No national statistics on sex differences in higher and lower levels of higher degrees. These were recently combined into one group in the Australian Bureau of Statistical Data. Women enrolled on doctoral programmes were 34.6 per cent for 1990.
Bulgaria: Women enrolled on doctoral programmes were 37.0 per cent for 1990.
Germany: All data from 1989.
Iran: One third of students enrolled on PhD programmes are women.
Russia: Data refer to 1989.
UK: In 1991–2 women were 31.5 per cent of PhD candidates at universities.

Sources

All categories: China: *Zhongguo funu tongji ziliao 1949–1989* (1991) (Statistics on Women in China 1949–1989), Beijing: Zhongguo tongji chubanshe, p. 172; and *Zhongguo tongji nianjian 1992* (1992) (Statistical Yearbook of China). Beijing: Zhongguo tongji chubanshe, p. 719.
France: Unpublished data from Ministère de l'Education nationale (questionnaire sur les statistiques de l'enseignement du 3° degré, année universitaire 1990–1991).
Greece: National Statistical Service of Greece, Ministry of Education (unpublished data).
Uzbekistan: Unpublished data provided by the contributors.

a. UNESCO (1992) *Statistical Yearbook*, Table 3.13, if not otherwise indicted.
Botswana: Figures for 1991 are compiled from the University of Botswana's admissions records.
Netherlands: Ministerie van oderwijs en wetenschappen (1991) *HOOP, Feiten en Cijfers*, Zoetermeer, Tables 80 and 81, 113.

b. UNESCO (1992) *Statistical Yearbook*, Table 3.14, if not otherwise indicated.
Netherlands: Ministerie van oderwijs en wetenschappen (1991) *HOOP, Feiten en Cijfers*, Zoetermeer, Tables 149–150, 185–86.

c. These figures are derived from the chapters in the book unless otherwise specified.
Australia: Department of Employment, Education and Training (1991) *Higher Education Series: Update No. 1*, 1991.
Germany: Fed. Rep.; Statistisches Bundesamt (1991) and BMBW 1991/92, p. 235. Dem. Rep.: *Stat. Jahrbuch der DDR* (1990), p. 344.
Iran: Minister of Culture and Higher Education (1988–89) *Iran Statistical Yearbook, 1367* (1988–89) Teheran, Islamic Republic of Iran, Plan and Budget Organization, Statistical Center of Iran, Tables 5–46.
Netherlands: Stimuleringsgroep Emancipatie Onderzoek (STEO) (1989) *Gepromoveerde Vrouwen in Nederland, 1980–1990*, Gravenhage.
Pakistan: University Grants Commission (1987) *Statistics on Higher Education*, Pakistan.
Poland: GUS (1992) *Higher Education in the Academic Year 1991/1992*, Warsaw.
Turkey: *The 1988–89 Academic Year Higher Education Statistics* (1989) Student Selection and Placement Center, Ankara.
UK: Lie, S S and O'Leary, V (eds.) (1990) *Storming the Tower: women in the academic world*, Kogan Page, London, Table 1.2.

Table 6 *Women's share of faculty positions in higher education, per cent*

Country	Year	Instructor/Lecturer (1)	Assistant Professor or equivalent (2)	Associate Professor Senior Lecturer (3)	Full Professor (4)	Women's share of faculty positions[a] (4 ranks)
Australia**	1992	38.5	17.8	10.9*	7.4	18.6
Botswana	1991–2	23.6	None	4.2	None	13.9
Bulgaria**	1991	44.0*	42.0*	25.0*	12.0*	30.8 (1989)**
China	1988	36.0	29.0	19.0	11.0	23.8
France**	1989–90	36.5	33.3*	33.3*	11.4	27.1
Germany**						
Fed. Rep.	1988	27.0*	20.2*	14.2*	5.2*	16.6
Dem. Rep.	1989	40.0*	17.3*	12.0*	4.9*	18.6
Greece**	1990	36.0	23.6	14.3	6.3	20.5
Iran**	1988–9	19.3	12.3	6.4	5.9	11.0
Netherlands**	1990	29.0	16.0	5.7	2.3	13.2
Norway**	1990	41.7*	29.3	16.3	9.3	24.2
Pakistan**	1987	18.4	16.1	8.2	4.2	11.8
Poland**	1992	44.3	33.7	16.9	16.9	31.7
Russia*	1986	37.0	25.0	NI	11.3	24.3
Turkey**	1989	30.3	26.8	22.7	20.0	25.0
UK**	1991	41.8*	25.2*	10.2*	4.9*	20.5 (1987–8)**
USA	1989–90	NI	38.1	26.0	14.0	26.0
Uzbekistan		NI	NI	NI	NI	NI

Notes

a. The figures in this column represent unweighted averages of the top four academic ranks in each country.

Australia: Category 3 *reader*.

Bulgaria: Category 1 *researcher/lecturer*; 2 *assistant*; 3 *docent*; and 4 *professor*.

France: *Assistant and associate professors are considered together*.

Fed. Rep.: Category 1 *lecturer*; 2 *reader, university lecturer*; 3 *senior lecturer*; and 4 *professor*.

Dem. Rep.: Category 1 *tenured teaching assistant*; 2 *senior lecturer*; 3 *assistant professor*; and 4 *professor*.

Norway: Scholarship holders and research assistants are regarded as junior staff.

Russia: Data refer to the former USSR.

UK: These figures apply to existing universities only, see relevant chapter for data on polytechnics = new universities. Category 1 *others*; 2 *lecturer*; 3 *senior lecturer/reader*; and 4 *full professor/chair*.

Sources

Information provided by the contributors if not otherwise indicated:

Australia: Australian Bureau of Statistics *Tertiary Education*. Catalogue no 4218.0, Australian Government Publishing Service, Canberra.

Bulgaria: National Institute of Statistics (1992) *Higher and College Education*, Sofia, 11. *Women's share of faculty*, see text.

France: Ministère de l'Education Nationale, *Note d'information 91–48*.

Germany: Fed. Rep.: Statistiches Bundesamt (Hg.) (1990) pp. 371, 373 and BMBW (1990) pp. 154f, 216. Dem. Rep.: Hildebrandt (1990), p. 9 (see text for full citation).

Greece: Ministry of Education, National Statistical Service of Greece (unpublished data).

Iran: Plan and Budget Organization (1367) (1988–89) *Iran Statistical Year Book*, Teheran, Iran and Ministry of Culture and Higher Education, Centre for Educational Planning (1368) (1990–91).

Netherlands: WOPI 1991, Kengetallen universitaiv, Personeel (peildatum: 31–12–90) and *VSNU*, Utrecht, September 1991.

Norway: Norsk offisiell statistikk (WOS C42) (1992) *Utdanningsstatistikk. Universiteter og høgskoler*, 1 Oktober 1990, Oslo-Kongsvinger.

Pakistan: Ministry Grants Commission (1987) *Statistics on Higher Education*, Pakistan.

Poland: GUS (1992) *Higher Education in the Academic Year 1991/1992*, Warsaw.

Turkey: Lie, S S and O'Leary, V (eds) (1990) *Storming the Tower: Women in the academic world*, Kogan Page, London, Table 1.3.

UK: For the category on the *women's share of positions* (1987–8) the data is from: Lie, S S and O'Leary, V (eds) (1990) *Storming the Tower: Women in the academic world*, Kogan Page, London, Table 1.3.

Uzbekistan: *Women in Uzbekistan* (1992).

Table 7 Introduction of Women's Studies and centres for research on women, by year

Country	Introduction of Women's Studies courses/research [a]	Establishment of Women's Studies programmes [b]	Women's Studies Chairs/Professorships [c]	Establishment of Women's Studies research centres [d]
Australia	1969	1974	No	No
Botswana **	1992	1992	No	No[2]
Bulgaria	No	No	No	1992–94[3]
China **	1987[4]	NI	No	1987[4]
France **	1972	1982[5]	No	No
Germany */**	1979[6]	1972/84[6]	1984[6]	1974/83[6]
Greece **	1989	No	No	1983[7]
Iran **	1972	1975[8]	No	1972[8]
Netherlands **	1974	1974[9]	Yes	1985[9]
Norway	1973[10]	1983[10]	1993[10]	1983[10]
Pakistan	1989[11]	No	No	1989[11]
Poland	1989	1991[12]	No	1991[12]
Russia	1991[13]	1990[13]	No	1991[13]
Turkey	1981[14]	1993–94[14]	No	1990[14]
UK **	1970[15]	1980[15]	1988[15]	1985[15]
USA **	1960s	1969[16]	No	1974[16]
Uzbekistan **	No[17]	No	No	No

Notes

Germany: Refers to the former Federal Republic of Germany only.

a.

(4) Beijing Foreign Studies University.
(6) As section of the German Association for Sociology.
(10) University of Tromsø.
(11) Quaid-e-Azam University, Islamabad and Karachi University.
(13) Centre of Gender Studies, Russian Academy of Sciences.
(14) Middle East Technical University.
(15) Various undergraduate courses since early 1970s; Lancaster University (1979).
(17) There have been several theses, supported or written, and publications on various aspects of female status in society, but they have not been united by any kind of general research programme.

b.

(5) Ministère de la Recherche et de l'Industrie (Colloquium on Women, Feminism, Research).

(6) Free University of Berlin.
(8) According to Mrs Mahnaz Afkhami, Director of Center for Research, Women's Organization of Iran, Women's Study courses had been proposed by the National University, but were not actively taught; as a result of the revolution they were eliminated.
(9) University of Amsterdam, Utrecht and Nijmegen.
(10) University of Oslo.
(12) University of Warsaw.
(13) See a.(13).
(14) Istanbul University and Middle East Technical University; both plan to admit students to graduate programmes in Women's Studies in this academic year.
(15) MA in Women's Studies, University of Kent.
(16) San Diego State University.

c.

(6) See b.(6).
(10) University of Oslo; Center for Women's Research.
(15) University of Queens, Belfast, Northern Ireland.

d.

(2) The Women's Studies research is done at the University of Botswana, National Institute of Research and Documentation. There is only one research fellow, and Women's Studies/research is done by interested faculty members and coordinated by the research fellow.
(3) In the framework of the Bulgarian Association of University Women, a project was started: 'The Women's Information and Training Center', financially supported by the Commission of European Communities.
(4) Zhengzhou University.
(6) See b.(6).
(7) KEGME (NGO) and Women Studies Group, University of Thessaloniki.
(8) See b.(8).
(9) Leiden University.
(10) University of Bergen.
(11) See a.(11).
(12) See b.(12).
(13) See a.(13).
(14) Istanbul University.
(15) Centre for Research and Education on Gender: University of London, Institute of Education.
(16) Radcliffe College.

Sources

Information provided by the contributors if not otherwise specified.
Botswana: Unpublished university policy drafted by the University Gender Committee.
China: (a) 'Women's Studies course', *China Daily*, October 12, 1988, and information supplied by Grace C L Mak. (d) 'A new way for women', *China Daily*, 3 May 1988.
France: Lagrave, R M (1990) 'Recherches féministes on recherches sur les femmes?', *Acts data Recherche en Science Sociales*. June 1990, pp. 27–39.
Germany: (b and c) Bock, U (1992) *Frauenforschungsprofessuren an Unterstät in Deutschland*, Zentraleinrichtung zur Förderung von Frauenstudien und Frauenforschung an der Freien Universität Berlin. Extra, Info 15. 12, Berlin. (d) *Frauen und Politik*, No. 49/1990, p. 12.
Iran: The Women's Organization of Iran (1975) *The Iranian Women, Past and Present*, Offset Press, Teheran.
Netherlands: Brouns, M (1988) *Fourteen Years of Women's Studies in the Netherlands* (an overview, September 1988). Zoetermeer.
UK: Klein, R D (1984) 'The intellectual necessity for Women's Studies', in Acker, S and Warren Piper, D (eds) *Is Higher Education Fair to Women?* (Guildford: SRHE and NFER-Nelson), and documents issued by individual universities.
USA: Chamberlain, M (ed) (1988) *Women in Academe: Progress and Prospects*, Russell Sage Foundation, New York.
Uzbekistan: Unpublished information provided by the contributors.

Biographical notes on contributors

Feride Acar is an Associate Professor at the Department of Public Administration, Middle East Technical University, Ankara. Her areas of academic interest are social and political change, social movements, and Women's Studies. She has participated in several international projects of a cross-cultural nature. Dr Acar has co-edited books and published many articles on conditions and characteristics of academic women in Turkey and Jordan, women and Islam and political parties in Turkey.

Felicity Allen is a Senior Lecturer in Applied Psychology at Monash University, Australia. Her PhD thesis assessed women's opportunities to attain professorships. As a consultant, she evaluates large-scale innovations including the introduction of new technology and the implementation of new legislation. With a colleague, she has written two detective novels about academic life: *Unable by Reason of Death* and *Not in Single Spies*.

Helen S Astin is Professor of Higher Education and Associate Director of the Higher Education Research Institute at UCLA. She has been President of the Division of the Psychology of Women of the American Psychological Association. Her major books include: *The Woman Doctorate in America*, and *Women of Influence. Women of Vision: A Cross-Generational Study of Leaders and Social Change* (with Carole Leland).

Julia Balaska is a graduate in Political Science and Social Psychology. Currently she is preparing her doctorate at the Panteion University of Athens, on 'Women's Cooperatives: Towards a New Psycho-social Women's Identity?'. Since 1990, Julia Balaska has been a member of the Mediterranean Women's Studies Centre (KEGME) research group.

Jacqueline Feldman is Senior Researcher in Sociology at the Centre National de la Recherche Scientifique, Paris. Doctor of Physics, she has published widely on the mathematical methods of the Social Sciences, the evolution of science, women and science, and feminism. She is the author of *The Sexuality of the Petit Larousse: a Game on Dictionary* and *An Unconventional Journey through Knowledge and Science* (in French).

Malgorzata Fuszara is an Associate Professor and Director of the Center for Socio-Legal Studies on the Situation of Women at the University of Warsaw, Poland. She has published on sociology of law, family and women's issues. Her major English works on women's issues include: *Will Abortion Issues Give Birth to Feminism in Poland?*; *Legal Regulation of Abortion in Poland*, and *Abortion and the Formation of the Public Sphere in Poland*. She is a member of the Advisory Board of Signs.

Susanne Grimm is Professor of Sociology at the University of Munich. She held a scholarship from the German Science Community (DFC) (1972–4) and was a founding member of Women's Studies of the German Sociological Association. Currently she is President-Elect of the Association of European Women in Science (EWIS). Central publications include: *Die Bildungsabstinenz der Arbeiter*; *Fernstudium und Studienabbruch*; and *Soziologie der Bildung und Erziehung*.

Beate Grudzinska has her degree in Scandinavian Studies from the University of Poznan. A freelance translator and researcher, she is an active feminist working to protect abortion rights in Poland.

Unni Hagen holds the degree *cand.polit.* in sociology of education, Oslo. Having worked as a research fellow (1992) on the Educational Leadership International project at the Institute for Educational Research, University of Oslo, she is now doing her PhD on 'Decentralization and educational austerity: the changing role of head teachers in Norway, Russia and Scotland' at DISE, Institute of Education, London.

Duncan Harris graduated in physics at bachelor level and by research at master's level at Nottingham University. His doctorate was in education from the University of Bath. He is currently Professor and Head of Education at Brunel University, London. His current interests include educational technology, assessment and evaluation. He has written and edited several books including a *Dictionary of Instructional Technology* (with H Ellington) and *Evaluating and Assessing for Learning* (with C Bell).

Tahereh Alavi Hojjat is Assistant Professor of Economics and Finance at Allentown College of St Francis de Sales. Among her publications are: *Economic Outlook of Iran in 1990s*; *As Cold War Ends*; *Positive and Negative Aspects of Investment in Eastern Europe*; she is co-author (with Mehdi Hojjat) of *Europe Without Frontiers: strategic planning for Europe 1992*. She is on the editorial board of the International Society for Social Studies and Economics.

Neelam Hussain is Principal of Lahore Grammar School, Pakistan. She has written extensively on educational and gender issues in the Asian context. Hussain is currently enrolled as a doctoral candidate at Brunel University, London, researching gender and higher education in Pakistan.

Suzanne Stiver Lie is Professor of Education, Institute for Educational Research, University of Oslo, Norway. She is a former Director of Women's Studies for the Social Science Faculty and former Vice-Director of the Equal Opportunities Council, University of Oslo. She has authored or edited several books on women in higher education and on women immigrants in Norway. Among her latest books are: *Storming the Tower: women in the academic world* (co-editor with Virginia O'Leary).

Grace C L Mak is lecturer in Comparative Education and Sociology of Education at the Chinese University of Hong Kong. She has published several articles on women's education in China and in Hong Kong and is currently working on a volume entitled *Women, Education and Development in Asia*.

Lynda Malik is an Assistant Professor at Villanova University, Pennsylvania, USA. A former Fulbright scholar, Dr Malik teaches in the Women's Studies Program at Villanova and publishes on current issues in the Islamic world.

P T M Marope is a lecturer at the University of Botswana's Department of Educational Foundations. She is the Deputy Chairperson of Botswana Educational Research Association, and an established Setswana novelist. She acquired her PhD in curriculum and instruction from the University of Chicago.

Uta Meier is Professor of Family Sociology, currently working at the German Youth Institute in Munich and at the Ludwig-Maximilians-University of Munich. She has published widely in Women's Studies, family and youth sociology.

Annie Morelle is Assistant Researcher at the Centre National de la Recherche Scientifique, Paris. She has worked in several fields: Latin-American studies, political science and sociology.

Marina Yu Morozova is a research scientist (PhD) at the Institute of Oriental Studies, Russian Academy of Sciences, Moscow. She specializes in socioeconomic problems of modern Pakistan and is the author of several publications including the book *Modern Pakistan Village*.

Railiya Mukhsinovna Muqeemjanova is a leading scientist (Doctor of Science) at the Institute of Oriental Studies, the Russian Academy of Sciences in Moscow, where she specializes in the foreign policy of Pakistan and international relations in South, South-East and Central Asia. Her major works include: *The U.S.A. Policy in Pakistan; Pakistan, South Asia and the U.S. Policy; Foreign Policy of Pakistan in South-East, South and Central Asia* and articles on the educational system of Pakistan.

Greta Noordenbos is Assistant Professor at the Department of Women's Studies at Leiden University. She has published widely on women and work, mentor relations and career development. She is co-editor of *Is Alma Mater Sympathetic to Women?* and *Career Development of Women.*

Gulnara Tukhlibaevna Quzibaeva is an Assistant Professor (Candidate of Science, equivalent to PhD) in the Tashkent Medical Paediatrics Institute in the Republic of Uzbekistan, where she specializes in economics. She is the author of several publications including articles on the labour resources of Uzbekistan.

Nicolina Sretenova, PhD, is a Research Fellow at the Centre for Science Studies at the Bulgarian Academy of Sciences. She has numerous publications on philosophical foundations of general theory of relativity and quantum physics, as well as on the history of Bulgarian physics. She is a newcomer in the field of gender studies.

Margaret B Sutherland, Professor Emerita of Education, University of Leeds, was editor of the *British Journal of Educational Studies*, 1974–85. A Fellow of the Scottish Council for Research in Education, she is currently engaged in writing and research in comparative education and women's education. Among her recent publications are *Women Who Teach in Universities* and *Theory of Education.*

Mari Teigen is a researcher at the Institute for Studies in Research and Higher Education, the Norwegian Research Council for Science and the Humanities. She has published widely on Norwegian women in politics, in the public sector and in research.

Bibliography

Compiled by David W Schlosser

Aasen, E (1993) 'Fra posisjon til avmakt: Kvinner og ledelse i kulturhistorisk perspektiv', *Nytt om kvinneforskning: Kjønn i organisasjon og ledelse*, **1**.

Acar, F (1983) 'Turkish women in academia: roles and careers', *METU Studies in Development* **10**, 4, pp. 409–46.

Acar, F (1990) 'Role priorities and career patterns of women in academe: a cross-cultural study of Turkish and Jordanian university teachers', in Lie, S S and O'Leary, V (eds) *Storming the Tower: women in the academic world*, Kogan Page: London.

Acar, F (1991a) 'Women in academic science careers', in Stolte-Heiskanen, V *et al.*, (eds) *Women in Science: token women or gender equality?*, ISSC-UNESCO-Publication, Beng Publishers: London.

Acar, F (1991b) 'Women in the ideology of Islamic revivalism in Turkey: three Islamic women's journals', in Tapper R, (ed) *Islam in Modern Turkey*, IB Taurus: London.

Acker, S, Megary, J, Nisbet, S and Hoyle, E (1984) 'Women and Education', *World Yearbook of Education*, Kogan Page: London.

Afshar, H (1985) 'Women, state and ideology in Iran', *Third World Quarterly*, **7**, 2, 256–96.

Alavi, H (1983) 'Class and state', in Gardezi, H and Rashid, J (eds) *Pakistan: the roots of dictatorship*, Zed Press: London.

Alexander, J (1983) *The Modern Reconstruction of Classical Thought: Talcott Parsons*, University of California Press: Berkeley.

Alexander, J (1988) 'The new theoretical movement', in Smelser, N J (ed) *Handbook of Sociology*, Sage: Beverly Hills.

Allardt, E (1990) 'Challenges for comparative social research', *Acta Sociologica*, **3**, 33, 183–93.

Allen, F C L (1990) *Academic Women in Australian Universities*, monograph no 4, Affirmative Action Agency, AGPS: Canberra.

Almanac of the Kliment Ohridski University of Sofia, 1888–1939 (1988) Kliment Ohridski University Press: Sofia.

Amirahmadi, H (1990) 'Economic reconstruction of Iran: costing the war damage', *Third World Quarterly*, **12**, 1, p. 29.

Amjad, R (1983) 'Industrial concentration and economic power', in Gardezi, H and Rashid, J (eds) *Pakistan: the roots of dictatorship*, Zed Press: London.

Anderson, D (1992) 'Access to university education in Australia 1852–1990: changes in the undergraduate social mix', *Higher Education Review*, **24**, 2, 8–36.

Andors, P (1983) *The Unfinished Revolution of Chinese Women 1948–1980*, Indiana University Press, Bloomington.

Arat, N (1989) 'Turkiye' de kadinlarin ve kizlarin egitimine genel bir bakis (A general look at the education of women and girls in Turkey)', in *Turkiye'de Cocugun Durumu (The Conditions of Children in Turkey)*, Turkish State Planning Organization and UNICEF: Ankara.

Argumenty i facty (The Arguments and Facts), weekly, Moscow, 19 November 1990; 2 November 1993; 3 November 1993.

Arnaoudov, M (1939) *History of Sofia University St. Kliment Ohridski during the First Half Century of the University (1888–1938)*, Court Publishing House: Sofia.

Arnot, M and Weiner, G (eds) (1987) *Gender and the Politics of Schooling*, Hutchinson: London.

Association pour l'emploi des cadres (APEC) (1981) *Les femmes cadres*, Paris.

Astin, A W, Korn, W S and Dey, E L (1991) *The American college teacher: national norms for the 1989–90 HERI faculty survey*, Higher Education Research Institute, University of Los Angeles.

Astin, H S (1984) 'The meaning of work in women's lives: a psychological model of career choice and work behavior', *The Counseling Psychologist*, **12**, 4, 117–26.

Australian Bureau of Statistics (1982) *Cross-classified characteristics of persons and dwellings*, Cat. No. 2452.0, AGPS: Canberra.

AUT (Association of University Teachers) (1991) *Pay at the Top of the University Ladder*, United House: London.

Aynshteyn, V (1991) 'Vysshaya Shkola: chrezvychaynaya situatsiya (Higher school: the state of emergency)', *Moskovskaya Pravda*, 19 April.

Ayoob, M (1979) 'Two faces of political Islam: Iran and Pakistan compared', *Asian Survey*, June, p. 535.

Baar, M, de Löwensteyn, M, Monteiro, M and Sneller, A A (1992) *Anna Maria van Schurman (1607–78): an exceptionally learned women*, Walburg: Zathphen.

Bacock, J and Temple, M (1990) 'Equal Opportunities, Management Strategies and Access to Higher Education', paper, Council of Europe Conference on Equal Advances in Education Management: Vienna.

Balaska, J (1991) *Report on Family Situation and Policy in Greece*, Gefam Geselleschaft für Familienforschung e.V.: Bonn (unpublished).

Baldwin, G (1985) *Women at Monash University*, Monash University Press: Melbourne.

Bammé, A, Holling, E and Lempert, W (1983) *Berufliche Sozialisation*, Beck: München.

Bataillon, A-M *et al.* (1991) 'Presence des femmes au CNRS', *L'homme et la societe*, 1–2.

Baudelot, C and Establet, R (1992) *Allez les filles*, Le Seuil: Paris.

Bechuanaland Protectorate, (1939) *Annual Report of the Director of Education for the Period: 1st January 1939 to the 31st March 1939*, West Rand Publications Ltd: Krugersdorp.

Beekes, A (1991) 'The hurdle race: developments in the arrear of women compared to men at universities in the Netherlands in the period 1960–1985', thesis, ISOR, Faculty of Social Sciences, State University of Utrecht.

Beijing daxue yanjiusheng yuan (Graduate School of Beijing University) (1991) *Yanyuan shilin (Profiles of Advisors for Doctoral Students at Beijing University)*, Beijing daxue chubanshe: Beijing.

Bellah, R N, Madsen, R, Sullivan, W M, Swidler, A and Tipton, S M (1985) *Habits of the Heart: individualism and commitment in American life*, University of California Press: Berkeley.

Berger, P and Luckmann, T (1987) *The Social Construction of Reality: A treatise in the sociology of knowledge*, Penguin Books: Harmondsworth.

Berggreen, B (1992) *Da kulturen kom til Norge*, Aschehoug forlag: Oslo.

Bernard, J (1981) *The Female World*, Free Press: New York.

Bernard, J (1987) *The Female World from a Global Perspective*, Indiana University Press: Bloomington, IN.

Bernard, J (1989) 'Educating the majority: the feminist enlightenment', in Pearson, C S, Shavlik, D L and Touchton, J G (eds) *Educating the Majority: women challenge tradition in higher education*, American Council of Education, Macmillan: London.

Birt, M (1985) 'The organization of tertiary education in Australia: the need for rearrangement', *Journal of Tertiary Education Administration*, **Z**, 1, 21–35.

Blix, K, Schytte, W and Gulbrandsen, L (1993) 'Småbarns familiers økonomi og bruk av barnetilsyn', *INAS Notat*, **93**, 2.

(BMBW) Der Bundesminister für Bildung und Wissenschaft (1974) *Grund und Strukturdaten 1974/75*.

(BMBW) Der Bundesminister für Bildung and Wissenschaft (1990) *Mädchen auf dem Weg zum Abitur*, Aktuell Bildung Wissenschaft, 6/90.

(BMBW) Der Bundesminister für Bildung und Wissenschaft (1990) *Frauen in Bildung and Wissenschaft*, Aktuell Bildung Wissenschaft, 12/90.

(BMBW) Der Bundesminister für Bildung und Wissenschaft (1990) *Hochschulpolitische Zielsetzungen der Bundesregierung*, Aktuell Bildung Wissenschaft, 14/90.

(BMBW) Der Bundesminister für Bildung und Wissenschaft (1990) *Grund- und Strukturdaten 1990/91*.

Bosch, M (1988) 'A female hegemony in Baarn: professor dr. Johanna Westerdijk, director of the

Laboratory Willie Commelin Scholten', in Loosbroek, *et al.* (eds) *Learned Women. Ninth yearbook of women's history*, Sun: Nijmegen.

Bourdieu, P (1984) *Homo academicus*, Minuit: Paris.

Bourdieu, P (1988) *Homo academicus*, Polity Press: Cambridge.

Bradburn, N (1963) 'Interpersonal relations in Turkish organizations', *Journal of Social Issues*.

Braun, I (1904) *Historia rozwoju ruchu kobiecego (The History of Women's Movement)*, GiW: Warszawa.

Brouns, M and Schokker, A (1990) *Labour Questions and Gender*, Trendrapport STEO: The Hague.

Bruyn-Hundt, M (1988) *Women in the Labour Market: the Dutch situation in the years eighty and ninety*, Spectrum: Amsterdam.

Burieva, M R (1991) *Rozhdaemost v Uzbekistane (The Birth Rate in Uzbekistan)* USSR govt: Tashkent.

Burki, S J (1980) *Pakistan under Bhutto 1971–1977*, St Martin's Press: New York.

Burton, E M (1912) *Notable Women of China*, Fleming H Revell Co: New York.

Cachelou, J (1979) 'Les femmes chercheurs au CNRS', *Courrier du CNRS*, **32**, 30–36.

Caclamanakis, R (1984) *The Position of Greek Woman in Society and Politics*, Castaniotis: Athens.

Cacoullos, A (1991) 'Women, science and politics in Greece: three is a crowd', in Stolte-Heiskanen, V (ed) *Women in Science: token women or gender equality?*, Berg Publishers: Oxford/New York.

Caragiorgas, S a o (1990) *Dimensions of Poverty in Greece*, National Center for Social Research (EKKE): Athens.

Cass, B, Dawson, M, Temple, D, Wills, S and Winkler, A (1983) *Why so few?: women academics in Australian universities*, Sydney University: Sydney.

Cavounidis, J (1990) *Young Women and Vocational Training*, Mediterranean Women's Studies Institute: Athens (unpublished).

Chamberlain, M K (ed) (1988) *Women in Academe: progress and prospects*, Russell Sage Foundation: New York.

Chen, Q (1973) *Zhongguo jiaoyushi (History of Chinese Education)* Commercial Press: Taipei.

Cheng, Z (1936) *Zhuongguo xiandai nuzi jiaoyushi (History of Women's Education in Modern China)* Zhonghua shuju: Shanghai.

Chenyan (1983) 'Trend of sex discrimination in job allocation for university graduates must be corrected', *Zhongguo funu*, **6**, 15.

China Daily, 9 March 1984; 25 February 1991; 9 November 1992.

Chirenje, J M (1977) *A History of Northern Botswana 1850–1910*, Fairleigh-Dickinson University Press: New Jersey.

CIA World Factbook (1992) US Government Printing: Washington, DC.

Cindoğlu, D, Muradoğlu, G and Çulpan, O (1992) 'Turkish women in a non-conventional field of academia; women academicians in finance and accounting education', paper presented at the ASA meeting: Pittsburgh.

Çitçi, O (1981) *Kadin Sorunu ve Türk Kamu Göreulisi Kadinlar (The Woman Question and Turkish Women Public Employees)*, TODAIE Yay: Ankara

Clark, B R (1986) *The Higher Education System Academic Organization in Cross-National Perspective*, University of California Press: London.

CNRS (1990) *Bilan Social*, Paris.

Coale, A C (1991) 'Excess female mortality and the balance of the sexes in the population: estimate of missing females', *Population and Development Review*, **17**, 3.

Colclough, C, Cumming, C and Sekgoma, G (1988) *Investment Options in Post-secondary Education*, University of Botswana: Gaborone.

Cole, J R (1987) *Fair Science: women in the scientific community*, Columbia University Press: New York.

Cole, J R and Zuckerman, H (1987) 'Marriage, motherhood and performance in science', *Scientific American*, **256**, 2, 15–22.

Council of Europe (1990) *The Fortunes of Highly Educated Women*, Council of Europe: Strasbourg.

Craig, J E (1981) 'The expansion of education', *Review of Education Research* **9**, 151–213.

Dahrendorf, R (1965) *Gesellschaft und Demokratie in Deutschland*, Piper: München.

David, M (1989) 'Prima donna inter pares? Women in academic management', in Acker, S (ed) *Teaching, Gender and Careers*, Falmer Press: London.

Davies, B (1982) 'Discrimination, affirmative action and women academics; a case study of the University of New England', *Vestes* **25**, 15–22.

Davis, D, and Astin, H S (1990) 'Life cycle, career cycle and gender stratification in academe:

breaking myths and exposing truths', in Lie, S S and O'Leary, V (eds) *Storming the Tower: women in the academic world*, Kogan Page: London.

Davis, F (1991) *Moving the Mountain: the women's movement in America since 1960*, Simon & Schuster: New York.

Dawkins, J (1987) *Higher Education: a policy discussion paper*, AGPS: Canberra.

DEET (1991a) Department of Education, Employment and Training Higher Education Staff Collection, AGPS: Canberra.

DEET (1991b) Department of Education, Employment and Training *Selected Higher Education Statistics*, AGPS: Canberra.

Delavault, H (1986) 'Les femmes dans les cadres de l'enseignement superieur et de la recherche', *Diplomees* **138**, 96–108.

Demenint-de Jongh, M (1989) 'Labour Duration, Organization and Emancipation: concerning the quality of part time work', thesis, University of Leiden.

Department of Planning, Ministry of Education, the People's Republic of China (1984) *Achievement of Education in China*, People's Education Press: Beijing.

DES (Department of Education and Science) (1966, 1977, 1982, 1990, 1991) *Statistics of Education*; Statistical Bulletins 11/90, 2/91, HMSO: London.

Dinkova, M (1978) *1000 Questions to the Modern Young Woman (Sociological and Psychological Analysis)*, Narodna Mladezh: Sofia.

Döbbeling, K, *et al.* (1990) 'Wozu forschungen über frauen im hochschulwesen?', *Forum Wissenschaft*, **1**, 25–9.

Domozetov, C (1985) *Reflections of the Equality of Rights*, Profizdat: Sofia.

Doorne-Huiskes, A van (1990) 'Women in Dutch Universities: analysis and politics', in Hicks, E K and Noordenbos, G (eds) *Is Alma Mater Friendly for Women?*, Van Gorcum: Assen, Maastricht.

Duru-Bellat, M (1990) *L'ecole des filles: quelle formation pour quels roles sociaux?*, L'Harmattan: Paris.

Educational Statistics Yearbook of China 1989 (1990) People's Education Press: Beijing.

Eeg-Henriksen, F and Pedersen, T B (1991) 'Women's studies in Norway', in Bergman, S (ed) *Women's Studies and Research on Women in the Nordic Countries*, 35–38 Painotalo Gillot Oy: Turku.

EKKE: National Center of Social Research (1988) *Research on the Political Behavior of Women in Greece*, Athens.

Eliou, M (1991) *Steps Ahead, Steps Backwards*, Porea: Athens.

Elutin, V P (ed) (1967) *Vysshaya shkola SSSR za 50 let (Higher education of the USSR during 50 years)*, USSR govt: Moscow.

EOC (Equal Opportunities Commission) (1988) *Women and Men In Britain*, HMSO: London.

Erkut, S (1982) 'Dualism in values toward education of Turkish women', in Kağitçibaşi, Ç (ed) *Sex Roles, Family and Community in Turkey*, Indiana University Press: Bloomington.

Feldman, J (1984) 'La science en mutation', in Armattde, M *et al*, *Le Sujet et l'Objet: confrontations*, Editions du CNRS: Paris.

Friedan, B (1963) *The Feminine Mystique*, Dell: New York.

Fürst, E (1988) *Kvinner i Akademia – Inntrengere i en Mannskultur?*, NAVF: Oslo.

Fuszara, M (1991a) 'Legal regulation of abortion in Poland', *Signs*, **17**, 1.

Fuszara, M (1991b) 'Will abortion issues give birth to feminism in Poland?' in Maclean, M and Groves, D (eds) *Women's Issues in Social Policy*, Routledge: London.

Fuszara, M (1993) 'Abortion debate and political scene in Poland' in Funk, N and Mueller, M (eds) *Gender, Politics and Post-Communism: reflections from Eastern Europe and former Soviet Union*, Routledge: London.

Gardezi, F. (1990) 'Islam feminism and the women's movement in Pakistan: 1981–1991', *South Asia Bulletin*, **10**, 2.

Gaudar, D (1991) *Women in Science: from token women to gender equity in science*, International Social Science Council and UNESCO – Social and Human Sciences Sector.

Gazette (1937) 'Decree on election of members of municipal councils' (Royal decree N8 of January 15th, 1937), N11: Sofia, 'Decree on election of members of Parliament for Ordinary National Assembly' (Royal decree N264 of 21 October, 1937), N234: Sofia.

Gazette (1944) 'Decree on equality of rights of two sexes', Ministry of Justice, N227: Sofia.

General Secretariat for Equality of the Two Sexes (1986) *National Report to the Committee of United Nations for the Elimination of all Forms of Discrimination against Women (CEDAW)*, Athens.

Geißler, R (1992) *Die Sozialstruktur Deutschlands*, Westdeutscher: Opladen.

Genchev, N (1988) *Bulgarian Culture, XV–XIX c.*, Kliment Ohridski University Press: Sofia.

Goffmann, E (1959) *The Presentation of Self in Everyday Life*, Doubleday: Garden City, NY.

Göle, N (1991) *Modern Mahrem (Modern Seclusion)*, Metis Yay: Istanbul.

Government of Pakistan Economic Survey 1986–87, Government of Pakistan Finance Division, Economic Advisors Wing: Islamabad.

Government of Pakistan Economic Survey 1991–92, Government of Pakistan Finance Division, Economic Advisors Wing: Islamabad.

Government of Pakistan, Ministry of Women's Development (January 1992) *Handbook*.

Government of Pakistan, University Grants Commission (1981) *Higher Education News*, 1, 1, 5.

Government of Pakistan, University Grants Commission (1987) *Statistics on Higher Education*, Islamabad.

Government of Pakistan, University Grants Commission (1989) *Statistics on Higher Education*, Islamabad.

Government of Pakistan and UNICEF Country Program of Cooperation (1988–89) *Situation Analysis of Children and Women in Pakistan*, Islamabad, Pakistan, 1987, 24.

Grimm, S (1987) *Soziologie der Bildung und Erziehung*, Ehrenwirth: München.

Grimm, S (1992) 'Zur aktuellen Rechtslage der Frauenförderung an den bundesdeutschen Hochschulen', *Konsens*, 8, 2, 4–8.

Grimm, S, Nitzinger, E and Heyn, S (1992) 'Zum Stand der Frauenförderung an den Hochschulen in der Bundersrepublik Deutschland: Eine nationale Dokumentation in Bayerisches Staatsinstitut für Hochschulforschung und Hochschulplanung' *Beiträge zur Hochschulforschung*, 2, 211–54.

Guangming ribao 26 March 1989.

Günlük-Şenesen, G (1992) 'An economic analysis of female participation in university administration: the case of Turkey', paper presented at the International Conference on Business and Economic Development in Middle Eastern and Mediterranean Countries: Malta.

Guojia kewei rencai ziyuan yanjiusuo (Human Resources Research Center, State Science Commission) (1986) *Voices from Women in Science and Technology Rencai tiandi (World of Qualified Personnel)* 3, 3–5.

Guojia tongjiju (State Statistical Bureau) (1992) *Zhongguo tongji nianjian 1992 (Statistical Yearbook of China 1992)*, Zhongguo tongji chubanshe: Beijing.

Gustafsson, I (1987) *Schools and the Transformation of Work: a study of four productive work programs in Southern Africa*, University of Stockholm: Stockholm.

Halsey, A H (1990) 'Long, open road to equality', *The Times Higher Education Supplement*, 9 February.

Han, C (1988) 'Education and route to achievement of women in China', *Renkou yu jingii (Population and Economics)* 5, 41–4.

Hansen, T (1989) 'Kvinner i akademia: hva forteller egentlig data?', *Tidsskrift for samfunnsforskning, Debatt*, 30, 289–47.

Harding, S (1986) *The Science Question of Feminism*, Open University Press: Milton Keynes.

Harper, J (1987) *Survey of Academic Staff, Part 1: report on women*, University of Melbourne: Equal Opportunity.

Hawkins, A C (1990) 'The perception of their work situation by female and male scholars working in Universities in the Netherlands', in Hicks, E K and Noordenbos, G (eds) *Is Alma Mater Sympathetie to Women?* Van Gorcum: Assen, Maastricht.

Hawkins, A C and Noordenbos, G (1990) 'Blocks in the moving up of women to higher functions at the university', *University & High School*, 36, 269–97.

Hayes, L D (1987) *Crisis of Education in Pakistan*, Vanguard Books: Lahore.

Hernes, H (1987) *Welfare State and Woman Power: essays in state feminism*, Norwegian University Press: Oslo.

Hicks, E K and Noordenbos, G (eds) (1990) *Is Alma Mater Sympathetic to Women?*, Van Gorcum: Assen, Maastricht.

Ho, P (1964) *The Ladder of Success in Imperial China*, Wiley: New York.

Hobson, K (1991) 'University is leading way in EEO drive', *Canberra Times*, 8 February p. 14.

Hochschild, A (1989) *The Second Shift: working parents and the revolution at home*, Viking Press: New York.

Hofstede, G (1980) *Culture's Consequences: international differences in work-related values*, Sage Publications: Beverley Hills.

HOOP, Facts and Numbers (1991) 'Ministry of Education and Science: higher research and education plan', The Hague.

Horstkemper, M (1987) *Schule, Geschlecht und Selbstvertrauen*, Beltz: Weinheim.

Huisman, J (1981) *Women in Men's Jobs: experiences, backgrounds and careers*, Anthos: In den Toren, Baarn.

Hulewicz, J (1939) *Sprawa wyzszego wyksztalcenia koviet w Polsce w wicku XIX (Women in Higher Education in Poland in XIX century)*, PAU: Krakow.

Hyman, H H, Payaslioglu, A and Frey, F (1958) 'Values of Turkish college youth', *Public Opinion Quarterly*, **22**, 3, 275– 91.

Ilieva, N (1991) 'The women's work under the condition of transition to market economy', paper presented before the conference The Women during the Transition to Market Economy (Theory, Social Practice, Information), 11–12 June 1991, Institute of Demography at Bulgarian Academy of Sciences: Sofia.

INSEE (1987) *Donnees Sociales*, Paris.

INSEE (1991) *Les femmes*, Paris.

Iqbal, J (1988) 'Crimes against women in Pakistan' paper presented in Urdu in Triennial Conference of All Pakistan Women's Association, Karachi, Pakistan. Nasira Igbal translation.

Iran Statistical Yearbook (1367/1988–9) 'Islamic Republic of Iran, Plan and Budget Organization', Statistical Center of Iran: Tehran.

Irfani, S (1983) *Revolutionary Islam in Iran*, Zed Books: London.

Jacobs, A (1978) *Memories*, SUN: Nijmegen.

Johnson, K A (1983) *Women, the Family and Peasant Revolution in China*, University of Chicago Press: Chicago.

Jones, J M and Castle, J (1989) 'Women in higher education – changes in the '80s?' *Australian Universities' Review*, **32**, 2, 6–8.

Jones, J M and Lovejoy, F H (1983) 'Discrimination against women academics in Australian universities', *Signs*, **5**, 3, 518–26.

Kağitçibaşi, Ç (1970) 'Social norms and authoritarianism: a comparison of Turkish and American adolescents', *Journal of Personality and Social Psychology*, **16**, 3, 444–51.

Kağitçibaşi, Ç (ed) (1982) *Sex Roles, Family and Community in Turkey*, Indiana University Press: Bloomington, IN.

Kağitçibaşi, Ç (1990) 'Women's intra-family status, education and employment in Turkey', *Improving Employment Prospects for Women in a Changing Society*, Turkish Employment Organization Pub: Ankara.

Kandiyoti, D (1982) 'Urban change and women's roles in Turkey: an overview and evaluation', in Kagitcibasi, C (ed) (1982) *Sex Roles, Family and Community in Turkey*, Indiana University Press: Bloomington, IN.

Karimov, I A (1992) *Uzbekistan, Svoy Put Obnovleniya i Progressa (Uzbekistan, Own Way of Renovation and Progress)*, USSR govt: Tashkent.

Kelly, G P and Slaughter, S (eds) (1991) *Women's Higher Education in Comparative Perspectives*, Kluwer: Netherlands.

Kendall, K W (1968) 'Personality development in an Iranian village: an analysis of socialization practice and the development of the women's role', PhD dissertation, University of Washington.

Kjeldstad, R and Lyngstad, J (1993) *Arbeid lønn øg likestilling*, Universitetsforlaget i samarbeid med Statistisk sentralbyrå: Oslo.

Kobieta w Polsce (Women in Poland) (1968, 1975, 1985) GUS: Warszawa.

Koker, E D (1988) 'Turkiye'de Kadin, Eğitim ve Siyaset: Yuksek Öğrenim Kurumlarinda Kadinin Durumu Üzerine Bir ijnceleme (Women, education and politics in Turkey: an investigation on the conditions of women in higher education institutions)', PhD dissertation, Ankara University, Institute of Social Sciences: Ankara.

Kokorev, V (1992) Supplied statistics for Moscow State University, tables 2 and 5.

Kozan, K (1993) 'Conflict management in Turkish organization' in Afzal and Blum (eds) *Global Perspectives on Conflict Management*, Praeger: New York.

Krasuski, J (1985) *Historia wychowania (History of Education)* WSiP: Warszawa.

Kurin, R (1985) 'Islamization in Pakistan: a view from the countryside', *Asian Survey*, **25**, 8, 852–62.

Kyvik, S (1988) *Vitenskapelig publisering blant kvinnelige og mannlige universitetsforskere*, Melding, Norges almennvitenskapelige forskningsråd: Norway.

Kyvik, S (1990) 'Motherhood and scientific productivity', *Social Studies of Science*, **20**, 1, 149–60.

Kyvik, S and Teigen, M (1993) 'Kvinner ved universitetene. Hva har skjedd på 1980-tallet?', *Rapport*, NAVFs utredningsinstitutt.

Lambiri-Dimaki, J (1974) *Towards a Greek Sociology of Education*, National Center of Social Research: Athens.

Lazaris, K (1989) 'Greek Women in Politics', Mediterranean Women's Studies Institute: Athens (unpublished).

Le Doeuff, M (1991) 'Un extreme desir di apprendre', *Diplomees*, **158**, 97–9, Paris.

Leninsky District-Moscow: Female Population of R & D (1987) *Institutions and Higher Education*, *Special Report*, January 18.

Le Monde de l'Education (1990) 'Les filles et l'école', July–August, 18–36.

Lie, S S (1978) 'Trenger vi flere kvinnelige forskere? (Do we need more women researchers?)', *Samtiden*, **1**, 26–41.

Lie, S S and O'Leary, V (eds) (1990) 'The juggling act: work and family in Norway', in Lie, S S and O'Leary, V (eds) *Storming the Tower: women in the academic world*, Kogan Page: London.

Lie, S S and O'Leary, V (eds) (1990) *Storming the Tower: women in the academic world*, Kogan Page: London.

Luukkonen-Gronow, T (1987) 'University career opportunities for women in Finland in the 1980s', *Acta Sociologica*, **30**, 193–206.

Lutz, J G (1971) *China and the Christian Colleges, 1850–1950*, Cornell University Press, Ithaca.

Mack, K (1990) 'Women in universities', *Legal Services Bulletin*, **15**, 5, 211–14.

Macquarie University Council (1986) 'Procedures for promotion to the grade of Senior Lecturer', Macquarie University.

Maier, F (1991) 'Patriarchale Arbeitsmarktstrukturen und das phänomen geschlechtsspezifisch gespaltener Arbeitsmärkte in Ost und West', *Feministische Studien*, **1**, 107–16.

Majaha-Jartby, J and Kann, U (1982) *Women, Education and Employment: the case of Botswana*, UMEA Universitet Pedagogiska Institutionen Weed-Projektet, working paper no. 3.

Mak, G C L (1991) 'The impact of educational reforms on women: a case study of the People's Republic of China', PhD dissertation, State University of New York at Buffalo.

Malik, L (1982) 'Measuring consensus in Pakistan', *Journal of South Asian and Middle Eastern Studies*, **7**, 1.

Malik, L (1993) 'The Islamic resurgence in Iran and Pakistan: revival, revolution or realignment?', *Contemporary Pakistan: socioeconomic and political problems*, Russian Academy of Sciences, Institute of Oriental Studies.

Malik, L and Pattnayak, S (1994) 'Gender and class as predictors of normative conformity in Pakistan', *Journal of South Asian and Middle Eastern Studies*, March.

Mannathoko, C (1991) 'Profile of Women and Development in Botswana', unpublished document.

Marchand, O and Thelot, C (1991) *Deux siecles de travail*, INSEE: Paris.

Mashika, T A (1989) *Zanyatost zheschchin i materinstvo (Women's occupation and motherhood)*, USSR govt: Moscow.

Meier, U (1991) 'Zwischen risiko und chance – der umbruch weiblicher normalbiographien in der ehemaligen DDR', *Sozialökonomische Beiträge*, **2**, 2, 65ff.

Mertens, L (1991) *Vernachlässigte Töchter der Alma Mater*, Duncker & Humblot: Berlin.

Mgadla, P T (1986) 'Missionary and colonial education among the Bangwato: 1862 to 1948', unpublished doctoral dissertation, Boston University.

Mikhova, G (1991) 'The unemployed mother and her family', paper presented before the conference The Women during the Transition to Market Economy (Theory, Social Practice, Information), 11–12 June 1991, Institute of Demography at Bulgarian Academy of Sciences: Sofia.

Ministère de l'Education Nationale (MEN) *Notes d'informations* (1988) 88-32; (1989) 89-39; (1991a) 91–43; (1991b) 91-48; (1992) 92-18, Paris.

Ministry of Education and Religion, Bureau of Statistics *Higher Education Statistics* (1930, 1937, 1940, 1955, 1960, 1962, 1970–71, 1980–81, 1989–90): Athens.

Ministry of Education and Science: Government Amendment (1986a) *Selective Shrinkage and Growth*, The Hague.

Ministry of Education and Science: Government Amendment (1986b) *The Process of Task Distribution and Concentration in Scientific Education*, The Hague.

Ministry of Finance and Development Planning (1984) *Botswana Education and Human Resources*

240 DAVID W SCHLOSSER

Sector Assessment, Tallahassee: Educational Efficiency Clearing House Learning Systems Institute.

Moghadam, V M (1991) 'The reproduction of gender inequality in Muslim societies: a case study of Iran in the 1980s, *World Development*, **19**, 10, 1337–44.

Mohr, W (1987) *Frauen in der Wissenschaft*, Dreisam: Freiburg.

Moi, T (1991) 'Appropriating Bourdieu: feminist theory and Pierre Bourdieu's sociology of culture', *New Literary History*, Autumn, 1017–49.

Molokomme, A (1987) *A Summary of Women's Legal Status under Botswana Family Law*, Gaborone.

Molokomme, A (1989) *Women and the Law in Botswana: report from a seminar*, University of Oslo: Oslo.

Montreynaud, F (ed) (1989) *Le XX Siecle des Femmes*, Nathan: Paris.

Moore, K (1987) 'Women's success and opportunity in higher education: toward the twenty-first century', *Comparative Education*, **23**, 23–4.

Morée, M (1987) 'The cosmetics of harmonious inequality, *Journal of Sociology*, **14**, 2, 290–311.

Morrison, A M (ed) (1987) *Breaking the Glass Ceiling: can American women reach the top of America's largest corporation?*, Addison-Wesley: Reading.

Moskovskaya Pravda (The Moscow Truth), daily, Moscow, 5 April 1990; 14 March 1992; 17 October 1992.

Moscow State University (1992) *Statistics*, Moscow.

Moss Kanter, R (1977) *Men and Women of the Corporation*, Basic Books: New York.

Mourik, A van and Siegers, J J (1982) *Developments in Sex Segregation of Men and Women in the Netherlands, 1973–1979*, Research Report Economic Institute: State University Utrecht.

Myzhuev, P G (1906) *Zhenski vopros i zhenskoye dvizhenie (Women's question and women's movement)*, USSR govt: St Petersburg.

Narodnoye Khozyaystvo SSSR za 70 let (National economy of the USSR during 70 years) (1987) USSR govt: Moscow.

Narodnoe Khozyaystvo Uzbekskoy SSR v 1979 godu (1980) *(Economics of the Uzbek SSR in 1979)*, USSR govt: Tashkent.

Narodnoe Khozyaystvo Uzbekskoy SSR v 1990 godu (1991) *(Economics of the Uzbek SSR in 1990)*, USSR govt: Tashkent.

Naselenie Sredney Azii (1985) *(The Population of Central Asia)*, USSR govt: Moscow.

Nashat, G (1981) 'From bazaar to market: foreign trade and economic development in nineteenth century Iran', *Iranian Studies*, **14**, 1–2, 91–104.

Nashat, G (1983) 'Women in pre-revolutionary Iran: a historical overview', in Nashat, G, *Women and Revolution in Iran*, Westview Press.

National Census of Population and Housing (1365/1988) Islamic Republic of Iran, Plan and Budget Organization, Statistical Center of Iran, Teheran, Table 21.

National Statistical Service of Greece (ESYE) *Statistical Yearbook of Greece* (1928, 1951, 1981, 1991); *Education Statistics* (1930, 1940, 1955, 1962).

National Institute of Statistics (1991) *Bulgaria and the World in Figures*: Sofia.

National Institute of Statistics (1992) *Higher and College Education*: Sofia.

NAVF (1992) *Handlingsplan for Likestilling i NAVF 1993–1995*, Norges allmennvitenskapelige forskningråd.

NAVF 'Research personnel register', unpublished data.

NAVF Norges allmennvitenskapelige forskningsråd 'Research Personnel register', unpublished data.

Nicolaidou, M (1981) *Labour and Emancipation: women in Greece*, Castaniotis, Athens.

Nickel, H M (1990) 'Geschlechtertrennung durch Arbeitsteilung' in *Feministische Studien*, 1.

Noordenbos, G (1990) 'A comparing study to the career development of male and female scholars' in Hicks, E K and Noordenbos, G (eds) *Is Alma Mater Friendly for Women?*, Van Gorcum: Assen, Maastricht.

Norges, Barne-og familiedepartementet (1991–92) *St meld Nr 70*, Likestillingspolitikk for 1990-åra.

Norges, Kirke-, utdannings-og vitenskapsdepartment (1992–93) *St meld Nr 36*, Forskning for fellesskapet. Om forskning.

Norges offentlige utredninger, NOU (1988); *28 Med viten og vilje.*

Norway Ministry of Cultural and Scientific Affairs (1989) Report No 28 to the Norwegian Storting (1988–89) on research.

Norwegian Statistical yearbook (1989).

O'Leary, V and Mitchell, J (1990) 'Women connecting with women's networks and mentors in the United States' in Lie, S S and O'Leary, V (eds), *Storming the Tower: women in the academic world*, Kogan Page: London.

Öncü, A (1981) 'Turkish women in the professions: why so many?, in Abadan-Unat, N (ed) *Women in Turkish Society*, E J Brill: Leiden.

Ott, M (1985) *Cinderellas and Princes: a research of the minority position of female police officers and male nurses*, SUA: Amsterdam.

Oudijk, C (1983) *Social Atlas of Women in 1983, Social and Cultural Studies, 3*, Social and Cultural Plan Office, State Publisher: The Hague.

Over, R (1981) 'Women academics in Australian universities', *Australian Journal of Education*, **25**, 2, 166-76.

Over, R (1982) 'Research productivity and impact of male and female psychologists', *American Psychologist*, **37**, 2, 24–31.

Over, R and Lancaster, L (1984) 'The early career patterns of men and women in Australian universities', *Australian Journal of Education*, **21**, 3, 309–18.

Over, R and McKenzie, B (1985) 'Career prospects for women at Australian universities', *Journal of Tertiary Education Administration*, **8**, 1, 27– 42.

Ozkalp, E (1990) 'Kamu Hizmet Sektorunde Calisan Kadinlarin Calisma Nedenleri ve Sorunlari', in *Prof. Ilhan Cemalcilar'in Hatirasina Armagan*, Eskisehir, Anadolu Universitesi, IIBF Yayinlari.

Pakistan Times Overseas Weekly, 22 February 1977.

Papanek, G (1967) *Pakistan's Industrial Development: Social Goals and Private Incentives*, Oxford University Press: Oxford.

Parsons, N Q (1984) 'Education and development in pre-colonial Botswana to 1965 in Crowder, M (ed) *Education for Development in Botswana*, Macmillan Botswana Publishing: Gaborone.

Parsons, T (1951) *The Social System*, Free Press: Glencoe, Ill.

PC Globe (1992) Tempe, AZ.

Petersen, T, Becken, L E and Snartland, V (1993) 'Lønnsforskjeller mellom kvinner og menn i privat sektor' (unpublished report), Department of Sociology, University of Oslo.

Pilkington, H (1992) 'Russia and the former Soviet republics. Behind the mask of Soviet unity: realities of women's lives' in *Superwomen and the Double Burden*: London.

Poiner, G and Burke, R (1988) *No Primrose Path: women as staff at the University of Sydney*, University of Sydney: Sydney.

Portegijs, W (1990) 'Turnover of female and male scholars at universities in the Netherlands: 1986–1988' in Hicks, E K and Noordenbos, G (eds) *Is Alma Mater Sympathetic to Women?*, Van Gorcum: Assen, Maastricht.

Powles, M (1986) 'Chips in the academic wall? Women as postgraduate students', *Australian Universities' Review*, **22**, 2, 33–7.

Pulatov, S (1984) *Vissheei Strednee Spesialnoe Obrazovanie v Uzbekistane za let (Higher and Vocational Education in Uzbekistan for 60 years)*, USSR govt: Tashkent.

Quanguo fulian fuyunshi yanjiushi (Research Center for Women's Movement, All-China Women's Federation) (1986) *Zhongguo funu yundongshi (History of the Women's Movement in China)*, All China Women's Federation: Beijing.

Rendel, M (1984) 'Women academics in the seventies', in Acker, S and Piper, D (eds) *Is Higher Education Fair to Women?*, Society for Research in Higher Education: Guildford.

Rendel, M and Hartnett, O (1975) *Women's Studies in the UK*, London Seminars, London Institute of Education.

Renmin ribao, 23 February and 16 June, 1990.

Renzetti, C M and Curran, D J (1992) *Women, Men and Society*, Allyn T Bacon: New York.

Republic of Botswana (1985) *National Development Plan 1985–1991*, The Government Printer: Gaborone.

Republic of Botswana (1991) *National Development Plan 1991–1997*, The Government Printer: Gaborone.

Respublika Uzbekistan: Spravochnik (1992) (The Republic of Uzbekistan: Reference Book), USSR govt: Tashkent.

Richmond-Abbott, M (1992) *Masculine and Feminine: gender roles over the life cycle*, McGraw-Hill: New York.

Ries, P & Stone, A J (eds) (1992) *The American Woman 1992–93: a status report*, W W Norton & Co: New York.

242   DAVID W SCHLOSSER

Robbins Committee Report (1963) (a) App. 2A. 24, (b) App. 3, 18, HMSO: London.
Rocznik statystyczny szkolnictwa (Annals of Educational Statistics) (1985) GUS: Warszawa.
Rørslett, M B and Lie, S (1984) *På solsiden – kvinners kamp for kunnskap hvor førte den hen?*, Cammermeyer forlag: Oslo.
Ryan, G and Evans, S (1984) *Affirmative Action for Women: a policy discussion paper*, AGPS: Canberra.
Sanasarian, E (1982) *The Women's Rights Movements in Iran*, Praeger Publishers: New York.
Sanders, C (1992a,b) *Times Higher Education Supplement*, 4 September, 17 July.
Sawer, M (1984) *Towards Equal Opportunity: women and employment at ANU*, Canberra: ANU Press.
Sayari, S (1975) 'Some notes on the beginnings of mass political participation in Turkey', in Akarli and Ben Dor (eds) *Political Participation in Turkey*, Bogazici University Yay: Istanbul.
Schäfers, B (1990), *Gesellschaftlicher Wandel in Deutschland*, Enke: Stuttgart.
Scheuch, E (1966) 'Cross national comparisons using aggregate data: some methodological considerations' in Marritt, R L (ed) *Comparing Nations, the use of quantitative data in cross national research*, Yale University Press: New York.
Schiebinger, L (1989) *The Mind has No Sex? Women in the origins of modern science*, Harvard University Press: Cambridge.
Sefe, F T K and Rasebotsa, N (eds) (1991) *University of Botswana Calendar*, University of Botswana: Gaborone.
Sevost'yanov, G and Shtifanov, V (1991) *Ohrana truda. Trud zhenschchin. Trud molodezhi (Labour protection. Women's labour. Youth's labour)*, USSR govt: Moscow.
Shaheed, F and Mumtaz, K (1990) 'The rise of the religious right and its impact on women', *South Asia Bulletin*, **10**, 2.
Shaikhulislami, P (1972) *Zanan-i-Ruznamehnigar Va Andishmand-i-Iran (Women Journalists and Intellectuals in Iran)*, March.
Shangguan, L (1988) 'Lieshi leiji xiaoying – Xhongguo keji jieceng nuxin renkou fenbu de shehui xinli fengxi (A social psychological analysis of female professionals in science and technology in China)' M Soc Sc thesis, Chinese Academy of Social Science.
Sharafi, Z (1991) *Problems of Female Experts in Agricultural Ministry*. Ministry of Agriculture: Teheran.
Simons, L A, Simons, J, McCallum, J, Powell, I, Friedlander, Y and Heller, R (1991) 'Dubbo study of the elderly: sociological and cardiovascular risk factors at entry', *Australian and New Zealand Journal of Medicine*, **21**, 701–9.
Skjeie, H (1991) 'The uneven advance of Norwegian women', *New Left Review*, 187.
Skocpol, T (1979) *States and Social Revolutions*, Cambridge University Press: New York.
Sloan, J, Baker, M, Blandy, R, Robertson, F and Brummit, W (1990) *Study of the Labour Market for Academics*, Report prepared for DEET, AGPS: Canberra.
Social and Cultural Report (1992) The Hague.
Socialnoe Razvitie i Uroven Zhizni Naseleniya Uzbekoskoy SSR (1990) (*Social Progress and the Living Standard of Population of the Uzbek SSR*) Tashkent.
Social Trends 22 (1992): Central Statistical Office, London.
Sommerkorn, I (1966) 'On the position of women in the university teaching profession in England', PhD thesis: London University.
Spear, P (1975) *A History of India*, Penguin Books: Harmondsworth.
Sretenova, N (1993) 'Bulgarian science before the entry of social janus' in *Science and the Challenge of Social Change*, Bulgarian Academy of Sciences, Centre for Science Studies: Sofia.
State Institute of Statistics, Republic of Turkey (1988) *Census of Population: Social and Economic Characteristics of Population: 20-10 1985*, Ankara.
Statistical Yearbook (1988) CBS: Heerlen.
Statistisches Bundesamt (1990a) *Statistisches Jahrbücher 1990*, Wiesbaden.
Statistisches Bundesamt (1990b) *Zableu und Fakten*, Metzler und Poeschel, Stuttgart.
Stolte-Heiskanen, V, Acar, F, Ananiva, N and Gaudar, D (1991) *Women in Science: from token women to gender equity in science*, International Social Science Council and UNESCO – Social and Human Sciences Sector, Paris.
Stratigaki, M (1989) 'Technological development and gender specialties', *Quarterly Scientific Revue, Modern Issues*, **40**, 31–8.
Sutherland, M B (1985a) *Women Who Teach in Universities*, Trenton Books: Stoke-on-Trent.

Sutherland, M B (1985b) 'Whatever happened about coeducation?' *British Journal of Educational Studies*, **XXXIII**, 2, 155–63.
Sytuacja spoleczno-zawodowa kobiet (The Socio-Occupational Situation of Women) (1988, 1991) GUS: Warszawa.
Szkoly wyzsze w roku szkolnym 1991/1992 (High Schools 1991/1992) GUS: Warszawa.
Taksdal, A and Widerberg, K (1992) *Forståelser av kjønn: i samfunnsvitenskapenes fag og kvinne-forskning*, ad Notam Gyldendal AS: Oslo.
Tashkentskiy Gosudarstvenniy Universitet imeni V I Lenina Khronika Sobitiy Bibgraphicheskie spravki uchenih (1990) *(The Tashkent State University Named after V I Lenin Chronicle Biographic Information on Scientists)* Tashkent.
Teigen, M and Tvede, O (1993) *Framtid i forskningen. En undersøkelse av kwinnelige og mannlige forskerrekrutters situasjon og karriereveier*, Rapport 6/93, NAVFs utredningsinstitutt.
Tekeli, S (1986) 'Emergence of the feminist movement in Turkey' in Dahlerup, D (ed) *The New Women's Movement*, Sage: London.
Tekeli, S (1990) 'Women in the changing political associations of the 1980s' in Sirman and Finkle (eds) *Turkish State, Turkish Society*, Routledge: London.
Thurow, L C (1987) 'A surge of inequality' *Scientific American*, **256**, 5, 30–37.
Toren, N (1990) 'Would more women make a difference?' in Lie, S S and O'Leary, V (eds) *Storming the Tower: women in the academic world*, Kogan Page, London.
TÜSIAD (Turkish Industrialists and Businessman's Association (1990) *Türkiyede Egitim (Education in Turkey)*, Tüsiad Yay: Istanbul.
TÜSIAD (Turkish Industrialists and Businessman's Association) (1991) 'Türk Toplumunun Değerleri (Values in Turkish society), *Tüsiad Yay*, **91**, 6, 145.
UCCA (Universities Central Council on Admissions) (1992) *Twenty-Ninth Report*, UCCA: Cheltenham, UK.
UNESCO (1987) *Enquete sur la representation des femmes dans l'enseignement superieur, la recherche, la planification et la gestion de l'education* UNESCO: Paris.
Universities Statistical Record (1992) Cheltenham.
UGC (University Grants Committee) (1921, 1953) *Reports*, HMSO: London.
U S Department of Labor (1988) *Employment and Earnings*, January.
Uzbekskaya SSR v Tsifrah v 1988 godu (1989) *(Uzbek SSR in figures in 1988)*, USSR govt: Tashkent.
Verwey-Jonker, H (1981) 'Development in the position of women', in Weeda, C J (ed) *Women and Society Series: aspects of the society*, Van Gorcum: Assen, Maastricht.
Vetchernaya Moskva (The Evening Moscow), daily, Moscow, 16 September 1991; 22 January 1993.
Vianen, A E M van (1987) 'The selection-interview: concerning the role of sex-stereotypes', thesis, Leiden.
Wang, H (1991) 'Analysis of the competition facing female intellectuals at institutions of higher education in Wuhan', in Li X, and Tan, S (eds) *Zhongguo funu fenceng yanjiu (Study of Women in China by Social Strata)*, Henan renmin chubanshe, Zhengzhou.
Wang, W et al. (1989) *Zhongguo kexueyuan boshisheng daoshi jianjie (Profiles of Advisers of Doctoral Students at the Chinese Academy of Science)*, Zhongguo keda chubanshe: Hefei.
Weiss, A M (1985) 'Women's position in Pakistan: sociocultural effects of Islamization', *Asian Survey*, **25**, 8.
Weitzman, L J (1985) *The Divorce Revolution: the unexpected social and economic consequences for women and children in America*, Free Press: New York.
Wetterer, A (ed) (1992) *Profession und Geschlecht*, Campus: Frankfurt/M.
Wienecke, C (1988) 'Room at the top? An analysis of the position of senior women in college administration in New South Wales', *Journal of Tertiary Education Administration*, **10**, 1, 5–17.
Williams, T and Carpenter, P G (1990) 'Private schooling and public achievement', *Australian Journal of Education*, **1**, 3–24.
Wilson, M and Byrne, E (1987) *Women in the University*, University of Queensland Press: St Lucia.
Wolpert, S (1989) *Jinnah of Pakistan*, Oxford University Press: Delhi.
Woodsmall, R F (1983) *Moslem Women Enter a New World*, George Allen & Unwin: London (originally published in the Annual Report of the Ministry of Education, 1932–33).
Woody, T (1966) *A History of Women's Education in the United States (Vol I)*, Octagon Books: New York.
WOPI (1991) *Information about Personnel of Universities: net numbers concerning 12-31-1990*, VSNU: Utrecht.
World Bank (1985) *Development Report*, p. 114.

World Bank (1992) *Social Indicators of Development (1991–92)*, Johns Hopkins University Press: Baltimore.
World Bank (1993) *Social Implications of Development (1992–93)*, Johns Hopkins University Press: Baltimore.
World Bank (1993) *Turkey, Women in Development, A World Bank Country Study*, Washington, D C.
Wroczynski, R (1987) *Dzieje bswiaty polskiej do roku 1795 (The History of Polish Education until 1795)*, PWN: Warszawa.
Young, C (1989) 'Life cycle experience of women in the labour force', Ch 4, in *Australia's Greatest Asset: Human resources in the 19th and 20th century*, NSW: Federation Press.
Yusuf, Z (1989) 'Woman power?', *Newsline*, July.
Zakharova N and Rymashevskaya, N (1990) Zhenskaya Kar'era (Women's career) *Pravda*, 15 February.
Zhenschiny Respubliki Uzbekistan Statisticheskiy Sbornik (1991) (*Women of the Republic of Uzbekistan: Statistics*) Tashkent.
Zhenschiny Sovietskogo Uzbekistana (1984) USSR govt.
Zhenshchiny o samih sebe. – Rabonitsa (Women about themselves) (1990) 11 November.
Zhenshchiny v SSSR. Statisticheskiye materialy (Women in the USSR. Statistics) (1991) Moscow.
Zhongguo funu (Women of China) (1990), 9.
Zhongguo funubao (Journal of Women of China) 27 February 1985; 22 September 1986; 10 August and 14 December 1988; 18 December 1989; 6 June and 21 September 1990; 6 July 1992.
Zhonghua quanguo funu lianhehui (All China Women's Federation) (1984) *Fenfa ziqiang, kaituo qianjin (Work Hard, Self-strengthen and Make Inroads Ahead)*, Renmin chubanshi: Beijing.
Zhonghua quanguo funu lianhehui funu yanjisusuo (Institute for Research on Women, All China Women's Federation) *et al.* (1991) *Zhongguo funu tongji ziliao 1949–1989 (Statistics on Women in China 1949–1989)*, Zhongguo tongji chubanshe: Beijing.
Zhu, C and Jiang, Z (1991) *Zhongguo nuxin renkou (China's Female Population)*, Henan renmin chubanshe: Zhengzhou.
Ziller, A (1986) EEO Awareness Seminar, presented at Nepean CAE 8th August (transcript).
Ziogou-Carastergiou, S (1985) 'Approach to the history of women's education in Greece', in General Secretariat for Equality of the Two Sexes (eds) *Congress on Equality of the Two Sexes and Education*, May 1985, Thessaloniki, Athens.
Zlhenchiny Sovietskogo Uzbekistan Statisticheskiy Sbornic (1984) *(Women of Soviet Uzbekistan Statistics)*.
Zvezda Vostoka (The Star of the Orient) (1990) 12 November, Tashkent.
Zvezda Vostoka (The Star of the Orient) (1991) Nos 8 and 12, Tashkent.

Index

academic attainment 224
All Pakistan Woman's Association 132
Australia 13–23, 207
  administrative committees 22
  education system 14–15
  effect of domestic responsibilities on rank 23
  higher degrees by sex 15
  history and society 13–14
  incompatibility of academic employment and domestic responsibilities 20
  levels of turnover in universities 19
  participation in administration 22
  publications 21–2
  qualifications of academic staff 21
  reasons for women's poor career opportunities in universities 18
  relative academic merit 23
  role of interpersonal politics 20
  selection and promotion procedures 18, 22
  sex-based differences in academic merit 20–21
  teaching ability requirements 22
  tenured and untenured male and female faculty 17
  tertiary sector 15–22
    recent changes in 15–16
  women as academic staff 16–18
  women's poor representation in senior positions 23
  women's reluctance to apply for positions 19–20
  women's role in paid work force 14

Bogomil movement 33

Botswana 24–32, 209
  academic staff by field, gender and rank 30
  discrimination against girls 27
  gender disparities in post-primary education 28
  post-primary education for women 27–8
  primary education for women 26–7
  socio-economic, political and cultural profile 25–6
  student enrolment by field and gender 28
  under-achievement in science, mathematics and related fields 30
  university governance by gender and citizenship 31
  women as circumstantial beneficiaries 26–7
Bulgaria 33–45, 210
  brain drain 44
  decommunization 42
  frozen brain 44
  gender gap in postgraduate education 40–42
  hidden mechanisms of discrimination 37–42
  historical and cultural profile 33–4
  'non-scientific' selection 42
  position of women in
    after Second World War 35–6
    in education 34–7
  privatization 42
  role of university in 34–7
  'scientific' selection 40
  structure of universities after Second World War 36–7